The Working

The Working Voice is an accessible, go-to resource to help readers get to know, take care of, and develop their voice. An essential guide for anyone whose voice acts as an integral part of their professional role, this highly practical yet informative book provides the necessary insights to achieve real results, drawing on the experience of an expert speech and language therapist, and an accomplished actor and voice and communication coach.

Each chapter offers a wealth of information on a key element of voice, including posture, tension release, breathing, resonance, volume, intonation and effective communication, alongside advice and exercises to maintain your vocal health and empower your communication in the workplace.

The book includes self-assessment checklists, questionnaires and thought-provoking prompts to help you understand your voice better; identifying the challenges you face as a professional voice user. It also contains exercises to enhance your vocal ability. Expert advice on what to embrace and what to avoid ensures a safe and structured path towards vocal health, quality and authentic presence.

This crucial introduction to voice in the professional workplace will benefit anyone who speaks as part of their job, including education, law, media, health, entertainment and corporate professionals, whether communicating in person, online or to a large audience.

Stephanie Martin, a speech and language therapist, has a multifaceted career combining clinical practice, communication skills training for business leaders, research, lecturing and writing. She specialises in occupational voice disorders and holds an MA in Voice Studies from the Royal Central School of Speech and Drama (London). Her doctoral research at The University of Greenwich examined factors affecting vocal performance of newly qualified teachers and lecturers. Stephanie is a past president of the British Voice Association and represented the UK on the Standing Liaison Committee of EU Speech and Language Therapists and Logopedists. In 2005, she received a Fellowship of the Royal College of Speech and Language Therapists for research and teaching.

Olivia Darnley is an actor, voiceover artist and voice and communications coach. She studied English and Drama at Birmingham University and earned a master's degree in drama from The Royal Conservatoire of Scotland. Over her 20-year acting career Olivia has worked extensively on stage, including with the Royal Shakespeare Company and National Theatre, as well as on TV, in film, and in audiobooks and radio dramas. For over a decade, she has coached actors and business professionals in accent, voice and communication; supporting her clients to express themselves effectively and confidently.

The Working Voice

Vocal Health and Effective Communication

Stephanie Martin and Olivia Darnley

Routledge
Taylor & Francis Group

LONDON AND NEW YORK

Designed cover image: © Getty Images

First published 2024
by Routledge
4 Park Square, Milton Park, Abingdon, Oxon OX14 4RN

and by Routledge
605 Third Avenue, New York, NY 10158

Routledge is an imprint of the Taylor & Francis Group, an informa business

British Library Cataloguing-in-Publication Data
A catalogue record for this book is available from the British Library

Library of Congress Cataloging-in-Publication Data
Names: Martin, Stephanie (Speech therapist), author. | Darnley, Olivia, author.
Title: The working voice: vocal health and effective communication/
Stephanie Martin and Olivia Darnley.
Description: London; New York: Routledge, 2024. |
Includes bibliographical references and index.
Identifiers: LCCN 2023040186 (print) | LCCN 2023040187 (ebook) |
ISBN 9781032420813 (hardback) | ISBN 9781032420806 (paperback) |
ISBN 9781003361114 (ebook)
Subjects: LCSH: Voice culture. | Voice–Care and hygiene.
Classification: LCC PN4162 .M345 2024 (print) | LCC PN4162 (ebook) |
DDC 808.5/07–dc23/eng/20231025
LC record available at https://lccn.loc.gov/2023040186
LC ebook record available at https://lccn.loc.gov/2023040187

ISBN: 978-1-032-42081-3 (hbk)
ISBN: 978-1-032-42080-6 (pbk)
ISBN: 978-1-003-36111-4 (ebk)

DOI: 10.4324/9781003361114

Typeset in Galliard
by Deanta Global Publishing Services, Chennai, India

Access the Support Material: https://resourcecentre.routledge.com/speechmark

Acknowledgements

The Working Voice draws not only on the authors' knowledge and practical experience but also on the generous support received over many years from our friends, colleagues, students, clients and patients who added, and continue to add, to our insight into, and experience of, the field of voice. To you all, a huge thank you is due.

We particularly wish to reference the knowledge, wisdom and influence of Lyn Darnley, whose untimely death in 2020 was a huge loss to us and to the worldwide voice community. Lyn's work and collaboration with Stephanie over many years, addressed voice use in both clinical and educational settings and influenced the content of *The Working Voice*.

For Olivia, working alongside Lyn as an actor, observing her work with others and, in more recent years, delivering workshops on Shakespeare, voice and public speaking, was not only an enriching educational experience but had a significant influence on this publication.

For us both, our separate experience of working with Lyn allowed us to build on her legacy. Our hope is that she would approve of our collaboration in *The Working Voice*.

We would especially like to thank our families for their understanding and encouragement during the writing of this publication. We hope it reflects our joy in working in a field that is fulfilling, stimulating and endlessly rewarding.

The Working Voice is accompanied by a number of printable online materials, designed to ensure this resource best supports your professional needs

Go to https://resourcecentre.routledge.com/speechmark and click on the cover of this book

Answer the question prompt using your copy of the book to gain access to the online content.

Contents

Acknowledgements   v

Introduction   1

1   What Is Voice?   7

2   Posture   31

3   Relaxation and Release of Tension   48

4   Breathing   68

5   Constriction, Deconstriction and Smooth Onset of the Note   84

6   Resonance   97

7   Exploring Pitch   113

8   Muscular Flexibility   136

9   Working for Variety   162

10 Development and Control of Volume   183

11 Communication in the Workplace   203

Appendices   301
Appendix A: Your Voice Profile   302
Appendix B: Voice Diary   312
Appendix C: Voice Care Recommendations   312

Contents

Appendix D: Voice Warm-up 314

Resources: Organisations and Resources of Interest 317

References and Further Reading 320

Index 323

Introduction

This book is intended for anyone who uses their voice as an integral component of their occupational or professional role; in particular, if you are a teacher, lecturer, facilitator, negotiator, fitness instructor, a member of the clergy, a lawyer or barrister, in the media, in telesales, a team leader, a member of the medical profession, an actor or performer, a singer or broadcaster, if you conduct meetings online or to large live audiences, or offer information through the medium of video, if you work in hospitality, or in the business of sharing information and communicating with others with your voice, then you are, in effect, an occupational and professional voice user. So if you use your voice for a variety of purposes – educating, instructing, entertaining and informing individuals and /or groups, both large and small, indoors, outdoors or in a variety of settings, some of which may have little amplification and are vocally very challenging – this book is for you and your voice at work.

Voice is a critical factor in all these roles, and your continued employment may well be dependent on maintaining vocal effectiveness through vocal care and conservation. In addition if, for a variety of reasons, you feel that your voice does not adequately match your personality and status, does not reflect who you are and what you do, then this book will suit your needs as well.

What happens when an occupational or a professional voice user can no longer effectively, inspire, educate, encourage, explore, exchange ideas or concepts, or entertain, through the medium of voice? What has happened to affect our ability to use our voice? Voice is a critical indicator of both our physiological and psychological well-being and, as such, offers a particularly acute and effective gauge of our physical and mental health.

Many professions require significant use of the voice; most of us will speak at some point during our working day. Some of that speaking may be casual or social, and some of it may feel 'professional', a part of your job.

DOI: 10.4324/9781003361114-1

Possibly you have to make a report, update your team, network, pitch, or deliver a presentation. This book will be of value to anyone who uses their voice for work in these ways, or simply in their day-to-day life. However, in some professions voice use will be more fundamental to the role itself, and these 'professional voice users' are more likely to experience vocal damage than others. It's worth noting that anyone who uses their voice extensively, regardless of profession, may be at risk of vocal damage if they do not practise proper vocal hygiene and take care of their voice.

The Degree of Vocal Demand in Professional Settings

Level One	**Elite vocal performer** Even slight vocal difficulties would severely impact their work	Singers Actors Broadcasters Singers, and other performers who use their voice for extended periods of time, particularly in high-pressure performance situations, may be at risk of vocal damage. Actors and voice actors may need to use the full range of their voice, and for prolonged periods of time, often under pressure which may lead to vocal fatigue or damage. Broadcasters use their voices in pressurised settings, often in challenging environments, and for extended periods of time.
Level Two	**Professional voice user** Moderate vocal difficulties may prevent adequate job performance	Teachers Public speakers Politicians Call-centre operators Clergy Law professionals Salespeople Coaches Teachers and trainers may need to use increased volume or speak for extended periods of time, which can lead to vocal fatigue and damage. Those who work in call centres, telesales, booking lines or customer service may need to speak for prolonged periods of time daily, often in a loud and noisy environment, which can contribute to vocal strain and damage.

		Coaches or personal trainers who frequently shout instructions or encourage clients during training sessions in noisy gyms, across open spaces or using heavy equipment may find their voice compromised. Clergy and religious leaders may experience vocal fatigue, speaking to large groups in acoustically challenging environments, with a need for vocal dexterity. Lawyers, barristers, judges and solicitors who frequently argue in court may experience vocal fatigue or find they wish to have more options in how they use their voice. Tour guides who use their voice to communicate information and stories about historical sites or tourist attractions, often outside and on the move, may find that, even with amplification, the environment is challenging and can be vocally stressful.
Level Three	**Professionals who do not rely on their voices for work** Severe vocal difficulties may prevent adequate job performance	Healthcare professionals Hospitality staff Media/business relations specialists Beauty professionals Etc. While not necessarily vocally challenging, communication is a large part of these professions, and there may be environmental challenges. For example, hairdressers having to speak above the noise of the salon, receptionists sitting in chilly foyers with ergonomic challenges, therapists talking through emotionally charged situations. Many of these professionals will be required to talk for substantial parts of their working day and require vocal options to perform their jobs well.
Level Four	**Professionals for whom voice is not an essential part of their work** Work is not compromised even with severe vocal difficulties	Labourers Caterers Factory workers Admin staff Aerospace employees Transport workers Etc. While their role, by definition, may not be particularly vocally challenging, there may be environmental challenges in these workplaces and requirements of the job that may be vocally challenging.

Other professionals not mentioned in this chart may be vocally challenged by the environment in which they work. Your ability to work may not necessarily be impaired by vocal loading or damage; however, there is immense value in this book for these individual's vocal health and conservation. You will learn how to mitigate these challenging environments and care for your voice in the workplace.

Examples of Vocally and Acoustically Challenging Environments

Construction sites.
Factories or manufacturing plants.
Mining sites.
Airports or transportation hubs.
Music venues or recording studios.
Restaurants or bars.
Fire stations or emergency response centres.
Call centres or telemarketing offices.
Sports stadiums or arenas.
Hospitals or medical facilities (in certain areas, such as the emergency department or operating room).

Along with the environment in which you work, a multitude of factors can affect the voice, including emotional, physical, ergonomic and psychosocial factors. This book will frame the many vocal demands experienced by the professional voice user and link those demands to multiple factors that may have contributed to voice loss, both actual and psychological, through circumstance, illness, trauma or misuse.

Vocal health and effective communication are integral to how we communicate, and this book will look at the ways in which our voice reflects our individuality and our professional role, our status and our personality. The ability to express ourselves with passion and vocal authenticity, maintaining and improving vocal skills, depends on knowledge and practice, underpinned by practical work. In addition, aspects such as environmental and acoustic influences on the voice, illness, stress and anxiety, plus the effect of ageing on the voice, are explored. Information on the vocal demands of the occupational voice user, the process of producing voice and how to care for your voice, are included. Practical advice on aspects of clarity of delivery, specific qualitative changes such as resonance, articulatory skills, pitch, range and projection of the voice, all aspects that allow others to really 'hear' you, are included and are supported by exercises.

Some of the exercises in the book may be familiar to readers in another form or from other sources. It is always difficult to correctly attribute provenance to practical exercises but having worked with both Lyn Darnley and Myra Lockhart for many years, joint working, leading to a unity of approach and the development of a body of work, makes it almost impossible to attribute a specific practical exercise to a specific individual. The exercises in this book should therefore be considered as a joint endeavour and permission has been given to include them. We freely acknowledge the inclusion of some text and exercises from *The Voice Box* (Martin and Darnley, 2013), as we've been fortunate to receive much positive feedback from readers of that resource, over the years. The exercises have been carefully vetted to make sure that they are as clear and unambiguous as possible. However, the book is not intended as a substitute for medical advice and supervision, so any application of the recommendations in the book is at the reader's discretion and sole risk. Developments in medical research may impact the advice that is offered here; while that advice does relate, in so far as is possible, to the most recent findings or developments, it is not possible to guarantee that views may not change over time. No exercise is without risk, so please do not continue with any of the exercises if, in the unlikely event, you feel unwell, dizzy or have any physical discomfort.

This combination of information and practice is what allows us to know our voice, to own our voice, and while it does not replace professional 'hands-on' intervention, it does offer knowledge and skills to care and protect our voice in our role as occupational voice users.

The Working Voice is essentially a practical resource and, as such, the focus is on the challenges and experiences of the professional voice user, noting the effect that limited communication skills can have on outcome measures and communicative potential. There is a strong 'how-to' element, using checklists, self-assessment and self-reporting tasks, to allow you to monitor your vocal health and voice care. This is accompanied by a strong element of practical advice and easily assimilated, sound, information, allowing you to better understand your own voice with its unique qualities and inherent challenges – related to your physical, emotional and mental health.

The voice is multifaceted. To work on the voice means to work on the body, the breath and the sound, and, for best results, voice work should include all these elements. Although intended to be read in its entirety, each chapter in the book deals with distinct topics. This allows a somewhat 'pick-and-mix' approach, once you have the essential foundations, to focus on what you need when you need it. Each chapter provides an in-depth introduction to the topic, details why it is of importance to you and provides well-informed theory, self-reflection prompts, practical advice, exercises and resources to use throughout your professional career.

This approach is based on the knowledge that, for an adult, life experiences are rich resources for continued learning, particularly if that life experience relates to one of our most important emotional and intimate communicative tools: that of our voice.

1 What Is Voice?

How Does It Work? What Happens When It Goes Wrong?

Voice is one of the most powerful communication tools we have. Each of us has a voice that is unique, one that can be instantly identified as belonging to us, and we could say 'we are our voice'. Voice translates our private, silent thoughts into spoken words and, indeed, the sound of another's voice can influence our view of them, moving in a nanosecond from like to dislike, from admiration to ridicule, from support to rejection as soon as they speak. We can express a point of view and sabotage a promising interaction by turning a sentence of praise into one of doubt, or turning doubt into conviction, or sarcasm into praise through altering the volume, speed and pitch of our voice.

Anne Karpf says of voice (2006): 'It bridges our internal and external world, travelling from our most private recesses into the public domain revealing not only our deepest sense of who we are but also who we wish we weren't. It is,' she continues, 'a superb guide to fear and power, anxiety and subservience to another person's vitality and authenticity as well as our own.' That is why, for those who lose their voice through illness, disease, emotional or functional reasons, the loss is extreme.

One of the difficulties of envisaging how the voice works is that it is not 'on view', so making changes to it is challenging. For the professional voice user, an ability to influence, persuade, encourage, educate, inspire and reassure through the medium of voice is critical to their role, and their ability to fulfil it successfully. Professional and elite voice users are dependent on the health and effectiveness of their voice to support sustained and prolonged use in demanding situations and the ability to use it effectively in a variety of settings and to differing groups and numbers of people.

To maintain vocal health and efficiency, it is particularly important to consider not only the physical condition of the entire vocal tract but also the

DOI: 10.4324/9781003361114-2

structures and systems that are critical to the production of the voice, the breathing (respiratory), sound (phonatory) and tone and quality (resonatory) systems.

Each of these systems has a specific section devoted to them in this book, but if the condition of the vocal folds is compromised due to infection, disease or lack of care and attention, then, however good the supporting system is, vocal quality will be jeopardised. Voice is a very precise stress indicator; many stress-induced changes affect every aspect of phonation, both directly and indirectly, such as breath capacity, muscle function, reduced lubrication of the vocal folds, changes within the lining of the vocal tract and the tissue integrity of the vocal folds. While it is important to not become overly focused on your own voice, as that can have the effect of a loss of spontaneity in delivery and production, there are aspects of voice that we hope will be of interest to you, as a professional voice user. For example:

- Where does it come from?
- When and how does it change?
- How can you care for and conserve your voice?
- How do you recognise that your voice is not working as effectively as it should?
- What lifestyle choices should you avoid if you are a professional voice user?
- What lifestyle choices should you actively encourage/engage with, as a professional voice user?

So, Where Does Voice Come From?

Our focus in this book is on its application as a practical resource. In view of the wealth of information available online that illuminates anatomical detail with the greatest precision, the decision to avoid explaining the anatomy and physiology of the vocal tract in minute detail seems justified. For those who are looking for a detailed account, there are many excellent resources – both publications and online. In this section the aim is to offer a broad overview of the structures and functions central to the production of voice and where it comes from.

When we consider where the voice comes from, we need to say that the process is dependent on a lot more than just the actions of the larynx, or, as it is often referred to, the 'voice box'. Three different, but interrelated, systems work together to create your voice: namely, the respiratory (breathing), phonatory (larynx) and resonance (voice quality) systems.

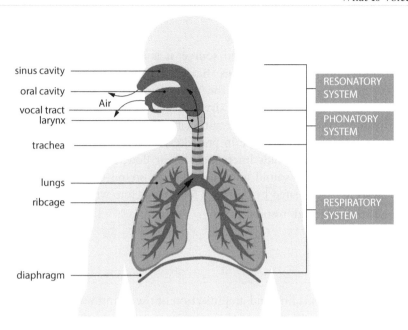

Figure 1.1 Schematic illustration of the three systems which create voice.

- The respiratory system, also known as breath support, includes the lungs, ribcage, chest muscles, diaphragm and vocal tract or windpipe, is primarily responsible for breathing.
- The phonatory system, also known as the larynx or voice box, where sound is produced includes the larynx and, specifically, the vocal folds. Historically the vocal folds were, and sometimes still are, known as the vocal cords. They are primarily responsible for producing sound.
- The resonatory system, also known as the vocal tract, includes the throat, nasal passages, sinuses and mouth, and is primarily responsible for shaping the sound.

Breath Support

Breath support comes from your respiratory system. Breath is the power behind voice production. When we want to speak, we take a breath (inhale) and then start speaking as we breathe out or exhale. It is this flow of air moving up the windpipe and through the voice box (between the vocal folds) that starts (and keeps) the vocal folds vibrating until you stop talking or run out of breath.

Phonation

Vocal fold vibration is the sound source: it is also called phonation. The vocal folds are two small muscles that have a flexible, lubricated surface, within the larynx. When you breathe in and out, the vocal folds are open to allow air to flow from your upper airway into your trachea and lungs. When you speak, your vocal folds close automatically, interrupting the outgoing breath and causing an increase in pressure that starts them vibrating. The vibration of the vocal folds interrupts the air flow, producing a buzz-like sound which doesn't sound anything like the sound of someone's voice! The buzzing tone created by the vocal folds turns into what we know as the human voice, through resonance.

Resonance

Resonance is the shaping and amplification of the sound waves of the vocal tone. The length and shape of the vocal tract influences the sound, along with the structures or cavities the sound waves may bounce off.

If you take a breath and hum on a steady tone for a few seconds, you can experience this sensation of resonance in the front of your face. In contrast, if you growl, you can feel that the resonance is farther down, in the back of your throat. Finally, once the sound-waves reach your mouth, you use your lips, teeth and tongue to shape the sound (articulation) into speech.

These vocal 'subsystems' need to share the work of voice production for the speaker to communicate effectively. The integrated nature of voice production is of particular importance and is the reason we never refer to voice – technically the buzzing tone produced by the larynx – in isolation. All contributory factors within your environment (here the term environment is

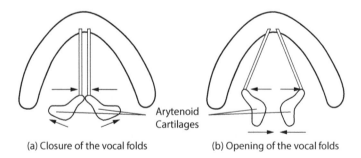

(a) Closure of the vocal folds   (b) Opening of the vocal folds

Figure 1.2 Schematic illustration of the movement of the arytenoid cartilages and consequent movement of the vocal folds.

used in its widest sense to encompass our vocal, social, physical and psychological environment) need to be considered to determine the possible impact of each of these, in terms of their collective contribution to, or maintenance of, a voice disorder. In most people, an adequate balance is achieved naturally, and a voice problem never develops. However, if the system is very out of balance or if voice use is intense, what is known as 'vocal loading', then a voice disorder can occur. As a result, 'voice work' (as found in the following chapters of this book) is especially important for all professional voice users.

Posture

Voice can never be seen in isolation but always as a combined effort of the respiratory, phonatory and resonatory system, and the effect of posture on the systems cannot be underestimated. Posture, in turn, is affected by the movement of the bony skeleton and the muscles that support the skeleton. The intimate connection of ligaments, tendons and bones within the body allows freedom of movement but it also means that the movement of one body part will affect another, either directly or indirectly. The interrelationship of head, neck, spine, back, pelvis will affect the ribcage and is consequently critically important for efficient and effective voicing.

Each of these systems (respiratory, phonatory and resonatory), plus posture, have a detailed chapter devoted to them, as do aspects of voice quality, such as pitch, volume and muscular flexibility. Each chapter includes advice and exercises to promote effective voice use, plus ways in which you can analyse, assess and apply what you've read.

When and How Does Voice Change?

Voice, from infancy to old age, is affected by anatomical and physiological changes – changes that are a consequence of several factors, which include the ageing process, hormonal changes, disease and disorder. The larynx in infancy, as opposed to its mature structure, is very unrefined, with short vocal folds (which determine the high pitch of the infant voice), and is positioned high in the vocal tract. The infant has limited control over the tension of their vocal folds and the air pressure needed for speech, which explains the short bursts of quite loud sound that the infant uses instead of speech! As the baby matures, the vocal folds modify and lengthen, and this continues into adolescence where hormonal changes in the male and female larynx bring about a notable alteration to the size and length of the vocal folds.

The greatest change is seen in the male larynx, where, due to the increase in the size of the larynx and the length of the vocal folds, the outline of the thyroid cartilage, or as it is sometimes known, the Adam's apple, becomes very prominent. These changes lead to the deeper pitch and resonance of the male voice.

Changes in vocal quality as a feature of ageing may occur for a variety of reasons throughout adulthood. In some cases, these are gender-specific: for example, because of female hormonal changes at puberty, during pregnancy and during, peri- and post-menopause. Permanent changes at menopause can also be the result of non–gender specific changes to the structure of the vocal folds because of ageing. As we age, we experience changes in the joints, muscles, blood supply and cartilages, and general degenerative changes. Equally, the larynx and the vocal folds are subject to change and deterioration, leading, in turn, to changes in the quality of the voice. We may hear a change in pitch, lower for women and for men often higher; as the tissues of the vocal folds become thinner and more fragile, reduced lubrication may cause a harsher sound and the voice may be less flexible. As well as changes in the larynx, ageing brings about changes in respiratory function, so a reduction in breath capacity and control will occur, affecting our voices. Importantly, however, the effects and process of ageing are very arbitrary, so ageing does not have to equal vocal deterioration. Health and lifestyle choices make a considerable difference; we all know older people who have retained vibrant and youthful-sounding voices into old age.

How Do You Recognise That Your Voice Is Not Working as Effectively as It Should?

All professional voice users should be aware of early warning signs and symptoms that will alert you to changes both to your voice quality and how your voice 'feels'. If you are using your voice 'a lot', placing a number of demands on it, for example, working for long hours, working in difficult physical and acoustic settings, talking for long periods of time, working while experiencing high levels of stress and tension, working while physically challenged through illness, extreme tiredness or burn out, working without breaks, smoking, drinking or using chemical stimulants in an attempt to 'keep going', you may be compromising your vocal health. Beware of all situations where you are placing considerable demands (what is known as vocal 'loading') on your voice, as a result of both your professional role and your personal circumstances. Feelings of a specific site of tension or generalised tension, rather than an inability to produce voice, may well be the first indicator of vocal misuse, although these symptoms are frequently ignored or seen as simply the result of stress, rather than effortful voicing being recognised as the cause of the physical tension. When voicing is effortful, it is also important to remember that some of that physical tension can come from poor habitual posture and muscular tension.

Tension and effortful voicing may also relate to the difficulty of monitoring your own voice. Without training, it is very difficult to assess volume levels accurately, particularly when there is significant background noise to deal with – a common occurrence for those working in education, or the hospitality, fitness and leisure sectors; often professional voice users, in an effort to increase the loudness of their voice, will try to 'push out' the voice. Fortunately, many professional voice users, while experiencing vocal tension daily, manage to avoid permanent vocal problems, but for some, vocal damage or a reduction in the range and robustness of their voice is the legacy of their professional role.

Early Warning Signs and Symptoms

An awareness of the following 'early warning' signs and symptoms in the vocal health inventory (VHI) is an important ingredient in recognising that your voice is not working as effectively as it should be.

Use the questions and record your answers to the VHI throughout your career, and don't ever dismiss vocal change as 'part of the job'. If you answer yes to one, or any, of the questions and they do not resolve within a period of two to three weeks, go and see a GP or seek medical advice.

Vocal Health Inventory

	Yes	No
Has the problem existed for longer than a month?		
Is it related to a cold or flu?		
Do you have asthma?		
Do you regularly use an inhaler?		
Are you ever short of breath?		
Do you have any recurring viral illness?		
Do you have any allergies?		
Do you regularly have acid reflux?		

	Yes	No
Can you remember anything that might have precipitated the voice problem, such as shouting or arguing or talking over loud background noise?		
Does it follow a pattern?		
Is it a recurring problem? For example, do you notice it occurring after you return to work after a holiday or time off? If you teach, does it occur at the beginning of term or after a half-term break?		
Have you changed – specifically, reduced – the amount of liquid that you drink each day?		
Have you changed your diet recently?		
Do you have any joint or mobility problems?		
Are you making postural changes to accommodate the positioning of your PC?		
Have you reduced heating and lighting in your home office or workspace?		
Could your individual working style be a contributing factor?		
Do you ever get a feeling that you have 'a lump in the throat'?		
Do you feel under professional or personal stress?		
Do you suffer from backache, neck-ache or other physical problems?		
Is there anything you do that helps to reduce the symptoms?		
Is the air quality in your workspace poor?		
Are you working in a poor acoustic environment?		

How Can You Care For and Conserve Your Voice?

For the professional voice user, caring for and conserving your voice is of critical importance and there is a lot that you can do to reduce vocal misuse using simple strategies.

The importance of a mind–body link has already been acknowledged, as we know the mind can affect the body in critical ways. Chapter 3, 'Release of Tension', gives more detail on the link between stress and voice, a critical factor, together with posture and postural issues, in the constellation of factors which can affect voice quality and vocal health. All these elements are essential to voice care and conservation, so it's important to identify any specific issues which may compromise your own voice. Completion of the vocal health inventory (VHI) above, will allow you to identify possible triggers related to vocal change, give you a clearer picture of both the onset and the progression of the changes in your voice quality and, in this way, certain factors, such as aspects of your physical health, your mental health or environmental factors that you may have not recognised as important, may emerge as being implicated in your voice problem.

14

In addition to completing the inventory, spend time thinking around your answers and trying to identify if they fit into a specific category such as stress and anxiety, physical health or environmental problems, as this will allow you to look at useful strategies to introduce into your daily practice.

At the back of this book, in the Appendices section, The Voice Profile (Appendix A) will offer you a profile of many factors that may affect your voice. Responding to the questions will build a personalised, full vocal profile to help you focus your practice. It is a useful tool which will allow you to examine potential areas of vulnerability or challenges that may contribute to your overall vocal quality. It offers you a point-in-time visual profile and may also be used to provide robust visual reinforcement of change over time as you use it to chart change.

Another great way to monitor your vocal use is to use the voice diary, below and (Appendix B), which will give you an overview of your vocal activity on a daily and a weekly basis.

Complete this chart every day using the following scale:

1 = voice rest, 2 = easy voicing, 3 = possible vocal stress, 4 = vocal loading /intense activity. Use the final column to assess voice quality.

Voice Diary

	Morning	Afternoon	Evening	Overall Voice Quality
Monday				
Tuesday				
Wednesday				
Thursday				
Friday				
Saturday				
Sunday				

Medical Referral

Within the UK there are currently considerable demands on doctors and consequent limits on consultation time, so it is entirely possible that voice problems are not always given the attention that they deserve. Identifying specific muscles or ligaments is difficult for all but the most skilled, so a voice problem, arising from muscular tension, may often, for example, be interpreted as a 'sore' throat. Anecdotal reports from professional voice users suggest that they went to their GP for help, but, because they were unable to articulate their voice problem clearly or describe the symptoms with precision, they left the surgery without the advice and help that they sought. On occasions, they complained that the GP's initial response had often been to write out a prescription, belying the true significance of the problem for the professional voice user. If you go and see your GP, bringing a completed vocal health inventory with you will help you to give a precise description of your symptoms, identify possible triggers and trace the progression of the vocal problem. All this provides useful information towards a diagnosis or an onward referral to a specialist speech and language therapist/speech pathologist or an ENT (ear, nose and throat) consultant.

Consultation with an alignment professional may be the most effective way of changing poor habitual posture. In addition to postural issues, it is important to monitor specific work postures which can become habitual and lead to chronic physical and vocal problems. An obvious problem arises from the extensive use of, tablets, laptops and mobile phones, and the significant periods of time spent looking down at these devices inevitably compromises head–neck alignment, sometimes known as 'tech neck'. Today's increased use of technology as a feature of work and leisure encourages individuals to spend considerable time sitting down, leading to a 'slumped' position, sometimes described as 'prawn posture' due to the jutting head position and curved spine. This position constricts the mid-portion of the body, which can lead to rib immobility and reduced breath capacity. Apart from the generalised stiffness and discomfort experienced, there is also an impact on the voice, as alterations in the head–neck–spine relationship can occur.

Changes in the position of the larynx within the pharynx and vocal tract can lead to a 'squeezed' vocal sound. The height differential that often exists when the professional voice user is communicating with their 'audience' – be this between members of the legal profession and their clients, judge and jury; barista and their customers; infant teacher and pupils; actor and audience; DJ and partygoers; clergy and congregation; telesales operator and PC – require the professional voice user to spend sustained periods of time leaning over or looking up. Good posture allows free muscular movement of the voice and respiration; the skeletal structure should support the muscular overlay not vice versa. The most effective standing position involves a long spine in which the natural curves are maintained and the head is balanced on top of the spine in a relaxed and easy manner. Good posture can be achieved equally well in a sitting as in a standing position. The 'sitting' bones may be used in the same way as the feet to support and balance the body. An easy, upright but not rigid spine is important so that the ribcage is free and lifted.

In the same way that you made an inventory of your voice, spend time thinking about your posture.

Posture Inventory

Standing Position	Check your standing position: is the spine long? the pelvis level? Try to prevent it thrusting too far forwards or backwards. Recruit the abdominal muscles to help to maintain this balance. Think of the pelvis as a cup filled with fluid; tilt too far in either direction and the fluid will spill over.
Knees	Check your knee tension: are your knees locked or relaxed? Is weight evenly balanced or are you leaning into one hip and preventing easy supported breathing for speech?
Weight	Is your weight evenly distributed? Weight should be well distributed across both feet, with knee joints flexible and unlocked. Imagine distributing your weight evenly across the triangle formed by the big toe, little toe and heels. Stand with your feet hip-width apart.
Tension	Release any tension in the lower back and abdominal muscles. Standing with arms crossed should be avoided, because breathing is restricted and the body tends to slump forward.
Back	Check that your back feels wide and free of tension. Imagine a space between the base of the ribcage and the abdominal area.
Head	Check your head position: is it well balanced on the top of the spine and free to move in the horizontal and vertical planes with ease? Check that your neck is free and lengthened. Check your eye levels: are they maintaining a forward 'level gaze'?
Shoulders	Thinking of the ears being 'over' the shoulders encourages this new head position. Is it possible to drop your shoulders? How much space is there between the base of your skull and your shoulders?

Returning to this 'physical inventory' will help you note change and progress, and act as a template for healthy and effective posture.

What Lifestyle Choices Should You Avoid If You Are a Professional Voice User?

The voice, when used efficiently and effectively, can 'work' for as long as necessary without presenting problems, providing the voice remains healthy and environmental conditions are reasonable. The list below is not exclusive, but it provides a useful checklist of voice-care recommendations. As a professional voice user, you should try to avoid:

- Talking above loud background noise at social or sports events or above office or machinery noise.
- Smoking or vaping.
- Chemical irritants or dusty conditions.
- Recreational drugs.
- Spicy foods and dairy products that may affect your voice.
- Excessive use of the phone, particularly whilst wearing headphones, as one of your feedback channels is restricted and can result in excessive volume.
- Drinks that cause dehydration, such as tea, coffee and carbonated soda drinks.
- Dry atmospheres.
- Eating a large meal just before going to bed, as it may cause reflux.
- Extensive voice use when emotionally challenged.
- Responding by shouting when upset or anxious.
- Whispering and continuing to talk if your voice is hoarse or you are losing your voice.
- The voice is closely linked with emotion and therefore vulnerable during periods of stress, emotional distress or psychological adversity. Try to avoid extensive vocal loading at such times.

What Lifestyle Choices Should You Actively Encourage/ Engage With, as a Professional Voice User?

Try to:

- Keep up your liquid intake but avoid excess alcohol.
- Be aware of the colour of your urine. Pale-coloured urine indicates a good level of hydration; however some medication and foods, can alter the colour of urine.

- Warm up the voice gently before prolonged speaking.
- Use a humidifier or water spray to moisten the air in centrally heated work rooms, offices or homes.
- If you have conventional radiators at work or at home, a wet towel draped over the radiator effectively humidifies the air.
- Steam when required and particularly before periods of prolonged speaking.
- Remain vigilant in terms of your voice quality.
- Monitor any change in your voice carefully and see a doctor if there is a persistent change in quality.
- If you are experiencing continuing vocal problems, ask your general practitioner (GP) to refer you to an ENT specialist or otolaryngologist.
- If you are prescribed new medication, be aware of any changes to your voice quality or any aspects that might cause irritation to your vocal folds, such as an increased tendency to cough or to feel dehydrated.
- Take preventative measures to reduce the effect of allergies, irritants and changes to the mucosal lining of the nose and lungs, such as asthma.
- If you suffer from hay fever and need antihistamines, be aware that they can cause dryness to your vocal folds.
- Some cold and flu remedies may also 'dry out' the vocal folds, so monitor your voice carefully if taking these over-the-counter medications.
- Try to sip water or swallow if you feel you need to clear your throat, as vigorous throat-clearing will damage your vocal folds.
- Try not to wear tightly fitting clothing that restricts your ability to breathe deeply. Wear layers of clothes so you can respond to the ambient temperature in the workplace and avoid getting too cold or too hot.
- Try and keep physically fit and mobile to maintain effective respiration, reduce areas of tension and encourage vocal flexibility.
- Try to avoid bringing the vocal folds together forcefully as this 'hard attack' at the beginning of words can damage the vocal folds.
- Rest your voice when possible.

The recommendations above are not mandatory, they are principally 'reminders', but they reflect the need to maintain vocal health and efficiency through the prism of the mind–body link, reflecting ways in which you can protect and look after your voice, through attention to your physical, mental and emotional health. Several warrant closer attention and are discussed below.

Postural Problems

In terms of your physical health, chronic pain from postural problems can be just as distressing as acute intermittent pain. Ongoing pain may feel less of a priority but will still affect your vocal quality. As a professional voice user, it is important that you invest in yourself and treat a chronic condition as you would an acute one. Treatment is important – a consultation with a qualified licensed practitioner, such as an osteopath or physiotherapist, or alternatively, working with a qualified Alexander, Feldenkrais, yoga or Pilates teacher can do a lot to improve the situation and prevent vocal problems.

When muscles are damaged, problems in the neck, upper back or shoulder area can easily occur, often initiating an instinctive protective response, which, in turn, leads to discrete changes within the skeletal and muscular frame that will affect your voice.

Liquid Intake

As a rough 'rule of thumb', the more an individual needs to speak, the more they should drink, to keep the vocal folds well-hydrated, to better withstand the intense demands of prolonged voice use. There remains some debate about the amount of fluid to drink daily, but our personal recommendation is to aim for at least 1 to 2 litres of water, bottled or tap, sparkling or still, per day, in addition to that contained in the normal intake of liquid through drinks such as tea and coffee. Tea and coffee have a diuretic effect and some specialists would suggest avoiding tea and coffee completely and substituting herbal teas, but that is a personal choice. The main thing is to maintain moisture within the body at an optimum level. Although drinking cannot directly lubricate the vocal folds, increasing fluid intake will 'top up' the general body fluid level and prevent dehydration. The 'pee pale' maxim is a good rule to follow; urine that is pale in colour indicates a good level of hydration in the body. For those on medication, it is important to remember that some medication can make urine darker in colour and some energy drinks contain riboflavin (vitamin B_2). Like all B vitamins, B_2 is water soluble: your body takes what it needs and discards the rest, so your urine can take on a yellowish tinge; similarly, some food such as beetroot can make urine dark red or dark pink in colour. It is particularly important to keep your fluid level topped up when your vocal folds are in any way vulnerable, to mitigate dryness of the tissue and membrane of the vocal tract. For example, in women of menopausal age, the vocal folds are subject to tissue change, as are those in individuals who are heavy smokers or drinkers. Introduce water gradually, however, as the fluid takes some time to be absorbed and to hydrate the vocal folds. Regular small amounts are a good policy, as if you drink a lot of water quickly, it will just mean you need to go to the loo before it is absorbed, defeating the whole purpose! Hydrate before heavy voice use, as well as during. Workplaces, for example, classrooms, are frequently artificially dry and overheated, yet teachers are often discouraged from drinking during class, not because of regulations imposed by the school but quite prosaically because the result of drinking more means leaving the classroom and going to the bathroom. Concern about the levels of dehydration among pupils, leading to reduced concentration and learning ability, has increased the number of water dispensers in schools. While that focus on hydration is very encouraging, many schools around the UK have a policy of locking school toilets during lesson times, while some even keep them shut in the short breaks between classes. As a result children try to reduce the amount they either eat or drink so that they don't have to use the loo regularly at school and draw attention to themselves (eric.org.uk).

Limiting atmospheric dryness in the workplace may be achieved through the use of a humidifier. Maintaining essential hydration can also be achieved with increased water intake, and using a steamer or steam room, if you have access to one. For those working in the world of fitness and leisure and dealing with air conditioning, pollution, pollens or chlorine, vocal care can be maintained through regular hydration, awareness of the acoustic environment, your vocal loading and regularly steaming. Those working in dusty environments or with irritants such as chemicals, paint, varnish, etc. can try to counteract the irritating effects on the vulnerable larynx by wearing masks, hydrating and steaming.

Steaming

Steaming is a very effective measure, alongside hydration, to prevent vocal damage or misuse. The effects of hydration on the vocal folds have been the subject of several well-regarded studies and many professional voice users steam regularly to keep the vocal folds lubricated and introduce moisture. Increased hydration levels will affect the speed and ease with which the folds move, which has a significant effect on voice quality. In the process of vocalisation, heat is generated by the action of the vocal folds, which increases dryness in the vocal tract and this, in combination with the drying properties of overheated workplaces, makes for a very challenging vocal environment for professional voice users. Steaming introduces moisture into the vocal tract, bathing the vocal folds and counteracting dryness. The tried-and-tested method of inhaling pure steam by leaning over a bowl of boiled water with a towel over one's head, while less than sophisticated, is still very successful; alternatively, steam inhaler cups are available at a very modest price from the high street or online. Another effective method is to have a long shower, remembering to inhale the steam, preferably through both the nose and the mouth, with the added benefit of relaxing the shoulders! Another and perhaps more practical alternative is a portable nebuliser, steam machine or facial steamer, but it is important to remember that these machines must be cleaned out meticulously after use because if they are not properly and hygienically maintained, fungal infections can occur. The use of distilled water is recommended and adding oils or herbal preparations is not advisable. Our professional and personal experience suggests that maximum benefit comes from steaming three times a day for five minutes at a time, but equally it may form part of your warmup. This is particularly important when you are using your voice professionally, but it is also an excellent maintenance tool. Any steam is good steam!

Smoking and Alcohol

The negative effects of smoking on the lungs are well known but perhaps less well known are the negative effects of smoking on the voice. Smoke irritates the respiratory tract and specifically affects the vulnerable vocal folds. Upper respiratory tract irritation and sinus and asthma problems can all be exacerbated by contact with smoky environments. In terms of vocal health, it is important not to smoke, but, if it is impossible to give it up, a reduction in the number of cigarettes smoked is recommended. In the same way that smoking affects the voice, so too do recreational drugs and cannabis; cannabis is associated with changes in the vocal fold appearance, respiratory symptoms and negative lung function changes. Vaping, which at one stage was advocated as safer than smoking tobacco, has been the subject of a recent report advising that hundreds of e-cigarette users have been affected by lung injury. Further research is needed to assess the long-term effects but certainly neither smoking nor vaping is conducive to good vocal health. It is worth considering how much smoke you are being exposed to in a passive way, including the smoke from candles, oil burners and open fires. Although there is an awareness of the relationship between smoking and vocal problems, there is less understanding of the impact of heavy alcohol consumption on the voice; it promotes dryness and irritation of the vocal folds and the vocal tract and can cause haemorrhaging of the small capillaries in the vocal folds, which leaves them additionally vulnerable.

Diet

Various types of food may contribute to thickened saliva and dryness of the mouth. Spicy food, for example, may result in thirst and a dry mouth, whereas foods with high carbohydrate content, or, for some, dairy products, may lead to sticky/thick saliva. A dry mouth and thick secretions will encourage regular throat-clearing, leading to irritation and potential damage to the vocal folds.

Increasing importance has been paid to the effect of gastro-oesophageal reflux disease (GORD) on the general condition of the vocal folds. This is where gastric acid from the stomach is regurgitated, spills into the larynx and bathes the laryngeal mucosa, resulting in irritation to, or inflammation of, the mucosal lining. Any change to the structure of the vocal folds alters their vibratory characteristics, leading to changes in vocal quality. In instances of gastro-oesophageal reflux, the structural change in vocal quality is perceived acoustically as hoarseness. This perception of hoarseness may encourage increased vocal effort to overcome it, which, in turn, compounds the vocal damage.

Digestive problems can occur without an individual being aware of them, so undiagnosed and untreated gastro-oesophageal reflux may well be present and unrecognised unless as part of a full vocal assessment. In instances where gastric reflux has been identified, it is particularly important to avoid eating late at night, to maximise the time spent during the digestive process in a vertical position. The distance between the upper end of the digestive tract and the larynx is approximately 20 cm, so, in a prone position, there is more likelihood for gastric acid to seep into the larynx and cause inflammation and ulceration. One remedy is either to sleep on raised pillows or to raise the height of the head of the bed. Spicy or highly seasoned food, fats, coffee, chocolate, smoking, alcohol and 'gassy' drinks can all aggravate the condition. For professional voice users – in particular, performers who do not want to eat before a performance and may wait until late at night before eating – this can be a problem. It is worth looking at meals and mealtimes and finding a solution that fits with your lifestyle while protecting your voice.

Voice-quality changes associated with the effect of acid reflux on the vocal folds may also occur because of frequent vomiting as a feature of bulimia. Changes in voice quality such as hoarseness, laryngeal pain, vocal fatigue, low pitch, recurring voice loss and phlegm are just some of the symptoms. For those suffering from anorexia nervosa, the process of starvation associated with this disorder can affect most organ systems and the important link between voice and anatomy, physiology, neuroanatomy and psychology leads to vocal change, manifested as either a loss of energy and delivery in the voice, or pain in the lower jaw or problems in chewing and opening or closing of the mouth, affecting both speech and resonance.

Throat-Clearing

Throat-clearing and coughing are often the presenting symptoms of vocal abuse. Many individuals are quite unaware of how often they cough or clear their throat, but the sensation of having a 'frog in the throat' or a 'tickle' is one that is frequently cited by those with voice problems. Unfortunately, the process of 'clearing' the throat in fact has the opposite effect, because in coughing, the vocal folds are brought together with considerable force. In turn, the vocal folds, trying to reduce the ensuing friction, become bathed in mucus, which the individual then feels the need to get rid of, by again clearing their throat, and so the problem continues. One way to limit this vicious circle is to keep a supply of water available and try to sip some water rather than clear the throat; the action of sipping the water appears to limit the need to clear the throat and gradually the problem becomes less acute. If it is not possible to sip water, try instead to swallow, rather than cough.

Hard Attack

'Hard attack', where the vocal folds come together forcefully at the onset of a word beginning with a vowel, is the result of a lack of coordination between taking in breath and starting to speak. It's a very common characteristic of the speech of stressed individuals, where the lack of synchrony between the muscles of breathing and the muscles of speech results in the vocal folds coming together with great force, even, over a period, damaging them. Later in the book there is a chapter on constriction, deconstriction and smooth onset of the note, which includes hard attack with sample exercises. The aim is to encourage a gentler onset of the note and to help the muscles of breath and voice 'remember' the appropriate posture and effort level required. Habitual vocal patterns tend to be strongly entrenched and, therefore, it often takes time to achieve vocal change, but it can be done.

Workplace Infections

There is always a conflict between taking time off work with what appears to be a rather trivial illness, such as a cold or cough, and 'soldiering on', but it is important to remember the damage that can result from 'forcing' the voice even for short periods. Inadequate ventilation contributes to the spread of infection and while there is a convention that 'it's only a cold so I can carry on', it is very important, particularly for professional voice users, not to 'carry on regardless'. Repeated colds are not only debilitating; the first indication of vocal deterioration is frequently cited as occurring after a bad cold. One of the positive outcomes of the COVID-19 pandemic was to discourage those with colds or coughs from going in to work, but the signs are that, as COVID-19 no longer requires isolation, there has been an increase in those disregarding the instruction to remain at home and many are continuing to work when sick.

The recommended vocal management in the case of a cold or respiratory infection is exactly as suggested in the lifestyle-choice advice proposed earlier in the chapter, in short, to:

–   Try and talk as little as possible at work and at home.
–   Take time off work to recover and not infect others.
–   Look after your voice by drinking plenty of water.
–   Steam your voice.
–   Get plenty of rest, and recover.

Cold Remedies

When thinking about 'voice recovery' strategies, it is worth discussing the use of over-the-counter cold remedies, which are designed to eliminate excess moisture and 'dry up' a cold. They are certainly effective but, for professional voice users, the drying effect on the vocal tract (cold remedies contain a high level of caffeine, aspirin and, often, antihistamine), is difficult to reconcile with the vocal demands of their role. If the voice is to be used strenuously and at a high volume over a period, it is advisable to use paracetamol and not aspirin as a remedy for colds and flu. The blood-thinning properties of aspirin can, in some circumstances, contribute to haemorrhaging within the vocal folds.

Sucking throat lozenges and pastilles should be kept to a minimum because they often contain strong dosages of decongestants that can affect the vocal tract. It may be worth noting that mentholated sweets that can be bought over the counter have a very limited effect on the mucosal lining of the nose and, although they may seem to 'clear' the nasal passages and produce saliva, they are often more of a panacea than a cure.

There are, of course, occasions when it is impossible to take time off work and so short-term remedial pharmaceutical measures can provide short-term symptom relief, but long-term use is not advised. Children's cough-and-cold medicines are a preferable option as they don't contain quantities of drying decongestants and caffeine.

It cannot be stated too forcibly that any vocal change persisting for longer than two to three weeks after a cold should be reported to a doctor.

Allergies

Given the increase in over-the-counter medication, it is not uncommon for individuals to self-diagnose and, without seeing a general practitioner, to self-medicate for a variety of conditions including hay fever or common nasal allergies. For many, these remedies work well but for others even a mild nasal decongestant may have a negative impact on the nasal mucosa. Frequent use of sprays for allergies, without advice from a pharmacist or general practitioner as to the pharmaceutical content, is not recommended. Professional voice users should ensure that medication is appropriate and does not have any unwanted side effects that may contribute to vocal attrition.

Physical Fitness

The link between voice and physicality was explored earlier in this chapter but it is important to remember that keeping flexible and mobile is very important, not only for long-term health, but also to underpin and maintain effective respiration, reduce areas of tension and encourage vocal flexibility. Counteracting some of the effects of ageing on the skeletal framework is also to be recommended, because effective and efficient use of the voice is possible into old age, providing that supple rib movement is maintained to support respiration and conserve good spine, pelvis, head and neck alignment.

Yoga and Pilates classes are particularly useful ways to focus on relaxation, breathing and general muscular flexibility. Low-impact aerobics, as well as encouraging physical fitness, will also contribute to increased respiratory function. Keeping fit has the added benefit of releasing endorphins, which influence mood swings and generally are thought to contribute to a feeling of well-being, as well as releasing tension.

For many people who find exercise classes tedious, a creative alternative form of exercise could be a dance class. If formal classes are not of interest, regular walking will improve breathing, strengthen muscles and bone and improve stamina.

Swimming will serve the same function and is particularly good for the muscles involved in respiration; swimming has the added benefit of being totally impact free, which is particularly relevant to those who are older or who may have osteoarthritic or rheumatic joint conditions. The caveat here is that you need to be aware of water purification compounds such as the elements bromine and chlorine that are added to pools, hot tubs/spas and water playgrounds to protect swimmers from the spread of germs. These, and other chemicals, react with organic matter to form hundreds of new chemicals that have been linked with asthma and allergies and can irritate the vocal tract and the vocal folds.

Warming Up

As with any form of intense physical activity, it is important for professional voice users to warm up vocally before beginning work, as once they begin work, they rarely do anything but the vocal equivalent of a marathon. To spend time gently 'stretching' vocally and making contact with the breath is important. Athletes perform an initial series of stretching exercises that gently encourage muscle movement and only then do they start to jog, or run slowly, but never do they run at full stretch as part of their warm-up routine. Voice users should do the same.

A vocal warm-up leads to an increase in blood flow to the muscles and an increase in nutrient deposition to the muscles used. As a result, exercised muscles have increased activation potential and, possibly, improved fine motor control; in effect, they work better. The voice work and warm-up exercises included in this book are recommended as useful preventive measures against vocal misuse. Warming up can be brief and subtle and can be carried out almost anywhere.

Workplace Responsibilities and Strategies

While advising the professional voice user to take responsibility for their own vocal health, it is also important to consider the overall responsibility of the employer. There are practical ways in which individual professional voice users could effect change in their workplace, to create an environment conducive to vocal health. Although it may take time for institutions to 'buy in' to change, if it prevents further vocal misuse, it would be worth 'beating a path' to the relevant door. It is important to work actively with employers to make the working environment less vocally challenging, through adaptation of the physical environment and addressing physical and mental health issues affecting voice production. While some professional voice users are not part of an organisation and work independently, many will have the support of a union or a support group. The following recommendations are offered in the knowledge that while some may not be possible, they might indicate a way forward for the future.

Well-Being

Changes in vocal quality and delivery can be some of the early indicators of mental fragility, demonstrated by lack of engagement, reduced sentence length, limited pitch range, altered intonation patterns and, if mental health issues are related to drug or alcohol addiction, a hoarse or husky vocal quality.

The following recommendations consider institution-wide factors that can mitigate vocal misuse, under the overarching categories of environmental health, physical health and mental health.

Environmental Health Recommendations

- Ensure that the workplace is kept at an even temperature.
- Ensure that windows and doors fit properly to avoid pollution and to maintain a consistent temperature in the room.
- Make sure that cleaning of the workplace is efficient and effective.
- Check that heating and ventilation systems are regularly serviced and properly maintained.
- Ensure that adjoining grounds in city or town centres, or near main roads, are regularly inspected for high levels of dust and debris.
- Monitor noise levels in open areas such as halls, walkways or recreation areas.
- If necessary, install sound baffles in open areas or in those near to large, noisy spaces.
- Provide acoustic material to reduce the level of sound reverberation in large rooms or practice halls.

Physical Health Recommendations

- If appropriate, encourage a voice-free period for a minimum of 30 minutes each day.
- Make sure that there are accessible free water dispensers throughout the workplace.
- If possible, provide a 'quiet' room for occupational voice users when off duty.
- Workplace policies should encourage a yell- or shout-free environment.
- Encourage a 'no talking above high levels of background noise' policy.
- Make sure protective masks are worn when working in dusty environments.
- Provide a humidifier for those working in dusty or polluted spaces.
- Discourage professional voice users from taking on extracurricular duties if they have a throat infection, laryngitis or an upper respiratory disorder.
- Provide occupational voice users with portable speech amplifiers when speaking to large groups.

Occupational health and safety policies provide support during times of mental fragility; however, for some professional voice users, mental health issues and the accompanying stress and tension will affect not only the individual's emotional state but also their ability to use their voice effectively, so they will need additional support.

Mental Health Recommendations

- If possible, encourage adherence to working-time regulations.
- Avoid setting unrealistic deadlines.
- Staff policy should encourage regular checks to see how much pressure colleagues are under.
- Encourage staff to take a statutory lunch break.
- Provide a 'safe space' where staff can go if they need to 'decompress'.

Continued

- Provide designated listening support for staff who are struggling with mental health issues and ensure follow-through.
- Provide staff with training for their mental well-being through cognitive behavioural therapy (CBT) or mindfulness training.
- Encourage behaviour-management training.
- Provide communication-skills training.

2 | Posture

Introduction

Posture is the way we position our body in space. There are two types of posture: dynamic posture is how you hold yourself when you are moving, like when you are walking, running or bending over to pick up something. Static posture is how you hold yourself when you are not moving, when, for example, you are sitting, standing or sleeping. In this chapter the focus will principally be on static posture.

The connection between posture and voice is a crucial aspect of effective communication. Our posture not only influences how we are physically perceived but also affects the quality and projection of our voice. The alignment and position of our spine, head and shoulders impact the resonance, clarity and power of our vocal delivery. When we adopt an upright and open posture, with the spine elongated and the chest expanded, we allow for optimal breath support and vocal production. Conversely, slouching or hunching can restrict the flow of breath and compress the vocal apparatus, leading to a weaker and less impactful voice. By consciously aligning our posture and incorporating proper breathing techniques, we can unlock the full potential of our voice, projecting confidence, resonance and clarity. This chapter explores the intricate relationship between posture and voice, offering practical exercises and techniques to enhance vocal performance and ensure our posture supports effective vocal communication.

Why Does Posture Matter to Me?

Why is posture important when the focus of this book is on your voice? In the previous chapter we looked at the importance of the mind–body link in terms of our voice and outlined the critical role that posture and postural issues hold in terms of caring for and conserving our voices.

DOI: 10.4324/9781003361114-3

'Sit up straight', 'Shoulders back!', 'No slouching!' Sound familiar? Undoubtedly, you will at some point have wondered ... 'Why does it matter?' 'How does it affect my voice?' Whoever it may have been who badgered you about 'good posture' was likely more concerned with how you looked rather than how you sounded. Appearing alert, attentive and 'professional' are indeed important aspects in sharing your message effectively. Posture can also alter how you feel about yourself in relation to communicating. There has been a lot of interest in the concept of power posing in recent years and the effect posture can have on your mood and self-esteem. If you haven't yet seen Amy Cuddy's TED Talk (2012) on 'power poses', it's worth a watch. Whilst there has been much debate about the science behind power posing, many people find it a powerful tool.

Consider for a moment the posture of defeat and that of victory, as well as the postures for well-being and depression. In defeat, the shoulders round forward, the spine slumps, the head drops and the eye level lowers. All this leads to a reduced space between the hips and ribs and results in diminished breath capacity. Feeling confident and positive on the other hand lengthens the spine and opens out the chest. The weight is now balanced, and the head is poised on the top of the spine, allowing the eye level to lift and open peripherally. There is also considerable space between the hips and lower ribs, allowing for breath to be full and low.

So, we know positive, healthy posture makes you look 'ready and willing' and makes you feel good, but, possibly more importantly, posture lays the foundation for effective and powerful voice and communication.

As we will often discuss in this book, there are many elements that need to be combined to use our voice successfully in the workplace. Thinking about this dependency and interdependency of several different factors in producing, sustaining and varying our voice to communicate effectively, we need to recognise the close connection between our voice and our physical condition. While posture is often discussed in terms of nonverbal communication – outlining the effect on the message of a closed posture, lowered eye levels and a general appearance of defensiveness reducing the effectiveness of a message, and an open posture having a positive effect on your audience – what is less often discussed is the effect on the voice of habitual slouching, hunching, neck jutting, misalignment and inactivity.

Poor posture can affect the quality, volume, pitch and resonance of your voice. When we are free from tension and our spine is in alignment, we can support our body without undue effort or stress, allowing free muscle movement which, in turn, improves our breathing and lets our voice function without restriction.

Sitting all day at a computer, or on your phone, feeling overwhelmed by work or the normal stresses and strains of life, can lead to slumped shoulders, a rounded back and a generally more contained, introverted posture, with accumulated tension in the shoulders, neck and jaw and consequences for your voice. Finding alignment, strength and ease in your posture is fundamental for effective and dynamic voice use.

What Is Posture, Exactly?

Most of us are born with 'good' posture. Work, clothing, use of technology, mental health, stress, fear, injury, illness, unconscious habits and life in general can change that.

Alignment is the key to a healthy and pain-free, vocally enhancing posture. The aim is to be flexible and fluid and without constriction, so as to discover the wonderful synchrony of breath, speech and movement.

Adults seldom correct or change the habits of adolescence; postural and movement patterns have been set and these continue to provide a pattern for adult life. Even when trying to absorb new patterns of alignment, the body 'prefers' the old pattern because it identifies and is comfortable with it, often rejecting the new posture as 'wrong'. For this reason, it is a very good idea to seek advice and to work with the help of an 'outside eye'. Once again, there are many people who can help, from physiotherapists, osteopaths, chiropractors, sports therapists, Alexander Technique and Feldenkrais teachers to Qi Gong, Tai Chi, Pilates and yoga instructors.

The exercises later in this chapter will give you the tools to assess your posture and the ability to adjust it when you notice it's not optimal. Many of the exercises will ask you to stand; however, it's still possible to optimise vocal function and effectiveness if you are not able to stand for long periods – if, for example, you are a wheelchair user or your job is mostly conducted in a sitting rather than a standing position. Remember, 'good' posture is not only important for preventing back pain, but it can also help improve your breathing, digestion and overall well-being.

How Can We Achieve 'Good' Posture?

'Good' is a subjective word; we can perhaps think of 'good' as meaning 'healthy' or 'helpful'. We might consider these elements of posture to be most conducive to easy and effective voice. We maybe need to start with understanding what doesn't work.

Unhelpful Posture

An off-balance, closed posture will reduce your ability to keep your ribcage relaxed and lifted to allow a virtual 'space' between the base of the ribcage and the abdominal area, so you can breathe more deeply.

If your habitual posture leads to tension, your muscles may end up over-working and this may lead to vocal tiredness or 'strain'. Lack of breath support results in more tension and the vocal result will often be tight, lacking engagement and volume.

If your spine is out of alignment, muscular stress will result, so keep your knee joints and thigh muscles relaxed when standing, and with your feet slightly apart. The 'sitting' bones, or ischium bones, serve the same function as the feet in terms of carrying the weight of the body when sitting. Remember to use these bones to provide adequate support and balance when sitting and check that your seating at work provides adequate support, as uncomfortable seating not only imposes back strain but also exerts pressure on the abdomen.

Breathing and voice production are impaired if the ribcage is 'slumped' or constricted, so keep your ribcage relaxed and lifted to allow a virtual 'space' between the base of the ribcage and the abdominal area.

If your eye levels are too high or too low it will affect the positioning of the head and may lead to neck tension, so keep your head well balanced, with the crown of your head the highest point, so that it can move effortlessly on the horizontal and vertical planes.

Poor neck alignment will create tension in the vocal tract, so by keeping your head level you will prevent a pull on the muscles of your neck and undue tension on your larynx.

Feeling shy, anxious or like an imposter can often make an individual avoid eye contact and adopt a lowered head position. This has a domino effect: the sternum becomes depressed, resulting in a lack of openness in the ribs and pressure on the abdomen.

A depressed sternum reduces the ability to achieve more than a very shallow breath, which in turn produces a monotonous vocal quality.

A rigidly fixed focus tends to correspond to a locked neck, clenched jaw and stiffly held shoulders, leading to an enormous amount of unuseful tension. This posture limits peripheral vision; the eyes do not scan, but look fixedly ahead, and can give an impression of aggression and rigidity. Tension limits the free exchange of breath and results in a vocal quality that is often strident, lacks flexibility and warmth and can even appear aggressive.

When the knees are locked, a lower abdominal tension is created, which impacts the breath.

Helpful Posture

A well aligned, open posture maximises your breath capacity and control and encourages warmth, energy and volume into your voice. The most effective standing posture involves a long spine in which the natural curves are maintained, with the head balanced in a relaxed and easy manner.

The pelvis should be level, with weight balanced over both feet, with your feet hip-width apart.

Shoulders should be in a neutral position, relaxed and lowered, counteracting any tendency to overcorrect or pull backwards; this will decrease any tension in the upper chest area.

Eye levels should be on the horizon to allow for a fuller breath and variety in the voice.

A 'long' and 'wide' alignment encourages peripheral vision; the individual can function within their world in an aware and integrated manner.

An area of the body that is not immediately associated with voice is the knee area. Most individuals brace their knees to steady themselves, particularly when they are under stress. Those unused to the experience of public speaking or performing often remark, 'My knees were shaking' or 'I went weak at the knees', which illustrates the body–mind connection and the ways in which tension and nervousness can manifest. We encourage you to remain aware of whether you are bracing or 'locking' your knees, and instead think about the knees being 'soft', unlocked and flexible as you stand in an open and balanced way.

Self-Assessment and Building Self-Awareness

How easy is it for you to assess your own body, breath and voice, in terms of posture? It is often very much more difficult that you might think. Try this exercise:

- Looking in a full-length mirror or videoing yourself, stand in your habitual posture, observing your feet, chin and eye height, neck length and shoulder height.

- Now gradually move from this posture by 'internally' adjusting the posture into a more balanced and open position, with the weight over both feet; drop the arms to the sides, lengthen the spine, open the rib cage, lower the shoulders and balance the head on the top of the spine. Try to 'sense' the muscles releasing and the body realigning. Avoid a sudden external correction. Notice where the eye level is now. Do not overcorrect.

In growing self-awareness around your body, which if any, of the following statements apply to you? Ask yourself the following questions and use the answers according to your current postural health. Consider this a reflective journal and think about the areas that you would benefit from improving and why.

Posture Self-Awareness

Do I notice any tension in my abdominal muscles?	
Does my back feel 'open' and 'wide'?	
Am I standing with weight balanced on both feet?	
Is my spine slumped or lengthened?	
Is there length in the back of the neck? Is my neck free and flexible?	
Do I have an old or new injury that may be contributing to poor postural habits?	
Can I sense space between the base of my skull and my shoulders? How much space?	
How slumped or upright is my posture when sitting? Do I sit in a supported and lengthened position at meetings or while relaxing?	
Are my shoulders relaxed or released to their natural level?	
Can my arms hang loosely from my shoulders with my hands and fingers free and relaxed?	
Do I find myself thrusting my head forward when reading or looking at technology?	
Is my head balanced and free to nod up and down with ease?	
Do I often suffer from back pain, stiff shoulders or stiff neck?	
Am I comfortable whilst working on my PC or at my workstation?	
Is my PC well positioned in terms of its height and is my chair at the right height?	
Do I remain in one position for long periods of time either when working or relaxing?	
Do I have problems with mobility due to health issues?	
Do I carry heavy equipment as part of my work?	
Do I work in extremes of temperature which I cannot alter?	
Is my home extremely cold much of the time?	
Do I need to lift or physically support family members, including small children, daily?	

Keep your answers on file and then you can return to this questionnaire in a month or six months; perhaps time spent using the exercises in this book might result in different answers.

Making changes to habitual and long-held postural settings will take time and may initially feel uncomfortable, as new 'muscle patterns' need to be established before they become familiar.

Making Change

Entering a situation with excessive physical confidence carries risks, as it might be interpreted as a signal of physical aggression by your audience. It is important always to be aware of the subtext of the language of your posture.

- If posture is slumped it might suggest a lack of confidence.
- If eye contact is not made, it might suggest insincerity or disengagement with the group.

Neither of these may be the case but could be interpreted negatively. While perceptions can be inaccurate, once established, they can be difficult to change.

- Your work may require you to perform repetitive and habitual postures; it is worth remembering, if needed, to bend at the knees rather than leaning towards people from the waist, wear comfortable shoes and monitor your posture during the day. If you are working at a computer all day create some sort of habit – an alert in your diary, or a note on your keyboard – to check in and assess your posture. Is it possible to find some length in your spine? Are you able to raise your eye level? The optimal position to strive for is a level gaze with peripheral vision.
- If during a presentation, speaking in an interview or delivering to an audience you are required to use a microphone, try to avoid 'poking' the head forward to direct the voice into the microphone. This will affect your vocal quality and detract from your ability to engage your audience. You can maintain an open posture whilst holding the microphone at a short distance from your mouth. Think about how you might spread your fingers out in an enthusiastic wave; the distance from thumb to little finger is generally a good distance from mouth to mic (approximately 18 to 30 cm). An advantage to this technique is that you are unlikely to hold the microphone too near your mouth, which distorts sound and can create unpleasant feedback and 'popping' on plosive consonants.

Exercises to Encourage 'Good' Posture

It is important to find someone who is qualified to work with the body therapeutically; practical help and advice need to be directed towards recognising the uniqueness of each individual and fulfilling individual needs. For this reason, the advice on alignment offers general principles, but working with a teacher/trainer in a 'hands-on' manner is strongly advised, if possible. If you experience any pain or discomfort with the exercises, stop the exercise and consult with a healthcare professional.

Exercises to Increase Spinal Movement and Achieve Flexibility of the Ribcage

N.B. Carefully watch out for neck tension, which can sometimes occur with these exercises.

EXERCISE ONE

- Stand with feet slightly apart and weight evenly distributed. The knees should be relaxed, slightly bent but flexible enough to allow for movement. Check that the pelvis is balanced and the thighs and calves are loose.
- Raise the arms above the head but do not extend them to their limit.
- Interlace fingers quite firmly, with the backs of the hands pointing towards the ceiling.
- Maintain this position but reverse the hands so that, still interlaced, they are now palms upward to the ceiling.
- Now begin to lift the hands towards the ceiling feeling the lift of the ribcage. You can imagine 'walking' the hands towards the ceiling by alternating raising each wrist slightly higher towards the ceiling, 'step by step'.
- Repeat this procedure three or four times. Again, notice the space between the lower ribs and the hips.

EXERCISE TWO

– Stand with the feet slightly apart and weight evenly distributed. The knees should be relaxed, slightly bent but flexible enough to allow them to move backwards and forwards. Check that the pelvis is balanced and the thighs are loose.

– Raise first one arm and then the other, with the heel of the hand extended towards the ceiling.

– Straighten the arms and gently punch, with alternate hands, the air above.

– Feel the ribcage move upward and away from the abdomen with this arm movement.

EXERCISE THREE

This exercise should be repeated 10 times initially, increasing to 20 times.

– Place the arms at mid-sternum level, in the classic starting position for swimming breaststroke. It is important that the shoulders are not raised and that the elbows are level.

– Breathe in and, as the breath comes into the body, move the hands forward and then out to the sides, keeping the bend in the elbow. At this point, movement in the ribcage can be felt as it moves slightly upward and outward.

– Breathe out through the mouth, and as you exhale, the hands return to the starting position.

EXERCISE FOUR

Repeat this exercise four times, pausing between repetitions and building up the number of repetitions as you grow more comfortable. Be careful not to breathe in and out too quickly.

– Standing in a balanced manner, raise the arms to mid-sternum level, as if holding a large beach ball, with fingertips touching and arms curved.

– Exhale through the mouth.

- Slowly sweep the arms out to the sides as you breathe in through nose. As the ribcage expands, the breath flows inwards.

- Ensure that your shoulders are relaxed and there is space between your shoulders and ears, feel an expansion in the abdomen as you breathe in.

EXERCISE FIVE

This exercise should be done with a Swiss ball, cushion or rolled-up towel, either lying or sitting. The exercise helps to stretch and release tension in the muscles of the upper back, shoulders and chest. It also encourages spinal mobility and can provide relief from stiffness or discomfort caused by prolonged sitting. Remember to listen to your body and modify the intensity of the stretch based on your comfort level.

- If lying, lie on your back and wrap your arms around the ball. Bring the knees up to touch the ball and feel your back open. If sitting, sit on a chair with the ball in your lap, wrap both arms around the ball and hug it.

- Now lie frontwards over the ball so that the lower and upper back opens. This may be followed by a floor exercise lying backwards, with your arms out to the sides, over the ball so that the chest opens.

- If you wish to perform this exercise in the workplace and don't have props, sit up straight in a chair with your feet flat on the ground.

- Take a deep breath in and, as you exhale, drop your chin towards your chest and gently draw your shoulder blades forward, bring your arms in front of your body and cross them over your chest. Give yourself a hug by gently placing your hands on the upper arms. Maintain this hugging position and take a few deep breaths, allowing the stretch to deepen with each exhale.

Exercises to Release the Shoulders

Most of us hold physical and emotional tension in the shoulders and this can very easily affect the voice because of their proximity to the larynx. Posture is a contributing factor in shoulder tension, as is being cold and carrying heavy bags and equipment. Identifying shoulder tension and remembering to relax the shoulders regularly throughout the day by shrugging them and realigning the head and neck will make a difference.

EXERCISE ONE

This should be done several times a day, whenever the shoulders become tense.

- Lift the shoulders up to the ears, hold this position for five seconds and then release. Repeat twice more.
- Then lift the shoulders in a brief shrug, making sure that they drop fully to a released position. Repeat twice more.
- Allow the breath to be released each time the shoulders drop.

EXERCISE TWO

- Lift the shoulders up to the ears, and then move them backwards, bringing the shoulder blades towards each other.
- Hold them in this position briefly, before releasing them and moving them forward and upward again.

Continue the cycle for at least six rotations.

EXERCISE THREE

- Raise both shoulders to their highest level, shortening the distance between chin and shoulders
- Hold them in this position for several seconds and then release them; from this position release them further to ensure that no residual tension persists.
- Repeat this exercise, but this time alternate the shoulders.

At the end of each exercise, check in a mirror that the shoulders are level and relaxed in a neutral position. Watch that they are not pulled back in a stiff manner.

EXERCISE FOUR

Start with the feet slightly apart. Look straight ahead, shrugging the shoulders up and down ten times.

- With the shoulders close to the ears, try moving them in a smooth, circular, gradual motion backwards, downwards, forwards and back to the starting position.

- Repeat this ten times and then change direction; starting, as before, with the shoulders close to the ears, roll them forwards first.

- Repeat the sequence first with one shoulder and then with the other.

EXERCISE FIVE

- Stand with the feet slightly apart and both arms stretched out to the side with palms facing upward.

- Rotate the arms forwards so that the palms are facing down, then backwards to face upward again.

- Repeat this ten times.

Exercises for Neck Release and Head Alignment

EXERCISE ONE

- Gently allow the chin to drop forwards onto the chest, feeling the extension of the back of the neck. Do not force or push the chin into this position but allow it to drop without any undue tension being felt at the back of the neck.

- Raise the chin slowly and gradually until the head is balanced easily on the neck and vertebral column. The crown of the head should be the highest point. Ensure that there is no overcorrection resulting in the chin being raised.

EXERCISE TWO

– Imagine the head is attached to the neck by a ball-bearing which is free to swivel. Taking care not to overextend, feel the length in the neck and allow the head and neck to bob and rotate freely like a marionette.

EXERCISE THREE

– Imagine there is a piece of chalk at the end of the nose and gently 'draw' a figure of eight, either vertical or horizontally, feeling the 'freedom' at the base of the skull. If this concept proves difficult, it can be helpful to visualise the 'nodding dog', where the dog's head moves up and down and from side to side.

Regular exercising will enhance your posture, your habits, and release tension which may be limiting you and affecting your voice.

Suggestions and Strategies

It is easy to fall into unhelpful patterns which may be holding you back in terms of breath capacity, easy voicing or physical discomfort, particularly if you sit in front of your computer for long periods of time. Use this checklist as a reminder of what will help in terms of breath, tension release and voicing until it becomes instinctive.

Sitting Checklist

– Are you sitting in a supportive chair? Choose a chair with good lumbar support or use a lumbar pillow.
– Are your buttocks evenly distributed and central on the chair?
– Is the height of your chair adjusted so that your feet can rest comfortably on the ground and your knees are at a 90-degree angle? Try and support your feet, to avoid placing undue tension and stress into your knees, thighs and psoas muscles; it might be worth using a footstool. This may help distribute your weight evenly and take pressure off your back.

- Is your back long and are your shoulders relaxed? Can you find more space between your shoulders and your ears?
- Is your computer screen at the right height? The top of your computer screen should be at or slightly below eye level.
- Are you aware of how you habitually use your phone? Aim to bring your phone to your eyes rather than your eyes to your phone.

Recommendations for Posture at Work

- Keep a reminder on your computer or set an alarm on your phone to take a moment to be aware of your posture a couple of times a day.
- Request an assessment of your computer set-up from a physiotherapist or occupational therapist or ergonomic specialist.
- Assess your home set-up – can you make some changes?
- Ergonomic chair: Invest in an ergonomic chair that provides proper lumbar support and can be adjusted to fit your body comfortably. Ensure that the chair allows your feet to rest flat on the floor and your knees to be at a 90-degree angle.
- Desk height: Adjust the height of your desk or workstation so that your forearms are parallel to the floor when typing or using the mouse. This helps maintain a neutral position for your wrists and reduces strain.
- Computer monitor: Position your computer monitor at eye level, directly in front of you. This prevents you from tilting your head up or down, promoting a more neutral neck position.
- Keyboard and mouse placement: Keep your keyboard and mouse close to your body, allowing your elbows to rest comfortably at your sides. This helps minimise strain on the shoulders and arms.
- If you are using a laptop, it can be helpful to invest in a separate keyboard so that you can raise the laptop to eye level but keep the keyboard at a good distance.
- Monitor distance: Sit at a comfortable distance from the computer screen, typically around an arm's length away. This ensures that you can see the screen clearly without straining your eyes or leaning forward.

Continued

- Lighting: Ensure proper lighting in your workspace to reduce eye strain, thrusting of the head and 'tech neck'. Avoid excessive glare or harsh lighting that may cause you to squint or strain your eyes and create excessive tension.

- Breaks and movement: Take regular breaks from prolonged sitting. Incorporate movement and stretching exercises into your routine to prevent stiffness and maintain flexibility.

- Posture reminders: Use visual cues or reminders, such as sticky notes or alarms, to prompt yourself to assess and adjust your posture throughout the day.

- Supportive accessories: Consider using supportive accessories like a lumbar pillow or cushion to provide additional support to your lower back, or a keyboard cushion for your wrists.

- Regular body awareness: Develop a habit of regularly checking in with your body and being mindful of your posture. Adjust as needed to maintain proper alignment.

- Use voice-controlled devices: Take advantage of voice-controlled devices or virtual assistants that allow you to perform tasks without straining your neck by looking down at screens.

- Adjust font sizes and display settings: Increase the font size and adjust the display settings on your devices to make the text more readable without the need to strain or squint.

- Are you taking breaks? It's important to take a break from sitting every 30 minutes or so. Stand up, stretch and move around. One recommendation for increasing vocal effectiveness at work is to think about using a break to focus on a brief internal body scan and check how you are feeling. Are you dehydrated, are you poorly seated in terms of your screen? We've included some suggestions in the section below that you can use to make your work situation more posture friendly and therefore more vocally friendly. It's useful to check in with this list regularly as it's very easy to get caught up with the daily 'busyness' of work and fail to acknowledge postural pitfalls.

- Are you moving? Exercise regularly: Regular exercise, especially exercises that strengthen your core and back muscles, can help improve your posture. Counteract the negative effect of sitting for long periods by getting up and changing your position every half an hour, even if only for a minute.

A Quick Note on the Psoas Muscle

It might be useful to spend a short time looking at the psoas muscle, reminding ourselves what it is and its relevance and importance in terms of our posture. The psoas muscle is among the most significant muscles that overlie the vertebral column. It is a long muscle on either side of the vertebral column and the brim of the lesser pelvis. The psoas is a deep muscle that originates from the lower back and pelvis and extends up to the inside surface of the upper part of the femur. The psoas tendon can get inflamed from overuse, muscle tightness and muscle weakness, resulting in a painful hip condition.

Symptoms of psoas muscle inflammation:

– Tension and pain in the lower back, hips, buttocks, pelvis or groin.
– Lower-back spasms.
– Snapping hip syndrome.
– Radiating pain down the leg.
– Sciatica.
– Lumbar-disc problems.
– Limping.

In the long run, maintaining a good posture at the desk can have significant benefits for the voice. By reducing unnecessary tension and strain, it helps prevent vocal fatigue, hoarseness and potential vocal damage. It also promotes overall vocal health and longevity, enabling the person to maintain a clear, strong and sustainable voice over time. Therefore, prioritising proper posture and ergonomic set-up when working at the computer is essential for preserving and enhancing vocal performance and well-being.

Quick Posture Prep Before Delivering a Speech, Pitch or Presentation

This exercise can be done in under a minute and helps you establish a grounded and confident presence before speaking. Remember to adapt it to your specific needs and preferences.

– Take a moment to relax your body and breathe deeply. Inhale slowly through your nose and exhale fully through your mouth.
– Imagine a string attached to the crown of your head, gently pulling you upward. Feel your spine lengthening and your body aligning.

Continued

- Roll your shoulders back and down, opening up your chest and creating space in your upper body.
- Soften your facial muscles and relax your jaw. Allow your face to express a calm and confident demeanour.
- Bring your awareness to your breath. Take a few deep breaths, feeling the expansion of your abdomen and the gentle rise and fall of your chest.
- As you continue breathing, imagine energy flowing through your body from head to toe, grounding you and filling you with a sense of inner strength.
- Take a moment to mentally affirm your confidence and readiness to speak.
- When you're ready, use this "relaxed but ready" quality to begin speaking.

Posture on the Move

If driving through busy traffic, in a queue or on public transport use the time to counteract the build-up of tension by lifting and releasing the neck and shoulders when an opportunity arises, e.g. at traffic lights or at a standstill. Good driving posture should include support to the lower spine, so as not to impose tension on the shoulder girdle and the maintenance of a released head and neck position. It is hard to dissipate tension, particularly if you experience it when going to work. Without dealing with it, the physical effects can remain for the rest of the working day.

Sound Bite

For the breath to flow in and out of the body to maximum effect, it is important to stand in a balanced and open manner, with the knees released and gently flexed (imagine that the big toe, little toe and heel form a supportive triangle) and the spine lengthened and the back widened, figuratively speaking.

3 | Relaxation and Release of Tension

Introduction

Most of us perform at our best when we are relaxed. We are more likely to deliver well, network easily or interview successfully if we can find a tension-free approach. This is also true of playing sport or cooking for friends. When it comes to our voice and speech, relaxation matters. The relationship between voice, emotion and physical state has long been known. In *The Voice of Neurosis*, written in 1954, Moses' thesis is that 'Voice is the primary expression of the individual, and even through voice alone, the neurotic pattern can be discovered' (Moses 1954). Moses identified the link between an individual's voice and their psychological state. Today this link is better known as a psychogenic voice disorder – where the vocal folds are essentially normal in structure and movement but the cause of the problem is psychological in origin.

Relaxation does not, however, mean being in a passive state; it is possible to be relaxed while moving, speaking and performing tasks. In the context of vocal use, relaxation implies the efficient use of muscular energy without the interference and restriction of additional non-productive energy such as an increase of tension. Work on relaxation is enormously beneficial in voice work, not only in reducing muscular and physiological tension but also in the accompanying psychological gains that arise from a reduction in stress and anxiety.

Breath support and control, volume, projection and vocal quality may all be affected by undue tension. A degree of muscular tension/tonicity is essential to support the body and to initiate and control movement. Excessive tension, however, affects smooth muscle coordination and will ultimately lead to tiredness, strain and poor postural habits. For some individuals, postural tension may arise from long-term, habitual and repetitive movement patterning in occupational roles: for example, dentists hunched over patients all day, hairdressers maintaining certain positions for prolonged periods with arms

DOI: 10.4324/9781003361114-4

above shoulder height, call-centre workers seated at a computer dealing with unhappy customers, administrative roles that rely on extended periods in front of a computer; in fact, any occupations that limit the opportunity to change position throughout the day.

Working from home can potentially result in people moving less, as they are not required to commute to and from work, which may have involved walking, cycling or other physical activity. Additionally, when working from home, people may spend more time sitting in front of a computer or on the couch, sitting in awkward positions which aren't supportive or may create tension.

Nervous tension, often unconscious, which arises from anxiety or conflict has the same effect on the muscles, interrupting the smooth integrated functioning of the vocal mechanism. You might notice feeling tight or tense; you may recognise that your jaw is clenched or your shoulders rise when in a difficult conversation.

'Relaxed readiness' is a term used by actors to describe a state of being both physically and mentally prepared for a performance while also maintaining a sense of calm and relaxation. It refers to the ability to be present in the moment, without physical tension or anxiety which can interfere with an actor's ability to perform successfully. It is useful for us to consider a similar relaxed, but ready, state, as professional voice users approaching any workplace task. Imagine approaching the lectern at a conference feeling ready (prepared, practised, warmed up) and relaxed (calm, present, able to make vocal and physical choices). Achieving relaxed readiness requires a combination of physical and mental preparation, warming up the body, vocal exercises and engaging in relaxation techniques.

Why Does Relaxation and Release of Tension Matter to Me?

As we said in the last chapter, breath support and control, volume, projection and vocal quality may all be affected by undue tension. Stress, anxiety and muscular tension within our personal, social and work environment can affect and compromise the way in which we use and produce our voice. Personality characteristics, emotional reactions to acute or chronic life stressors and emotional disturbances, such as chronic anxiety, affect the movement of our vocal folds through increased levels of intrinsic and extrinsic laryngeal muscle tension.

Stress responses, such as anxiety and depression or physical symptoms, are often the result of chronic demands such as professional or personal worries.

In any discussion of stress, it is important to try and define what is understood by the term 'stress', since 'tension', 'anxiety' and 'pressure' are words that can be, and are, used synonymously with 'stress'. Stress can be seen as both negative and positive. It affects everyone but not to the same extent, and it is not necessarily confined to those with, for example, heavy occupational responsibilities. Stress is not an illness; it is a state. Pressure and stress are different, even though they are sometimes used interchangeably. Pressure can be positive and a motivating factor, often used to help us fulfil our goals and perform better, but when demands become greater than our ability to cope, then we experience stress. Stress occurs as a natural reaction to too much pressure, but it also provides a necessary and essential warning sign of impending danger or that something is wrong.

In the UK the Health and Safety Executive (HSE) recorded figures for 2021/22 of more than 1.8 million people who were off work suffering from work-related ill health cases, both new and longstanding, with the primary causes of ill health being work-related stress, depression or anxiety (914,000), musculoskeletal disorders (477,000) and exposure to coronavirus at work (123,000). Around 30.8 million working days were lost due to stress, depression and anxiety. Similar figures can be found worldwide. For occupational voice users, stress is often cited as a considerable element in their work, notably evidenced by teachers in the UK giving stress as a reason for their series of strikes in 2023.

Thinking about your levels of stress and anxiety, how many, if any, of the following statements apply to you?

Levels of Stress and Anxiety Checklist

	Rarely	Sometimes	Often
I worry a lot.			
I consider myself to be a tense person.			
I have had a lot of stress in the past year.			
I feel unable to cope.			
I feel stressed by aspects of my life.			
I feel that in general there are too many demands placed on me.			
I get angry.			
I get into arguments with friends and work colleagues.			
I find it very difficult to wind down and relax.			
I have feelings of dread and/or panic without cause.			

If you answered 'often' to one or more of these statements, this may be affecting your relaxation, muscle tension and ability to use your voice with ease. Think about ways in which you could reduce your levels of stress and anxiety, perhaps by getting some professional support from the human resources department at work or from counselling support.

Stress and Exhaustion

As we've already mentioned, for some, stress is stimulating and exciting, whereas for others a similar degree of stress is insupportable and can result in sleeplessness, depression, anxiety attacks or a vocal problem. Whether stress is stimulating or insupportable, both responses activate (as part of the fight-or-flight response) the release of large amounts of adrenaline and noradrenaline, which help individuals to maintain a high level of activity, giving that extra 'buzz' that people experience when working at full stretch. However, unusually high levels of noradrenaline ultimately lead to an abrupt loss of energy, often accompanied by an overwhelming feeling of exhaustion unrelated to physical effort.

Our individual response to stress and tension cannot be absolutely anticipated; we can predict areas of 'danger', but we do not know what the effects will be. Some professional voice users demonstrate amazing vocal resilience for years, only to find that their voice 'disappears' without any apparent increase in vocal loading. Others experience mild vocal symptoms for years that never get any worse or become unmanageable. In terms of symptoms, however, very similar symptoms emerge as common denominators – a reduction in vocal flexibility, vocal range, vocal loudness and ease of voicing – all leading to an erosion of the concept of self. The inability to express feelings, emotions and thoughts properly because of voice loss is very alienating.

The Effect of Stress on the Voice

Physiological changes occur as the body, responding to the threat of stress, prepares for action by triggering the 'fight-or-flight' response and releasing several adrenal hormones into the body. The effect of these hormones leads to:

– Difficulty in swallowing.
– Aching neck and backache.
– Muscle tension and muscle pain.

- Tiredness and fatigue.
- Frequent need to urinate.
- Diarrhoea.
- Less efficient immune system.
- Over breathing – taking frequent shallow breaths.
- Indigestion.

The effect of these physical changes on our voice and the way in which we use our voice are many and various, so taking them in order:

- Difficulty in swallowing reduces the opportunity to move and reposition our larynx.
- An aching neck can lead to tension in the internal and external muscles of the larynx resulting in overall vocal challenges such as limited vocal range, pitch variability, voice fatigue and discomfort.
- Backache can affect the easy movement of the ribs and reduces the amount of air used to support the voice.
- Muscle pain tends to discourage movement so increasing stiffness and flexibility of both the ribs and the vocal folds.
- Fatigue leads to a loss of effective muscle function and consequently leads to reduced flexibility and movement of the vocal folds.
- Frequent urination and diarrhoea lead to dehydration and can affect voice quality.
- A less effective immune system leads to lowered resistance to infection and, in turn, upper respiratory infections are likely to occur more often – affecting vocal health.
- Over-rapid breathing leads to reduced breath support and may also cause dizziness and light-headedness.
- Indigestion may lead to gastro-oesophageal reflux, and this causes irritation and inflammation of the vocal folds, affecting voice quality.

While this is a very brief outline of the far-reaching physiological effects of stress, it shows how every aspect of our voice, from phonation, breath capacity, changes to the lining of the vocal tract and the lubrication of the vocal folds, may be affected by stress.

Environmental Factors

The influence of environmental factors as a source of stress can be overlooked. Conditions such as overcrowding and a lack of personal space in the workplace can significantly impact mental well-being. When we find ourselves in crowded environments, stress levels tend to escalate, leading to heightened feelings including those of aggression and potential violence. For instance, teachers may grapple with overcrowded classrooms, which in turn affects their teaching efficiency. The challenges of teaching a large class, meeting individual needs, and maintaining control can take a toll on their vocal and emotional well-being. This issue isn't limited to educational roles; it's crucial to recognise the far-reaching consequences of space and crowding on all professional voice users, from those in hospitality and call centres to the field of medicine. We recommend that workplaces seek professional guidance on the latest developments in ergonomics and strategies to mitigate overcrowding issues, thereby creating optimal working conditions that offer employees ample space, ergonomic efficiency and a more tranquil environment.

Most of us want to have a sense of a 'home' or a workplace with a designated space which we identify as our own territory. Many individuals like to mark their space with personal items such as family photos. The environment in which we work or learn has a powerful influence on mood and emotion, one that should be considered more robustly. With 'hot seating' or flexible workspaces which are so common today, finding a workspace of one's own is rare and personalising it is rarely, if ever, allowed. If you are lucky, you get a locker and a basket and can store a small number of things, but often even having a proper desk to work from is impossible to find. Mitigating the stress of hot-desking and not having a dedicated workspace may involve establishing a daily routine, using noise-cancelling headphones, adjusting your mindset to foster adaptability, communicating your needs to your manager and prioritising your work-life balance. These strategies help create a more manageable and less stressful work environment, even in shared or flexible spaces.

Work–Life Balance

The importance of achieving a satisfactory 'work–life balance' has and continues to receive considerable attention. A satisfactory work–life balance is the concept that suggests that individuals should try to divide their time and energy between work and the other important aspects of their lives.

Achieving work–life balance requires a daily effort to make time for family, friends, community participation, spirituality, personal growth, self-care and other personal activities, in addition to the demands of the workplace.

Work–life balance is obviously greatly aided by an employer's willingness to institute policies, procedures, actions and expectations that enable individuals to easily pursue more balanced lives. The pursuit of work–life balance reduces the stress that employees experience. When individuals recognise that they are spending most of their days on work-related activities while feeling as if they are neglecting the other important components of their lives, stress and unhappiness result. It is known that the COVID-19 pandemic had a considerable effect on our work–life balance, particularly when our home became our workspace and it was impossible to achieve either a mental or a physical separation. To deal with work-related stress, France introduced a law in 2017 stating that companies of 50 employees or more cannot email an employee after typical work hours. It is, however, difficult to fully reconcile differing demands such as personal, professional and monetary needs to work.

Strategies to Mitigate Stress

Strategies to mitigate or 'cope' with stress, known as stress moderator variables, are resources, skills, behaviours and traits that can reduce the negative impacts of stress. These may take the form of several interventions, from physical exercise to social support that can help protect someone from the negative effects of a stressful life event such as loss of a job. Positive strategies for coping include proactive, meaning-focused and social activities such as exercise, new hobbies or meditation, which can all be great ways of relaxing. It has been shown that someone using these strategies copes better in times of stress compared to someone who experiences the same life event without adequate coping skills or support. Obviously, everyone is different, and you may find that certain strategies work better than others, but when feeling overwhelmed, it's always helpful to reach out to others for support.

Lack of control over your personal and professional life is stressful, so identifying whether you have a strong internal or external locus of control can help you to manage your stress.

– If you have a strong internal locus of control, a belief that events in your life derive primarily from your own actions (Rotter, 1966), you will tend to praise or blame yourself and your abilities in respect to life events. This self-reflection and blame can add greatly to levels of stress when things 'go wrong'. For you, trying to recognise that you are not solely responsible for the overall outcome of an event or a problem is an important step in reducing stress. It is important to try to find someone else to look at the issue with you, someone who can isolate the personal and help you look at the diverse elements that have led to a particular outcome.

- If you have a strong external locus of control, a belief that your decisions and life are controlled by environmental factors which you cannot influence or that chance or fate controls your life, you will tend to praise or blame external factors in respect of life events. For you, trying to regain control is an important element in reducing stress when things 'go wrong'.

Additional Factors in Stress Management

Self-Efficacy

Self-efficacy, or your belief in your capabilities, determines how you think, motivate yourself and behave. Self-efficacy and self-esteem are linked to locus of control and have been proven to predict several work outcomes, specifically job satisfaction and job performance. (Judge et al. (2002) argue that the concepts of locus of control, neuroticism, self-efficacy and self-esteem measure the same single factor.) Under stress, as noted earlier in this chapter, your self-efficacy may become skewed, and it is important to meet with others either in work or outside to objectively reaffirm your capabilities. Essentially, take a step back and seek the opinions of others. This used to be much easier to achieve in a pre-pandemic climate, where there was an opportunity to meet up with colleagues in a much more ad hoc, casual way. When those opportunities are rare, there is a tendency to 'overthink' a problem, resulting in more self-focus and attribution of self-blame.

Self-Control

Self-control is influenced by the emotional brain, and during periods of stress, the amygdala, responsible for regulating emotions, can become less effective, potentially causing emotional outbursts or a 'meltdown'. It's important to monitor your emotional state and find constructive outlets for emotional tension through physical activities. Deep breathing, mindfulness and meditation, journaling, talking to a friend or therapist, creative outlets, self-care activities, taking short breaks, mindful distraction, progressive muscle relaxation, visualization, aromatherapy and sensory engagement can also help with emotional release. Choosing the most effective technique depends on individual preferences and can provide valuable tools for managing stress and emotional well-being.

Anxiety

Excess anxiety can manifest in several ways. It can affect mental processing, so try to be aware that anxiety may cause you to jump to conclusions before understanding exactly what has occurred, be this related to a professional or a personal issue. Make sure that you inform others of stressful situations or when you are in a state of anxiety. Do not try to protect others by 'soldiering on'.

Experience

When dealing with stressful situations, do rely on your life experience, both personal and professional, to navigate them effectively. You will learn to recognise physical sensations which may arise, such as discomfort, pain, tightness or stiffness that may signal tension, often accompanied by feelings of anxiety or stress. This recognition, knowing yourself, will allow you to take appropriate actions (many of which you will find in this book) such as hydrating, moving your body, mindfulness, warming up or muscle tension release. Additionally, recognising your past successful speeches or public speaking experiences can significantly benefit you by boosting your confidence, reducing anxiety and allowing you to be present in the moment. The phenomenon of 'cognitive reassurance' or 'cognitive relief' occurs when you recognise that you have previous experience and competence in handling a specific situation or challenge, leading to a sense of confidence and reduced anxiety about facing it again.

Self-Assessment and Building Awareness

One way to recognise areas of tension is to be mindful of your body throughout the day. Take breaks and check in with your body, paying attention to any sensations or discomfort you may be feeling. By doing this, you can develop greater awareness of your body and the areas where you tend to hold tension. Do you, for example, recognise personal issues triggered by stress? The answers to the questions below will give you a general idea of your level of relaxation and help you identify areas where you need to focus on reducing stress and promoting relaxation. Make a note of your answers and the date on which you answered the questions, and then revisit them again in three to four months' time to see if your answers have changed. Following the 'Practical Advice' suggestions should help you make the required changes and allow you to reduce your stress and anxiety levels.

Tension Self-Assessment

Ask yourself:

How often do you feel tense or anxious during the day?	
Are you drinking more alcohol than usual?	
Are you doing less exercise?	
How often do you take breaks during the day?	
Do you have trouble falling asleep at night?	
Are you eating more than usual?	
Are you more short-tempered than usual?	
How often do you feel overwhelmed by the demands of work or your personal life?	
How often do you engage in activities that help you relax?	
Do you have physical symptoms of stress such as muscle tension or stomach problems?	
How often do you take time for yourself to do something that takes you away from screens, such as reading a book or going for a walk?	
How often do you feel rested and energised after a night's sleep?	

Practical Advice

Release of tension is important to efficient vocal function as breath support and control, volume, projection and vocal quality may all be affected by undue tension. It is quite possible to be relaxed when moving around freely, speaking and performing tasks, but it is important to remember that releasing tension is a technique like any other and it does need to be learned. While a degree of muscular tension is essential to support your body and to initiate and control movement, too much tension will affect smooth muscle coordination, which in turn will lead to general tiredness, strain and poor postural habits.

Do remember that habitual tension becomes 'normal' after a period and, because it is familiar, it does not seem out of the ordinary. It can be difficult to identify the areas of the body that hold tension, so take time to develop an awareness of held tension before learning new techniques of relaxation.

If you are feeling tense or wound up, your voice and speech will be affected, so when thinking about releasing tension, the following advice may be helpful.

–   Check on your tension levels throughout the day – be aware of any tension building up and try to counteract it. Allow enough time during the day to do one or two exercises which release tension. Make sure you are doing them in a warm and comfortable space.

–   Listen. Monitor your own voice for any changes to pitch, variety and range, as they can be indicators of muscle tension.

–   Try to make sure that you allow yourself some time each day for your exercises.

–   If the time you have available for tension-release exercises is limited, put them off until another time; do not start your exercises in a hurry. Begin them when you are relaxed and quiet and do not rush them.

–   Quiet background music is helpful to aid the release of tension as you do the exercises.

–   Limit any distractions before you begin the release-of-tension session: turn your mobile to silent, use the bathroom, put a 'keep out' sign on the door.

–   Keep breathing slowly and steadily as you complete each exercise; do not breathe too deeply or too quickly.

–   When you relax, you need less oxygen and you breathe more slowly and more shallowly. Be aware of this happening as you relax.

–   Encourage family, friends and work colleagues to help you to 'monitor' your tension levels.

Exercises for Release of Tension

Exercises to Encourage General Release of Tension Through Imagery

EXERCISE ONE

Sit or lie in a comfortable position with your eyes closed. Think of a place which gives you a feeling of peace and relaxation. For example, this could be beside a warm fire or on a beach in the sunshine.

–   Remember the feeling of warmth and peace that you experienced there.

–   Add sounds to this image. Think of a favourite piece of music or the sounds of the waves on the shore.

–   Become aware of your breathing. Keep it slightly slower than normal and steady. Breathe in easily and breathe out in the same way.

–   Enjoy the sensation of relaxation and be aware of how comfortable you feel.

EXERCISE TWO

Lie or sit in a comfortable relaxed position with your eyes closed.

–   Begin by thinking of a quiet and relaxing place from your memory.

–   Imagine you are replaying a calming video of this peaceful place in your mind. Allow the sights, sounds and sensations to become vivid and real.

–   Use this calming image to encourage a deep sense of peace.

–   Keep this peaceful mental image firmly in your mind, holding onto it as you proceed.

–   Slowly shift your focus to your body, starting from your toes and moving upwards. Pay attention to each muscle group as you go.

–   As you focus on each muscle group, consciously release any tension you may feel there. Release the muscles one by one, until your whole body is tension free.

–   While maintaining this relaxed state, breathe in and out slowly and naturally. Your breaths should be slightly slower than your usual pace, but with no conscious effort at all.

Exercises to Encourage Progressive Whole-Body Release of Tension

EXERCISE ONE

Stand with your body well balanced.
N.B. Do not do this exercise if you suffer from vertigo or postural dizziness.

- Stretch your whole body upwards towards the ceiling, keeping your fingers extended.
- Feel the stretch in your spine and hold it for a few seconds.
- Start with the tips of your fingers, releasing the tension digit by digit.
- Allow your wrists to relax and flop, then your elbows, shoulders and head.
- Release tension through your spine, vertebra by vertebra, and allow your knees to 'give' a little.
- Allow your body to bob gently in this position.
- Reverse this sequence from the base of your spine, allowing each vertebra to build upon the preceding one.
- Finally, in a standing position, slowly raise your head and allow your arms to float weightlessly up to the starting position.
- You should experience a feeling of being light and stretched.

EXERCISE TWO

Lie on the floor with your head centred, your bottom flat on the floor and relaxed, knees drawn up and a little apart, arms at a slight angle away from your trunk with palms down.

Watch for any undue curve in your spine. If this happens, draw up your knees towards your chin, supporting them with your arms and slowly return your feet to the floor.

- Relax and ease out your shoulder joints, allow your back muscles to 'spread' gently. Do not press your back into the floor; instead, focus on relaxing and easing out your tension.
- Think about your spine lengthening along the floor, trying to extend it from top to bottom.

- Think of your neck becoming longer like your spine, but make sure that you remember that you are being held by the floor and supported. You do not need to do anything to support yourself.
- Lift your hands from the floor, gently shake your wrists and let them fall back slowly.
- Now slowly move your head from side to side, feeling the release of tension before returning to a central position. Press your head slightly back into the floor and then release. Feel the difference between tension and release in your neck muscles.
- Gently lower your chin towards your chest – do not force it, but feel a sense of lengthening in your neck and upper back.
- Once you have worked through the sequence, repeat it, remembering the order: back free, shoulders free, lengthen back, lengthen neck, hands free, wrists free, neck free.

EXERCISE THREE

Sit comfortably in a firm chair with your back well supported by the back of the chair or lie down comfortably. If you feel any discomfort in your back, try lying with your knees raised a little, feet flat on the floor, in semi supine position. Be careful not to press your feet into the floor, as this will create tension.

- Starting at your feet, curl your toes up as tightly as possible. Hold the tension for three to four seconds and then release it.
- Follow the same sequence of tensing, holding the tension briefly and then releasing while systematically working through your body, from the feet to the calves, to the knees to the thighs, buttocks, stomach, chest, back, hands, arms, shoulders, neck and, finally, the face and scalp.
- Remember that when you are thinking about your face you need to include the lips and tongue as well as the eyes and cheeks.
- Concentrate on achieving maximum tension each time and then maximum release.
- Repeat each sequence of tension and release from tension three times with each muscle group.
- When you move from one muscle group to another, try to remember to maintain the release of tension in the muscles. Periodically revisit the areas and monitor any tension that may have returned.

- As you work through your body, concentrate on how it feels in a state of tension release. Your feet and hands should begin to feel slightly tingly, heavy and warm.

- Your legs should rest heavily into the chair if you are sitting, or on the floor if you are lying. Your stomach and waist should feel loose, soft and free, your arms resting heavily on the chair or on the floor, and at all times you should feel supported by the chair or the floor. Embrace the support from the floor or the chair.

- As you work through your body from toes to scalp, become aware of your breathing. It should be slightly slower and steady. Feel the air as it flows in to fill your lungs and flows out as they empty.

- Sit or lie in this state of release from tension for a few minutes before moving, and then gradually bring yourself out of your state of released tension by first thinking of moving and then getting out of the chair or up from the floor. If you are moving from the floor, roll over on one side and then get up slowly, making sure that you bring your head up last of all.

- Try to maintain this state of mind for as long as you can.

Exercise to Encourage Release of Tension in the Shoulders and Upper Chest

- Stand or sit comfortably in front of a mirror.
- Raise your shoulders as high as possible, straight up to your ears.
- Hold that position for a few seconds, then relax.
- Let your shoulders return to their resting position, gently sloping downwards.
- Repeat this several times.
- Become aware of the different muscle sensation between a state of tension and a state of release from tension.

Exercises to Encourage Release of Tension in the Neck Muscles

N.B. Any neck exercise must be done slowly and gradually. Never force your neck.

EXERCISE ONE

You may sit or stand for this exercise.

- With your head up and looking straight ahead, keep your eyes, nose and chin level.
- Slowly and gently turn your head to one side, until your chin is over your shoulder.
- Do not let your head tilt forward or back. Be aware of where it is in relation to your body.
- Feel the stretch in the muscles of the side of your neck.
- Hold the stretch briefly, then slowly return to the midline.
- Repeat this sequence of movements to the other side.
- Repeat this three times on each side.

EXERCISE TWO

Sit in a comfortable chair with your back well supported.

- Drop your head slowly to one side towards one shoulder, feeling the muscle lengthen at the side of your neck.
- Now lift your head upright to the midline and repeat to the other side.
- Drop your head forward with your chin tucked to your chest and roll it to one side and then to the other.
- Now slowly lift your head and return to the midline.
- Repeat this sequence of movements three times.

Suggestions and Strategies

Releasing Tension Before a Speaking Event

Body scanning can be a useful tool for identifying areas of tension in the body. It involves systematically focusing your attention on different parts of the body and noticing any physical sensations or discomfort. There are many apps you can listen to which will guide you through a body scan, you can record the script yourself or simply memorise the steps of the exercise to use anywhere at anytime!

- Inhale to focus attention, exhale to release tension. Begin by bringing your attention to the top of your head. Notice any sensations or areas of tension or tightness. Take a moment to acknowledge them without judgement.

- Slowly move your attention down to your forehead and eyebrows. Notice any furrowing or tension in this area and consciously release it as you exhale.

- Continue to scan your face, jaw and neck. Release any tightness or tension you become aware of with each exhale.

- Direct your attention to your shoulders. Notice if they are raised or if there is any tightness. Take a deep breath in and, as you exhale, allow your shoulders to relax and sink down.

- Progressively scan down your body, bringing awareness to your arms, hands, chest, back, abdomen and hips. Release any tension you notice along the way, using your breath to facilitate relaxation.

- Continue scanning down to your legs, knees, calves and feet. Allow any tightness or discomfort to melt away with each exhalation.

- Take a few moments to focus on your entire body as a whole, observing any residual tension or areas that may need extra attention. Breathe into those areas, inviting them to relax and let go.

- When you feel ready, slowly open your eyes and take a moment to reorient yourself to your surroundings.

This body-scan exercise helps cultivate mindfulness and body awareness, allowing you to identify and release tension throughout your body. Regular practice can promote relaxation, reduce stress and enhance overall wellbeing. Feel free to adapt the exercise to suit your needs and preferences and remember to approach it with patience and self-compassion.

Recommendations for Dealing With Stress at Work

- Breathe: take a few moments throughout the day to engage in conscious breathing. This can help activate the relaxation response and reduce stress.

- Meditation: find a quiet space, even if it's just for a few minutes, to practice mindfulness or meditation, or simply be still and quiet. Close your eyes if you wish, focus on your breath, and let go of any racing thoughts. This can help clear your mind, reduce stress, and increase focus.

Continued

- Move: incorporate simple stretching exercises or brief physical movement into your routine. Release your neck, shoulders, arms and legs to reduce muscle tension and promote circulation. Take short walks or do desk exercises to get your blood flowing and increase energy levels.

- Prioritise and delegate tasks: organise your tasks and prioritise them based on importance and deadlines. Delegate responsibilities whenever possible to lighten your workload and reduce stress. This can help create a sense of control and prevent feeling overwhelmed.

- Breaks and time management: take regular breaks throughout the day to rest and recharge. Step away from your workstation, engage in activities that you enjoy or simply take a walk outside. Use effective time management techniques, such as the Pomodoro Technique (bursts of 25 minutes focused work followed by a short break) or workflow apps, to structure your work and build in dedicated breaks.

- Create a soothing workspace: if possible, personalise your workspace with calming elements, such as plants, photos or soothing colours. Use ergonomic equipment and ensure your workstation is organised and clutter-free. A visually appealing and comfortable environment can contribute to a more relaxed mindset.

- Mindset: be mindful of your internal dialogue and reframe negative thoughts. Replace self-criticism with positive affirmations or encouraging statements. Cultivating a positive mindset can help reduce stress and increase resilience.

- Support: connect with supportive colleagues or friends during breaks or lunchtime. Engage in positive conversations, seek advice or simply enjoy some social interaction. Building a support network can help alleviate stress and provide a sense of camaraderie.

- Health: pay attention to your eating habits and choose nourishing foods that support your well-being. Stay hydrated by drinking water throughout the day, as dehydration can contribute to increased stress levels and vocal fatigue.

- Set boundaries and practice self-care: establish clear boundaries between work and personal life. Taking care of yourself holistically can enhance your overall well-being and resilience to stress. It is worth looking at the work of Nedra Tawwab (2021) to help set boundaries.

Remember that everyone is different, so find what works best for you and adapt these strategies to fit your needs and work environment. It is important to prioritise self-care and make stress relief a regular part of your routine to maintain a healthy work–life balance.

Tools for Relaxation

There are many great ways to release tension and modern life provides us with lots of help. Some recommendations are:

— Portable massage gun – this needs to be used gently but can be a great aid for muscle tension to keep on your desk.
— Massage – a massage might feel indulgent, but if you find it reduces tension and is enjoyable, regular massage can be so helpful for the professional voice user.
— Heated pads for the back can help with muscle tightness, particularly if you spend long hours in one position.
— Electric foot massager – you can install one of these under your desk!
— An inversion table – this is a matter of personal taste of course, but an inversion table can relieve the pressure gravity puts on your spine and help lengthen and decompress your spine.
— Muscle rollers, spiky balls or massage roller sticks for muscle tension release.

Holistic Ways to Relieve Tension

— Tai Chi, Qi Gong, yoga.
— Meditation.
— Breathwork.
— Progressive muscle relaxation.
— Adequate sleep is vital for stress relief and tension reduction.
— Any regular exercise, such as walking, yoga or dancing, can help release tension and increase the production of endorphins, the body's natural mood-boosting chemicals.
— Holistic therapies such as acupuncture, massage, aromatherapy and reiki focus on restoring balance and promoting relaxation in the body. These practices can help alleviate physical tension, reduce stress and enhance overall well-being.

- Engaging in activities that you enjoy can often help relieve tension and promote relaxation. When you participate in activities that bring you pleasure or satisfaction, they can shift your focus away from sources of stress and tension, allowing your mind and body to relax and recharge.

- Building and nurturing healthy relationships, spending time with loved ones and seeking support from others can provide emotional support, perspective and a sense of belonging, which can help alleviate feelings of tension and stress.

Sound Bite

Professional voice users represent a group of individuals who are at high risk of external and internal stressors. Release of tension not only helps to counteract the physiological and psychological effects of stress but also helps to induce feelings of calmness and relaxation that can support your vocal performance. A relaxed and tension-free voice is more likely to perform optimally, delivering clear and controlled sound without strain or discomfort.

4 | Breathing

Introduction

In the strictest sense, a definition of 'breathing' might be as literal and as brief as, 'the exchange of gases upon which life depends'.

Breath has, however, many other amazing qualities. Breath offers a unique template for voice, and through its properties of control and support for the voice it has many roles. It supports both sung and spoken performance, it has a diagnostic role, it can offer an insight into an individual's physical and mental health, it can alert us to physiological changes associated with ageing and, most of all, it sustains life. Our priority is to equip you with the means to not only access your breath but also to harness it to empower your voice for rich and effective communication in a multifaceted and demanding world.

The way we breathe affects our voice quality – our volume, flow, tone and variety. Sustained speech and clear vocal quality, essential for the needs of the professional voice user, require good breath support, plenty of air and flexible and relaxed respiratory muscles as well as healthy and flexible vocal folds and uninhibited use of the resonators. Committed, meaningful speech tends to engage the breath and muscles in the most positive way and produces naturally energised language. Vocal colour and variety are heard when a voice is well connected with the breath, has range and is capable of pitch and volume change.

There are aspects of emphasis such as pause, pace, pitch and stress, all of which add natural colour, texture, energy and nuance to the voice. Their use, or lack of use, is usually an indicator of how open or happy the individual is about engaging the breath and voice freely and responsively, rather than being the result of a lack of specific technique.

Breathing for speech and singing are modifications of the main purpose of the respiratory system – that of maintaining life – but here breath is

DOI: 10.4324/9781003361114-5

referenced in terms of its role in initiating and sustaining voice and its role as a measure of vocal quality. The primary function of the vocal folds is to protect the airway, but the symbiotic relationship of breath and the vocal folds is critical to the quality of our voice and the way in which we use it. Our DNA determines our physiological inheritance which dictates the size and shape of the vocal tract which in turn determine the individual's unique vocal fingerprint, the vocal quality that distinguishes one individual's voice from another. The integrated nature of breath and phonation (speech sound) means that as voice and phonation change, so too does respiration, and vice versa.

As mentioned, breath can offer an insight into an individual's physical and mental health. As we age, we see changes in vocal quality through infancy, childhood, puberty, adulthood and older age, partly because of changes in lung capacity. Breath can make a radical difference to human functioning and the ability of an individual to express themselves.

Breath is much more than a physiological event; it is closely related to emotion. As April Pierrot (2009) notes, the vocabulary of breath is closely allied to our psychophysiology. We hold our breath when we are surprised, we catch our breath when we are astonished, we save our breath when we feel nothing we say will matter, we mutter under our breath in resentment, we give each other breathing space.

Breathing is generally taken for granted until we cannot breathe as efficiently as we used to, or we notice that we don't have the same control over our breathing as we used to, or we find that our breath is limited or laboured because of anxiety and stress, or we experience problems due to asthma or allergies.

Stress affects every aspect of phonation, including breath capacity; tension limits the free exchange of breath and results in a vocal quality that is often strident, lacks flexibility and warmth, and can appear aggressive. Not only does our breath have an impact on our voice, but also our health and well-being, emotions and mental state, which will in turn impact our breathing. Postural problems may also restrict or compromise our breathing, or this may occur due to disease or disorder. The recent pandemic both educated and informed us of the danger from respiratory problems.

In this chapter we will explore your breath and discover how to comfortably and confidently work with your breath to benefit your speaking voice and your overall well-being.

Why Does Breath Matter to Me?

Breath is responsible for the vibration of the vocal folds which, in turn, create sounds which we perceive as speech, and, if that breath is either not powerful enough to set the vocal folds in motion or not synchronised with the activity of voice, problems can occur. For the vocal folds to vibrate properly, they require a steady stream of air passing through them. An unsteady or ineffective stream of air can result in a weak or strained voice that may be difficult to hear or understand. In some cases, this can even lead to voice problems or damage to the vocal folds. Therefore, taking in sufficient air is important for maintaining a healthy voice and producing clear speech. For some readers, there may be a concern that they don't breathe 'properly', that their breath control isn't efficient enough to allow them to communicate effectively at work because they don't have enough air to sustain longer phrases or sentences, which can cause the voice to trail off at the end of a sentence or become choppy and interrupted. Some of you may experience a sense of 'shortness of breath' when under pressure; this can feel very uncomfortable, and indeed distressing, so then you become overly conscious of your breathing.

The need to breathe may be interrupting the flow of thoughts and meaning. If you don't breathe in at the right time, or if you feel you haven't taken in enough breath to allow you to finish a sentence, you may break up the fluency of your speech; in some cases you may feel you need to speak quietly in case you run out of air and this can give the impression that you lack confidence.

Alternatively, perhaps there is a concern that your voice is sounding strained or feeling tired. Lack of effective breathing can also cause tension in the throat and vocal folds. This tension can make the voice sound tight and may even cause vocal fatigue or damage over time.

Overall, inefficient or inadequate control over your breathing can have a significant impact on your voice quality and reduces the effectiveness of your communicative intent. If you can become familiar with, and learn how to modify, your breath outside of stressful situations, you can learn how to apply these methods during periods of stress. Breath is closely linked to our emotional life and so when we are under stress we are more likely to 'block' or inhibit the very natural and normal activity of breathing. By learning how to breathe correctly and practising the breathing exercises in this chapter, you can improve your breathing habits, promote better vocal health and communicate in the way you want to with the vocal quality you choose to employ.

What Is It Exactly?

If we look at breath in a conventional physiological way, we can see it as a system for maintaining life by the metabolic exchange of the gases oxygen and carbon dioxide. Breath enters the body, flows through the lungs where oxygen is taken into the blood stream through the alveoli and transported around the body by the action of the heart muscle. Carbon dioxide is expelled from the blood by the muscles of exhalation. In short, we are dependent on breath for life.

When we breathe, we take in oxygen and release carbon dioxide, which is essential for the functioning of our body's cells. In addition to providing oxygen to our body, breathing also plays a crucial role in regulating our nervous system. The act of breathing influences our autonomic nervous system, which controls many of the body's automatic processes such as heart rate, blood pressure, digestion and respiration. When we take slow, deep breaths our body's parasympathetic nervous system is activated, which promotes relaxation and reduces stress. On the other hand, rapid, shallow breathing can trigger the sympathetic nervous system, leading to a 'fight-or-flight' response and increased stress. Our impulse to breathe is controlled by chemoreceptors, which monitor levels of carbon dioxide and oxygen in the blood. The balance of oxygen and carbon dioxide is constantly changing with bodily activity and this balance is adjusted by the central nervous system – when carbon dioxide levels are too high and oxygen too low, nerve impulses are sent to activate inhalation.

Breathing exercises and techniques such as those in this chapter, and other wellness practices such as meditation, breathwork, yoga, Alexander technique and relaxation techniques, have been shown to help reduce stress, anxiety and depression. These techniques can also help improve concentration, increase energy levels and promote overall feelings of calm and relaxation. Incorporating breathing exercises into your daily routine can be a simple yet effective way to support your mental and physical health.

Self-Assessment and Building Awareness

Thinking about how easy you find it to breathe, in terms of your breath capacity and ability to breathe, how many, if any, of the following statements apply to you?

- Do you take any medication regularly?
- Do you have any allergies?
- Do you have any chest problems affecting your breathing?
- Do you have asthma?
- Are you ever 'short of breath'?
- Do you experience any chest tightness?

Continued

- Do you have any recurring viral illnesses?
- Have you ever had COVID-19 and if so, how many times?
- Have you ever been hospitalised with breathing problems?
- Have you ever had any open-heart surgery?
- Have you ever experienced an episode of intense uncontrolled coughing?
- Have you ever had to be nebulised?
- How far can you walk without experiencing any shortness of breath?
- Do you often work in conditions with poor air quality?

If you answered yes to any of the above questions, it is possible that breathing issues may well have contributed to or triggered a voice problem. These scenarios may have had an influence over your control, capacity and ease with which you breathe and produce voice. Some medication, poor air quality, historical medical issues and allergies can all impact your breathing. The exercises in this chapter will be of help but do speak to your GP if you are at all concerned.

Building Self-Awareness Around Breath

How often do you pay attention to your breath throughout the day?	
How does your breath affect your overall sense of well-being and mood?	
Have you noticed any patterns or triggers that affect your breath, such as specific environments, activities or emotions?	
How does your breath affect your ability to concentrate or focus on tasks?	
Do you feel in control of your breath, or does it feel out of your control at times?	
What role do you see your breath playing in your overall health and well-being?	
Do you feel that you 'don't breathe properly', or maybe you had an allergic reaction at some time and felt you were unable to 'catch your breath'?	
Describe your usual breathing pattern (e.g., shallow, deep, steady, calm, fast, slow).	
How do you feel when you take a deep breath? Do you feel relaxed or tense? Is this situation-dependent?	
How does your breath change when you are stressed or anxious?	
Do you find yourself holding your breath during certain activities or situations?	

As with the other self-awareness tasks, keep a note of your answers and ask yourself these questions again at a later date, noting change.

Practical Advice

Breathing exercises can produce unexpected and uncomfortable emotional responses. This is quite a normal response and unless it brings back distressing memories or revives emotions that you cannot deal with, there is no need to be concerned. Many others experience similar reactions, so do not feel in any way embarrassed or self-conscious.

You may feel sceptical about needing to 'learn' to breathe, but to support your voice you need plenty of air and for that reason working on breathing and using your lower back and abdominal muscles is important.

–   Use good, open posture, and allow free movement of your whole body. Keep your back, shoulders and neck free from tension for free and easy breathing.
–   Be careful not to overbreathe. Only take two or three deep breaths at a time until your body becomes used to this new pattern, otherwise you may feel light-headed.
–   If you suffer from asthma, work within your own limits so that you feel secure and safe.
–   Stop working on your breath if you feel tired, light-headed or short of breath. Take a moment to release physical tension until the sensation has passed.
–   If your posture is a problem, it is important to work on this before, or certainly alongside, work on breathing. Return to the exercises in the posture chapter and ensure your posture is giving you the opportunity to breathe well.
–   Make sure that your lower back and abdominal muscles are not locked as this will lead to tension and will limit the ease with which you can breathe. A body scan, as featured in the chapter on tension release, may be helpful.
–   Watch for any excess movement in your upper chest or shoulders. They should remain free from tension and still.
–   Concentrating too much on breathing 'in' can cause tension in the upper chest and vocal tract; instead focus on the 'out' breath and the 'in' breath will follow more naturally.

- Silent breathing indicates relaxed, open air passages. Noisy inhalation and exhalation are caused by tension. If this occurs, try yawning widely to stretch and release the muscles in the throat.
- Practising little and often is best.

Exercises for Breath

Introductory Breathing Exercises

EXERCISE ONE

Stand in front of a long mirror and place your hands on either side of your waist, with fingers spread and pointing towards the centre of your waist, thumbs behind and pointed towards the back.

- Press firmly with your hands, as though trying to make them meet in the middle, and breathe out.
- Maintain your hand position and take a breath in, feeling the forward and side expansion of your torso.
- Watch in the mirror as the gap between your fingertips increases.
- Monitor your shoulder movement at the same time – there should be no undue movement. This can also be achieved by placing one hand on your midriff and exerting some slight inward pressure. Breathe in and monitor the outward movement of your midriff. Breathe out on an /f/ sound. Feel your hand move inwards. Release tension and breathe normally. Repeat this several times. Remember that your hand moves 'out' as the breath moves 'in'.

EXERCISE TWO

Start with your feet slightly apart and arms out to the sides.

- On an outgoing breath, drop your arms. Then sweep them back up in front of you, with your palms uppermost. When they are at eye level in front of your body, allow your knees to bend.
- Drop your arms and sweep them back into their original position – out to the side – as you breathe in. Notice how the breath flows back into your chest. Return your arms to their forward position on the exhaled breath.

- Repeat for a maximum of 20 swings, or as many as are comfortable, always releasing tension and breathing normally between each attempt.

Exercises to Encourage Greater Awareness of Breath in the Lumbar Region

It is very beneficial to work on establishing the breath in the lumbar (lower back) region. This ensures the breathing is not limited to the front of the body and flexibility and openness of the back is encouraged. Because the area is not one commonly associated with breathing, back breathing can take time to establish.

EXERCISE ONE

The following exercise should be done as one unit and worked through as a sequence. Do not start halfway through the sequence.

- Lie face down, arms by your sides or hands folded under your head, with a heavy book placed on your lower back.
- Breathe in and think about the breath filling the lungs.
- Be aware of the book rising and falling as you breathe in and out, or the lower back widening. Remember this is due to the activity of the muscles which support breathing and not because the breath is reaching this area; the movement is the result of muscular activity.
- It can sometimes take some time to 'feel' this exercise and establish the movement.
- An alternative, or additional exercise, is to lie on your back in semi-supine position (knees bent and feet flat on the floor) and place the heavy book on your tummy. Register the sensation of the book rising and falling as you breathe in and out, and a feeling of expansion around your waist and lumbar area.

This exercise develops awareness of the breath as it reaches low into the lungs.

EXERCISE TWO

Start by giving yourself a 'hug'. Allow your spine to curve forward.

- Drop the chin to the chest.
- Breathe in through the nose. On the 'in' breath feel the sideways spread of your back, you may experience a sense of widening in your back. Breathe out through the nose or mouth.
- Take a few deep breaths in this 'hugging' position.

This exercise develops awareness of the breath as it reaches low into the lungs, and an understanding that movement is created in the back and that breathing has a 360-degree quality which isn't restricted to the front of the body. Over time and with practice you will begin to sense more movement.

Exercises to Encourage Breath Control

As speech is produced on an outgoing breath, it is important to distinguish between the 'held' breath and the released breath, so 'control' is the effective release of breath *without* tension rather than the release of breath *under* tension.

EXERCISE ONE

- Standing in a relaxed manner, breathe out and eliminate as much air as possible from the lungs.
- Feel the action in the centre of your body, but do not shorten your spine.
- Wait for a second or two.
- On the 'in' breath experience the sudden, dramatic and powerful inflow of air.
- Repeat this five to ten times.
- Stop if you feel at all dizzy or unwell.

EXERCISE TWO

- Breathe in through your nose and out through your mouth, gently and easily, until a smooth and relaxed rhythm has been established.

- Once you have achieved this, begin a silent count (at approximately one second intervals) of breathing in and breathing out. A count of three is a good rate to aim for.

- Maintain this silent count for several attempts and then begin to vary the length of the 'in' and 'out' breaths. For example, try a count of two for the 'in' breath and four for the 'out' breath.

- As this becomes more familiar, decrease the 'in' breath time and increase the 'out' breath time. This more closely mirrors the pattern of breathing for sustained and controlled phonation.

- Take in a breath quickly (on a count of two) and then breathe out on the sound /s/ for as long as possible but without strain. Make sure that you do not allow any tension to occur in your lips, tongue or neck. If you do feel any tension occurring, reduce the length of time over which you maintain the /s/ sound.

EXERCISE THREE

- Begin by releasing any held tension. Either sitting well supported in a chair or lying on the floor, rest your hand on your diaphragm – the area just above your waist – and become aware of the gentle inwards and outwards movement.

- If seated, you can use a mirror to monitor the movement and give yourself visual feedback. If lying down, ask a friend or family member to observe and comment, or video yourself.

- Gradually exaggerate the 'out' breath through gently pursed lips. Propel the air out, using your abdominal muscles; once 'empty', let the lungs refill naturally. Again, monitor the movement of the diaphragm as you do this – the diaphragm moves out with the 'in' breath and in with the 'out' breath. Aim to keep the shoulders low and relaxed during this process.

- As you become more used to this breathing pattern, exaggerate both the breathing in and breathing out movements. You should start to feel an increase in lung capacity.

- Use your hands to monitor the range of movement in your lower-back area and diaphragm. Be careful that there is no movement in your upper chest or shoulders.

- Once you feel confident that you can achieve a greater degree of control over your breathing pattern, alter the pattern in terms of the length of the breath.

- Gradually increase the length of the 'out' breath to three, four, five, six or as far as it is comfortable; the 'in' breath remains the same. Concentrate on these new patterns and sensations. Never 'force' the breath further than is comfortable.

Exercises for Breath Release (for Energised Speech)

EXERCISE ONE

Use different images to experiment with breath pressure, fitting the breath to the task.

- Imagine blowing a feather off your hand.
- Imagine blowing several feathers off your hand.
- Imagine blowing out four candles on a cake.
- Imagine blowing out six everlasting candles on a cake.
- Imagine blowing a feather off your hand and keeping it airborne.
- Imagine writing your first name and then your full name with your breath as if it were ink.

N.B. Never force the breath out or allow undue tension to affect the exercise.

EXERCISE TWO

- Take in a moderate amount of air on an inward count of two, and when you breathe out try to produce a long steady /s/.

- Do not produce the sound with any excess tension in your lips, tongue or neck. Do not force the air out, simply maintain a steady pressure and listen to the sound.

- As you become more competent you will find that you can maintain the /s/ sound for longer without undue effort.
- Begin to vary the loudness of the sound – make it quiet to begin with and then let it get louder – ssssSSSSSS.
- Begin with a loud but easy /s/ sound and let it become quieter over time – SSSSssss.
- Vary the loudness so that the sound is loudest in the middle – ssssSSSSSssss.
- Try to alternate periods of loudness and quietness – sSsSsSsSsS.
- Try using /f/ or /sh/ (as in 'hush') in place of /s/ for these exercises, although you will need a little more air pressure to maintain these sounds as they may not last as long.
- Always aim for quality of sound; do not compromise quality for quantity.

Suggestions and Strategies

Breath Diary

An alternative approach to 'thinking' about your breath is to become more aware of your breath through keeping a self-reflection 'diary'.

- Set aside a few minutes each day to focus on your breath. You may choose to do this in a quiet, relaxing environment or during a specific activity such as walking or yoga.
- During this time, pay attention to the physical sensations of your breath. Notice the rhythm, depth and quality of your breath, without trying to change it in any way.
- As you observe your breath, also take note of any thoughts or emotions that come up for you. For example, you may notice that you feel anxious or distracted or that you have a particular thought that keeps popping up.
- Write down your observations, noting both the physical sensations of your breath and any thoughts or emotions that arise.
- Over time, review your breath diary and look for patterns or insights that emerge. For example, you may notice that your breath tends to be

shallow and rapid when you are feeling stressed, or that you tend to hold your breath during certain activities, or that your breath is smooth and calm when you're relaxed.

- Use these insights to guide your breath practice, focusing on specific areas that you would like to improve or explore further.

By regularly observing and reflecting on your breath, you can develop a deeper understanding of the relationship with your breath and any issues you may be facing. This can help you develop more effective strategies for improving your breath and your overall well-being.

Keeping Your Voice in Good Shape

Once work begins, the professional voice user rarely does anything but the equivalent of 'running at full speed' vocally. As with any form of intense physical activity, it is important to spend time gently 'stretching' vocally and making contact with your breath and your voice. Breathing exercises are a very useful way to 'warm up' the voice. Use some gentle relaxation exercises to begin and then pick two or three breathing exercises that you feel help you to make contact with your breath, following up with engaging your voice and your breath. Try the exercise below. You can also try it in your own private space before starting work or on your way to work.

Breathing Out

- Sigh out to the count of five on an /f/. When the lungs empty, simply allow them to refill.
- Sigh out to a count of six on an /s/. Repeat the refill process.
- Sigh out to a count of seven on a /th/. Repeat the refill process.
- Sigh out to a count of eight on a /sh/. Repeat the refill process.

If you are in a private space (the car is ideal, if it is not overheated and your shoulders and neck are not locked in a state of tension because of traffic jams) you can begin to voice on the outgoing sigh.

- Sing out to a count of seven on /m/.
- Sing out to a count of eight on /v/.
- Sing out to a count of nine on /z/.

Count in your head while you voice the sounds. If you prefer, sing numbers from one to five, then start again from one and add a number until you reach your limit. Always be aware of tension in the muscles of the neck when you voice sound, particularly as you come to the end of the breath capacity.

Breathwork Techniques

By focusing on conscious breathing techniques, speakers can regulate their breath, enabling better control over their voice and reducing performance anxiety. Deep, diaphragmatic breathing promotes relaxation, activating the parasympathetic nervous system and reducing stress. This, in turn, helps speakers maintain a steady pace, project their voice effectively and sustain their energy throughout their presentations. Breathwork also enhances vocal resonance, ensuring a fuller and more resonant tone, while enabling smoother articulation and vocal dynamics. Incorporating breathwork into your preparation for speaking events can empower you to engage your audience with clarity, authenticity and a commanding presence.

Box Breathing

Box breathing, also known as square breathing, is a breath-control technique utilised by the Navy SEALs and other elite military units to manage stress, increase focus and enhance performance in high-pressure situations. By consciously regulating the breath, box breathing activates the parasympathetic nervous system, inducing a state of calm and reducing the body's stress response. It allows you to maintain composure, clarity and optimal cognitive function during intense or critical moments, promoting mental clarity, emotional stability and overall well-being.

1. Find a comfortable position and relax your body.
2. Inhale deeply through your nose for a count of four.
3. 'Pause' your breath for a count of four, maintaining your calm state.
4. Exhale slowly and fully through your mouth for a count of four.
5. Pause your breath again for a count of four, maintaining your relaxed and still state.
6. Repeat this cycle for several rounds, focusing on the rhythmic pattern and sustaining a calm and steady breath.

Relaxing Breathwork: Deeper Relaxation

The goal here is to stimulate your parasympathetic nervous system, promoting a state of rest and relaxation. This technique involves slow, deep breathing which causes the vagus nerve to signal your nervous system to lower your heart rate, blood pressure and cortisol.

1. Inhale through your nose for a count of 1–2–3–4.
2. Exhale through your nose for a longer count of 8–7–6–5–4–3–2–1.
3. Repeat this cycle for ten rounds, allowing each breath to be slow and deep, inducing a sense of relaxation.

The 4–7–8 Breath

The 4–7–8 breath activates the parasympathetic nervous system and induces a state of relaxation. The 4–7–8 breathing technique focuses on extending the exhale, which stimulates the parasympathetic nervous system and promotes relaxation. It can help calm the mind and reduce stress. Remember to practise this technique at your own pace and adjust the counts if needed to ensure comfort and ease.

Find a comfortable seated position, with your spine lengthened and your shoulders released.

1. Close your eyes and take a few deep breaths to settle into the practice.
2. Begin by exhaling completely through your mouth, making a whooshing sound.
3. Close your mouth and inhale silently through your nose to a mental count of four.
4. Pause your breath for a mental count of seven.
5. Exhale completely through your mouth, making a whooshing sound, to a mental count of eight.
6. This completes one breath. Inhale again and repeat the cycle for a total of four breaths, you can build on the repetitions over time.

If you are interested in diving deeper into breathwork there are many accredited courses you can take, you may be interested in the Wim Hof method, or working one-to-one with a qualified breathwork practitioner.

Rapid Strategies

When you are feeling anxious or unprepared for a meeting, here are some further ways in which you can quickly 'check in' with your breathing to ensure it will support your voice in a difficult or stressful situation.

–   Remember at the beginning to exhale gently and the inhalation will follow naturally.

–   Do a quick body scan, close your eyes and bring your attention to your breath. Slowly scan your body from head to toe, noticing any areas of tension, tightness or discomfort. As you come across these areas, mentally release, and soften any tension with an 'out' breath. Continue this body scan, focusing on the breath and using it as a tool to bring relaxation and ease to each area.

–   Remind yourself that you've 'got' this. Breathing is natural and it's important not to get overly 'breath-conscious'.

–   Silent breath. Place your hand gently on your midriff/diaphragm and take in two or three slow breaths through your nose, and with lips gently exhale through the mouth without any 'breathy' noise. This has the effect of slowing down your heart rate at the same time as your breath rate; this is very useful, as no one will know you are working on your breath and calming your nerves.

Sound Bite

Breath is the foundation of life, the key to all human activity; breath is as integral to effective human communication as it is to sustaining life. The way we breathe affects our voice quality, our volume, tone and vocal variety. When we approach speech with intention and awareness of our breath, we unlock the potential for meaningful and impactful communication. Working on, and with, your breath will reward you by benefiting you, your voice and your overall well-being.

Constriction, Deconstriction and Smooth Onset of the Note

Introduction

Constriction is the term used to describe tension in some part of the vocal tract, either in the jaw, the pharynx, the oral cavity (mouth) or the nasal cavity. Deconstriction, in brief, is the release of this tension. The 'onset of the note' refers to the initiation of a sound produced when we start singing or speaking, and this in turn is affected by tension. We have already considered postural tension and discussed the need to think about whole body tension arising from long term, habitual and repetitive movement patterning; however, tension that is specific to the vocal tract was not discussed and can sometimes make a more immediate impact on our vocal quality.

Constriction

The word constriction may conjure up images of tightness, something being squeezed or a small uncomfortable space. So, we can imagine vocal tract constriction having an impact on the sound of your voice – creating a 'squeezed' or 'tight' sound, something we can successfully counteract with release of tension.

Deconstriction

Deconstriction on the other hand refers to the process of releasing tension in the vocal tract. This can help to improve the resonance, tone and projection of the voice, making speech sound clearer and easier to understand. In addition, deconstriction can help to reduce vocal strain and fatigue, which can occur when the voice is forced or pushed beyond its healthy limits.

DOI: 10.4324/9781003361114-6

In this chapter we will be looking at ways to release tension specific to your vocal tract, and how to remain tension free as you begin to speak. We will focus on constriction and deconstriction in the first half of this chapter and move on to onset in the second half.

Why Do Constriction and Deconstriction Matter to Me?

Overall, deconstriction is an essential element of healthy vocal technique, allowing us to use our voice in a way that is efficient, effective and sustainable over time. The importance of deconstriction is both to focus on relaxing the muscles in the throat and jaw, allowing the vocal folds to vibrate freely, and to prevent your voice from reflecting qualities that may be heard by listeners as harshness, nasality and a lack of flexibility around the note, which can sound very monotonous and even aggressive. On occasion, listeners may well transpose how your voice sounds into how you are as a person and align your voice quality to character traits such as anger, anxiety and aggression, none of which may reflect who you really are. Despite your best efforts and awareness of your vocal health, some workplaces' acoustic and ergonomic environments have a significant impact on the constriction of the voice. Organisations often have limited awareness of the effect of these environmental features on the voice. Some staff may be unwittingly exposed to irritants, such as dust or chemicals, that can, in turn, cause inflammation or irritation of the vocal folds, once again leading to constriction and other voice-related issues. In workplaces with powerful air conditioning or where the air is dry or where people may not have easy access to water, dehydration can be a problem. This can cause the vocal folds to 'dry out' and become irritated, leading again to tension and constriction, plus other vocal problems.

Volume

In many work environments, for example, those of education, hospitality, accident and emergency, call centres, security, policing or on building sites, staff may need to speak at a higher volume to be heard over background noise or to communicate with people at a distance. When you speak more loudly and breath support is lacking, people often compensate by substituting technique with constriction in the throat and neck, to try to produce a louder sound. This can lead to a feeling of tightness and strain in the throat, which can cause further compensatory tension in the muscles of the neck and shoulders as well. To avoid this and promote good vocal health it is important to develop proper breath support and vocal technique, including deconstriction.

Vocal Loading

Staff who work in jobs that require a lot of talking, many of whom also work in acoustically challenging environments, are very likely to be prone to vocal fatigue and strain; the length of time speaking, allied to speaking loudly, further compounds the vocal damage, leading to tension and, in turn, constriction of the voice.

Stress

Work-related stress, as we discussed in Chapter 3, can lead to constriction and other far-reaching and significant vocal problems.

Generally, the workplace can be a challenging environment for maintaining good vocal health, and it is important for people to take steps to minimise the impact of these factors on their voice. This may include taking breaks when possible, staying hydrated, using amplification devices to reduce the need for shouting, and practising techniques to reduce stress and tension in the throat and neck.

What Are Constriction and Deconstriction, Exactly?

The reason that you notice change due to constriction is because the pharynx has two muscular layers, wrapping around the larynx. The outer layer, which forms the major part of the pharynx, is formed of three pairs of constrictor muscles – the superior, middle and inferior constrictors. These muscles form the back and side walls of the pharynx, while the front of the pharynx forms a link to the nose, mouth and laryngeal sections of the pharynx. These linkages are known as the nasopharynx, the oropharynx and the laryngopharynx. The constrictor muscles literally constrict the pharynx when we swallow or gag and these systems are directly affected by posture, which, in turn, is affected by the movement of the bony skeleton, muscles and tendons. Tension in one area of our body quickly promotes tension in another, and this domino effect ultimately spreads to the jaw, oropharynx, pharynx and larynx. This, in turn, results in a throaty, tight, harsh, nasal-sounding voice which, to the listener, can translate as belonging to an angry, apprehensive and/or possibly antagonistic individual.

Self-Assessment and Building Awareness

The questions below aim to guide you towards a clearer picture of your voice and your vocal health, particularly in relation to constriction.

Constriction Self-Assessment

Do you ever feel like your voice is strained or 'forced' when you speak?	
Does your throat feel tight or constricted when you speak?	
Do you ever experience hoarseness or raspiness in your voice?	
Do you find it difficult to project your voice or speak at a higher volume?	
Do you experience vocal fatigue or discomfort after speaking for a prolonged period?	
Do you find it challenging to reach high or low notes when singing or speaking?	
Do you tend to clear your throat frequently when speaking?	
Do you ever experience pain or discomfort in your throat or neck when speaking?	
Do you feel like you need to strain or 'push' your voice to be heard in noisy environments?	
Under stress do you feel your voice is higher pitched and more nasal than normal, or lower and more muffled?	

If you answered yes to one or more of the above questions you are likely to benefit from the deconstriction exercises in this chapter.

Thinking about other aspects of your physical and vocal health, ask yourself if any of the following statements regarding habitual tension apply to you? If so, this may be the result of, or may cause, constriction.

- I wake up in the morning with my teeth clenched.
- My dentist has commented on the fact that I grind my teeth.
- I carry my tongue high in the mouth, so it is bunched rather than lying gently against the lower front teeth.
- I notice that my tongue is stuck to the roof of my mouth because my mouth is very dry, and I don't have very much saliva.
- I find that my head is often thrust forward.
- I sometimes find that my neck is 'locked' at certain points during the day.
- I am aware that I often hold my breath, although I am not conscious of doing so at the time.
- My shoulders are locked or raised and sometimes habitually rounded unless I constantly review my position.

87

If you agreed with any of these statements, work on tension release, and the exercises in this chapter will help. You can return to both these questionnaires after working on the deconstriction exercises and changing your daily habits, to monitor whether you are still in need of vocal tract tension release.

Practical Advice

Making changes to the way in which you use your voice requires careful attention and consistent effort. When thinking about your 'working voice', the following advice may be helpful.

- If you feel very tense and anxious, first address your posture, release tension, work on your breath, and only then work directly on your voice.
- Remember it is important to be gentle with your vocal folds; they will work very well if they are not ill-treated.
- Excess tension in the internal musculature of the vocal folds will stop them moving together smoothly and increase the effort needed to produce sound. Release tension first.
- Monitor any excess tension in your chest and shoulders, neck, and jaw. Ensure you warm up physically, using the exercises from the chapter on posture (Chapter 2) and the chapter on release of tension (Chapter 3).
- Make sure that you have enough air to support your voice before you start to speak.
- Think carefully about how you are coordinating your breath with your voice. As you let the breath out, begin speaking immediately to retain volume and power.
- Try not to 'punch' or 'force' the first sound out.

Exercises to Release Tension and Constriction of the Vocal Folds and the Surrounding Muscles

Use the following movements to help release tension and constriction.

N.B. Be gentle and gradually the tension will reduce. Releasing tension in the throat will ease constriction and is dependent on the shoulders, neck and jaw also being free and the tongue root being released. If your muscles are very tense, the exercises may be slightly uncomfortable at first as you stretch and/or release this tension.

Some of these exercises may feel more comfortable and beneficial than others; try them all but use the ones which help you best regularly.

- Imagine your favourite scent is wafting under your nose – a flower, perfume or freshly baked cookies. Breathe in gently through the nose, with your eyes closed and a contented smile, as you savour this beautiful scent. Notice a sense of expansion in your throat as you feel your throat release. Repeat this several times with normal breaths in between.

- Imagine you have been given a wonderful surprise and you open your mouth wide in an expression of amazement. If you hold this for a couple of seconds you may feel a yawn! Yawning is good; enjoy it, don't suppress it.

- Remember the feeling of coming home after a long, tiring day. As you settle into your favourite chair and kick off your shoes, you take in a deep breath and sigh out a long and loud breath (just breath, no voice).

- Breathe in, then yawn widely and loudly. Feel the release of tension and constriction as you yawn.

- Holding an imaginary glass or large mug, tip the contents slowly over the back of the tongue and down the throat, feeling the additional space that has been created.

- The yoga lion: suddenly (and simultaneously) stretch fingers forward with eyes wide open while stretching the tongue out of the mouth. Hold the position briefly and then gently release; the jaw and tongue will slowly return to their natural positions where they remain free of tension and neutral. Experience the space inside the mouth and the back of the throat. This is a silent activity, don't vocalise a roar!

- Inner pharyngeal posture: yawn and then feel the sense of space between the upper and lower molars. Lift the soft palate by imagining hot food in the mouth.

- Place one hand in the centre of the body over the diaphragm and breathe out silently onto an imaginary mirror held in your other hand as if you were misting up the mirror. Make sure that the breath enters and leaves the body silently.

Exercises for the Temporomandibular Joint (TMJ/Jaw Hinge)

We release the jaw for greater flexibility, resonance, articulation and vocal clarity. The temporomandibular joints, or TMJs, are the two joints that connect your lower jaw to your skull. You can easily feel them: they are the joints that slide and rotate in front of each ear and consist of the lower jaw and the temporal bone, the side and base of the skull. They are among the most complex joints in the body and, along with several muscles, allow the lower jaw to move up and down, side to side and forward and back. When they are properly aligned, smooth muscle actions, chewing, talking, yawning and swallowing can take place, but if any of the structures, muscles, ligaments, jawbone and temporal bone are not aligned or when the movement is not synchronised, several problems can occur, such as temporomandibular disorders (TMD) and chronic facial pain. Myofascial pain, internal derangement of the joint and degenerative joint disease may also occur.

- Work on the jaw joint by using both knuckles to stroke the jaw downwards slowly and creating space between the back teeth. Look into a mirror staring directly ahead and very slowly stroke downwards, keeping the movement slow and in synchrony with your mouth slowly opening. Don't rush this exercise as if you do you may find you are opening your mouth too quickly, ahead of your knuckles.

- Try to imagine chewing a piece of toffee or gum which increases in size with every chewing movement. When the exercise is completed, you may sense that you have 'worked' the jaw joint – the mouth will feel more open, and you may notice a change in resonance.

- Tuck the tongue tip behind the lower front teeth and and keep it there while you bulge the body of the tongue out of the mouth – feel the opening of the jaw and a release in the tongue root. Please note: as with all the exercises, only do this if it feels comfortable.

Introduction to Onset of the Note

We've looked at the effect of tension in the vocal tract and how to mitigate it under the 'deconstriction' label earlier in the chapter, but now we're thinking of tension in terms of the synchronisation of breath and voice, under the 'onset' label.

What Is It, Exactly?

Onset refers to the moment when the vocal folds start vibrating and interrupt the air which flows through the larynx, signalling the beginning of sound production during speech and song. The onset of the note can be classified in different ways, depending on the specific characteristics of the sound produced. For example, a 'hard onset' is when there is a sudden and forceful onset of sound, while a 'soft onset' is when the sound starts more gradually and softly. A 'breathy onset' is when air escapes through the vocal folds before they start vibrating, creating a breathy or whispery sound. Modifying the onset of the note can reduce constriction and is particularly helpful in counteracting tension, and it gives you options for the sound you produce.

Why Does Onset Matter to Me and My Voice?

Some readers who experience 'soft onset' may find their voice doesn't 'connect' straight away, and you may become conscious of the sound you are producing as opposed to what you are saying. This can make you feel less assertive, or not listened to. Alternatively, you may feel that with a hard onset your voice is too harsh when you begin a presentation, possibly giving the wrong first impression, and you find that your audience turns off.

The onset of the voice can also be affected by various factors, including vocal technique, health and emotion. For example, a singer might use a specific vocal technique to achieve a smooth and controlled onset of the voice, while someone experiencing anxiety might have a shaky or abrupt onset of the voice due to tension in the throat. Many people experience this at the beginning of a meeting, for example, and feel frustrated that they can't begin speaking as smoothly as they had hoped, that it was different when they practiced at home, or feel they didn't make a good first impression.

The exercises in this chapter will help you have options when it comes to your onset quality, the atmosphere you want to create and how to adjust your vocal quality and tone.

Practical Advice

Much of the preliminary work needed to establish smooth onset is the same as that required to achieve deconstriction but it is worth repeating here:

– If you feel very tense and anxious, then think about working on your posture, releasing tension and working on your breathing, before working directly on your voice.

- Making changes to the way in which you use your voice requires careful attention and consistent effort.
- Remember it is important to be gentle with your vocal folds; they will work very well if they are not ill-treated.
- Excess tension in the internal musculature of the vocal folds will stop them moving together smoothly and increase the effort needed to produce sound.
- Monitor any excess tension in your chest and shoulders.
- Keep your neck and jaw relaxed.
- Make sure that you have enough air to support your voice before you start to speak.
- Think carefully about how you are coordinating your breath with your voice.
- Try not to 'punch' or 'force' the first sound out.

Exercises for Smooth Voicing

Awareness Exercises

Some of these exercises may feel more beneficial than others; try them all but use the ones which help you best regularly.

- Visualise a smooth, flowing stream of water. Imagine that the sound of your voice is like the flow of water, starting gently and gradually increasing in strength. Start with the sound /hah/. Notice the moment your vocal folds begin to vibrate; maybe gently put your hand on your neck to feel the vibration. Does this smooth flow feel familiar?
- Pay attention to the sensations in your body as you begin to speak or sing. Focus on your throat, jaw and tongue, and try to release any tension you might be holding in these areas. Make a note of any points of tension; perhaps try some of the relaxation techniques from Chapter 3 and try the exercise again. Do you notice any difference in onset?
- Think about the voice of someone you enjoy listening to. Maybe bring up a clip on YouTube or listen to a podcast. Can you make a judgement about what quality of onset they have?
- Self-reflection: after vocalising, take a moment to reflect on your performance. Rate your perceived smoothness of the onset of your voice on a scale of 1–10, with 1 being very abrupt and 10 being very smooth. Repeat this step after the following exercises.

Exercises to Promote Smooth Voicing

You will notice many of these exercises use an initial /h/ sound. During the production of an /h/ sound, the vocal folds do not fully come together, so limiting the potential for damage. Using a voiceless /h/ sound before a voiced vowel encourages auditory and kinaesthetic awareness of the difference between smooth onset of the voice and hard vocal attack.

   N.B. It is important to be aware that the /h/ sound should be produced with minimal tension. Imagine your breath misting up a window on a cold day.

EXERCISE ONE

–   Breathe in and then out on /h/ (a gentle breath as if sighing). Repeat this several times and then add /ah/ so that the sound /hah/ is heard. Repeat this several times. Listen to the sound carefully, noting any tension in the voice. Can you find a way to produce more smoothly?

–   Repeat this exercise but use different vowels such as /ay/ /oh/ and /eye/. Try to avoid the use of /ee/ as this can sometimes cause undue tongue and lip tension, as the tongue is high and the mouth is almost closed for this sound.

–   Try the following: /hey/ /hi/ /hoe/ /hoo/ /hah/.

–   Place /h/ before the following words: I, old, own, all, it.

–   Once this has been tried several times, try to omit the /h/ and repeat the word on its own. Think of the 'action' of /h/ but do not say it.

–   Using the following word list, try to bring the vocal folds together very gently which will ensure the gentle, smooth onset of the note that is required so as not to damage the vocal folds. Initially linger on the /h/ in front of the following words (these may not make sense) and then say the word without the /h/.

h–at	at	h–it	it	h–over	over
h–ever	ever	h–oppose	oppose	h–awful	awful
h–ooze	ooze	h–easy	easy	h–ugly	ugly

– As an alternative to /h/, using words that start with /sh/ can also encourage the vocal folds to come together gently and smoothly. Here is a list of words to try.

show	oh	shy	eye	shaft	aft
shame	aim	shop	op	shell	elle
shout	out	sheer	ear	shame	aim

The following short sentences can be used to practise smooth onset of the voice for an extended period.

How heavy is Henry?	How are you?	Who hears the hall clock?
How hungry is Hannah?	Happy birthday Harry!	Have you had any ham?
Shall I shave, shortly?	Sharon shoved Seamus.	Should we share?

EXERCISE TWO

Smooth onset of the note can also be achieved through the use of imagery, such as using an image of tiptoeing onto a vowel. For example, walk around the room and conjure up an image of stepping lightly while vocalising quietly. Use the following words which begin with a vowel, avoiding hard vocal attack. If this is difficult, go back to putting an /h/ or a sh/ in front of the word to ease onset.

isolate	even	over
ant	upper	eery
everlasting	organise	agile

EXERCISE THREE

The following sentences may be used to achieve smooth onset of the vowel.

I am an ostrich.	I am an Eskimo.	Aunt Aleesha is agreeable.
I am an extrovert.	I am an excellent organist.	Forever and ever and ever.
Over here Ella.	Easier and easier and easier.	Over and over and over again.
Over eleven artists use oil on their easels.	Even otters are allowed the occasional ice-cream.	I'm always eager to elevate my experience.
In April I am off to Australia, Africa, India and Istanbul.	In Orpington older organisers arrange amazing outings.	Are other uncles and aunts as agreeable as Alan and Amy?

Strategies and Suggestions for Deconstriction and Onset of the Note

Before any performance, ensure you release tension and constriction. Use the exercises from this chapter, and some from the release of tension chapter (Chapter 3); find your favourites and build them into your preparation routine.

Three Stages of Preparation for Deconstriction and Smooth Onset

Preparing in Advance

In advance of an important meeting or presentation try to find time to warm up and practice. Speaking a short poem aloud is a great way to warm up the voice and practice smooth onset, or you could try the following extract from a speech by Amelia Earhart where the opportunities for smooth onset have been highlighted.

> The impetus of the sociological evolution of the last half century should be largely credited to those who have toiled in laboratories, and those who have translated into practical use the fruits of such labors.
>
> Among all the marvels of modern invention, that with which I am most concerned, is of course, air transportation. Flying is perhaps the most dramatic of recent scientific attainment. In the brief span of thirty-odd years, the world has seen an inventor's dream, first materialized by the Wright Brothers at Kitty Hawk, become an everyday actuality. Perhaps I'm prejudiced, but to me it seems that no other phase of modern progress contrives to maintain such a brimming measure of romance and beauty, coupled with utility as does aviation.
>
> *A Woman's Place in Science* (1935)

An alternative approach may be to look at the opening remarks of a recent or upcoming presentation and notice where you need to pay attention to ensuring smooth onset. It's useful to record or video yourself and listen carefully to any incidents of hard attack or constriction.

Preparing En Route

These can be performed as you walk to work, in the lift or the loo!

– Clean your teeth with your tongue for tongue release. Run your tongue around the outer surface of your teeth keeping your lips gently closed/together.

Continued

- Sigh as if very content – feel the 'width' in your throat.
- Yawn! Reducing tension in the throat, jaw and neck.
- Gently massage the jaw joint.

Preparing in the Meeting Room

- Be aware of your posture and shoulder tension; ensure you are sitting in a balanced and comfortable position with both feet on the floor.
- Take in a breath and, as you let it out, imagine that your breath is following the path of a channel of water flowing upwards from your belly button, through the chest, neck and out of the top of your head. As you do that, sense the openness and length of the throat and vocal tract and the width in the back of the neck. This is also good for your eye line, and prevents constriction.
- Breathe out gently to create a mist on your glasses or phone, as if to clean them, to encourage smooth onset.
- As you walk into a room, or begin to speak, feel the 'inside smile' to aid deconstriction. With lips lightly together, breathe in through the nose. Ensure the jaw is not clenched and there is space between your upper and lower teeth. Begin to softly smile, and feel the apples of your cheeks rising. With that you will feel the space increasing and widening at the back of the mouth, almost as if you are smiling from that place. This is known as the 'inside smile', which increases awareness of this area and encourages a more open setting.
- With your mouth closed imagine you are singing like an opera singer. This in turn may produce a yawn.
- Use your greetings to 'warm up' – "Hi, Hey! Hello! How are you? Hope you're well! How's it going?" Be aware of the smooth onset you can achieve.

Sound Bite

Deconstriction and smooth onset allows the vocal folds to function optimally, to release tension within the vocal tract and to improve resonance, tone and projection of the voice. Increased vocal clarity will reduce the listening demands of your audience and allow you to focus on the essential elements of your presentation.

6 | Resonance

Introduction

Resonance plays a crucial role for professional voice users, enabling effortless message delivery and amplification while minimising vocal strain and fatigue. Vocal resonance is essentially the sound of the note, or 'laryngeal buzz', augmented and modified by the shape and size of your distinctive resonating cavities, the throat, mouth and nasal passages. These cavities determine the specific qualities and nuances of your tone, timbre and the richness of your voice.

Very simply put, the intensity, or quality, of the sound you hear when you speak or sing is caused by the reverberation of sound waves from your vibrating vocal folds, which are enhanced by the air-filled resonators through which it passes. There are six main resonating areas in the body – the larynx, the pharynx, the oral cavity, the nasal cavity, the upper skull cavity and the chest – which modify and enhance the sound.

In this chapter, we will look in detail at how to find more resonance and utilise the natural resonator available to you: your body and, specifically, your vocal tract.

What Is It, Exactly?

The resonatory system modifies and amplifies the fundamental note and consists of:

– The chest.
– The pharyngeal, oral and nasal cavities.

DOI: 10.4324/9781003361114-7

The resonators above the larynx can alter in size, shape and tension through the movement of the base of the tongue and the soft palate. In addition, further modification can occur through contraction of the pharyngeal and extrinsic laryngeal muscles.

Although the larynx is obviously the primary contributor to the production of voice, without the acoustic influence of the resonators the voice would sound very thin indeed. Most of the quality and loudness characteristics associated with the voice are the result of the resonators. In the same way that the weak vibrations of the strings of a musical instrument are altered by the resonating body of the instrument, so the tone that is produced at the level of the larynx, the laryngeal buzz, is altered by the resonators. The airway above the larynx acts like an acoustic filter, which can suppress or maximise some sounds as they pass through. Alterations can also occur in the configuration of the vocal tract by varying tongue positions, raising or lowering the soft palate, and as an effect of the degree of relaxation or tension present.

The mouth or oral resonator, being the resonator capable of most flexibility of size and shape, is able to enhance natural resonance by producing optimal shapes and so reinforce vibration. Additional resonance can be developed through vowels and the voiced nasal consonants /m/, /n/ and /ng/ that add nasal resonance. For the skilled professional voice user, effective use of the resonators can be a powerful tool in increasing the range, power and tonality of the voice.

Each resonating space has a different characteristic and their effect on the voice changes depending on the size, shape, type of opening, composition and thickness of their walls, surfaces, and combinations of the above. These factors also determine which frequencies (pitch) are enhanced. Larger resonators respond most to low frequencies; resonators which experience less 'damping' create a brighter sound. If we think of musical instruments, we can use them as an example to link to the sound produced by physical resonators; for example, think of a piccolo or a violin and the sound it makes in contrast to a drum or double bass. Resonators which are flexible and mobile are more universal in how they enhance the sound; the mouth or pharynx is more flexible than the nose or the sinuses.

Balanced resonance promotes a more robust vocal tone that encompasses both lower and higher frequencies, resulting in a well-rounded and resonant voice, which in turn can be effective in engaging the attention of your listener. To achieve this balance it is important that all resonators work in concert. While change is possible, resonance does somewhat depend on the size, shape, flexibility and structure and physiology of your body, so someone with a long, thin and fine nasal cavity will not produce the same nasal resonance as someone with a small, short, thick nose.

Any imbalance in the resonators can disproportionately affect vocal quality and will be heard by your listeners; it can also detract from other vocal aspects which may be completely fine, for example:

- You may have a very flexible and mobile tongue and jaw, but too much oral resonance is making your voice sound 'thin' and 'high' in pitch.
- Neglecting oral resonance, which involves the shaping and amplification of sound within the oral cavity, can result in a lack of clarity, warmth and projection.
- If someone heavily relies on throat resonance, their voice may sound strained, constricted or 'throaty'. The lack of balanced resonance from other areas can lead to vocal fatigue and limited pitch range.
- Overemphasising nasal resonance can result in a nasal tone quality where the sound is overly focused in the nasal cavity. This can make the voice sound pinched, nasally, or lacking depth.
- Depending excessively on chest resonance alone can create a heavy and boomy sound. While it can provide depth and richness, a disproportionate reliance on chest resonance may hinder vocal agility, flexibility and the ability to produce higher notes with ease, and navigate more sensitive situations.
- Neglecting head resonance can lead to a lack of brightness, clarity and sparkle in the voice. The upper range may suffer, sounding dull or strained, and the voice may lack the projection and presence needed for certain styles of singing or public speaking.

Why Does Resonance Matter to Me?

When we consider voices that we admire and enjoy listening to, they often possess common qualities such as richness, a wide range of movement and vibrational energy.

Resonance extends beyond mere vocal quality; it encompasses the notion that sound, or your message, can travel and have a profound impact. Just as the sound of a bell can reverberate and travel through a building, a resonant voice can reach the far corners of a room. When we say that someone's message resonates with us, we may mean that their voice brings their message to life in a way that touches us emotionally or intellectually. By understanding and cultivating resonance in our own speaking voices, we too can enhance the power of our message, creating a captivating and memorable experience for our listeners.

Resonance is invaluable in the workplace as it aids volume, amplification, projection, clarity and vocal variety. By cultivating a rounder and more embodied sound, we can convey a sense of confidence that has the potential to make listeners feel assured and at ease. Actors, often excellent communicators off stage as well as on, do not rely solely on high volume in order to be heard. The use of high volume *without* resonance can result in a vocal quality that may be perceived as forceful, empty, domineering, insincere or insensitive. This can cause complications in the workplace; your audience cannot sense the true meaning of your message if the heart of the message is missing.

The voice comes alive through resonance, as sound reverberates within the body, infusing it with meaning and vitality. It can help us sound more powerful, dynamic and commanding or nurturing and comforting.

Humans are naturally drawn to resonant voices for several reasons, which can be both physiological and psychological. Considering this, as professional voice users, understanding and harnessing the power of resonance can be highly advantageous in our communication endeavours. Here are some possible explanations as to why resonant voices hold this natural appeal:

– A resonant voice is often associated with qualities such as confidence, strength and authority. When someone speaks with a resonant voice, it can convey a sense of power and command, which can be appealing and influential to others.

– Resonant voices can evoke emotions in listeners. A voice that vibrates with rich, full tones can be emotionally captivating and create a sense of warmth or comfort. It can also be perceived as more genuine and trustworthy, leading to a deeper emotional connection with the speaker.

– Resonance can enhance the clarity and projection of speech, making it easier to understand and follow. A resonant voice can cut through background noise and be heard clearly in various environments, which can be advantageous in communication and public speaking settings.

– Societal norms and cultural conditioning can also influence our preference for resonant voices. In some cultures, or societies, a deep, resonant voice may be associated with desirable traits such as leadership or assertiveness, leading to a preference for such voices.

It is important to note that preferences for voices can vary among individuals and are also influenced by personal experiences, cultural backgrounds and individual perceptions.

Self-Assessment and Building Awareness

Know Your Resonance

Making changes to the resonance or overall tonal quality of your voice will take time as it can be difficult to fully identify different resonant qualities in your own voice. Vocal self-knowledge is an important aspect of this process; to begin, ask yourself the following questions.

Resonance Self-Awareness

Has anyone ever asked you if you had a cold when you haven't?	
Have you ever felt that your voice didn't carry far in a large space?	
Have you ever felt that your voice sounded a bit 'thin'?	
Have you ever felt that your voice sounds a bit too childlike?	
Do people ever comment on your voice in a negative way?	
Do you feel that you can't get enough 'warmth' into your voice?	
Do you feel that people tend to ignore you when you are trying to get attention in a group?	
If you are speaking to someone new who cannot see you, do you feel you are perceived as being younger than you are and/or given less status?	
Do you ever find it difficult to sound authoritative in professional and personal exchanges?	
Are you ever uncomfortable listening to your own voice?	
Generally, do you think your voice gives a poor impression of you to other people?	

The solution to affirmative responses to the above questions is often found in enhancing resonance in other parts of your voice, which maybe you're not currently doing; working on all the exercises in this chapter will lead to more balanced resonance and help you become more familiar with your voice. Whilst resonance may play a factor in sounding childlike, or as if you have a cold, or your voice not carrying well or lacking in authority, it is important to remember that this may not be the only reason. Your communication style will play a big factor in how you are perceived by others, and some solutions are provided in Chapter 11. Remember that your own perception of your voice may not be accurate.

The discomfort and dislike we experience when hearing our own voices in audio recordings can be attributed to a combination of physiological and psychological factors. When we hear our voices in our heads, the sound is transmitted through a blend of air conduction and internal bone conduction via our skull bones. The sound from a recording, however, is filtered through technology first, and then reaches our ears through air conduction.

Psychologically, the discrepancy between our self-perception and the reality of our recorded voice can be jarring. Our voice is a unique and integral part of our self-identity and realising that others have been hearing a different version of our voice can be unsettling. Additionally, we are more accustomed to hearing ourselves in a certain way, so the unfamiliarity of our recorded voice can contribute to our discomfort.

Research has shown that individuals tend to rate their own recorded voices more negatively compared to objective assessments. This suggests that our own self-criticism and judgement can play a role in our dislike of our recorded voice. It is important to recognise that we may be overly harsh in evaluating our own voices and that others may perceive our voices differently and more positively than we do.

When a voice is resonant, it is more likely to be vibrant, engaging and, therefore, have more carrying power. Many people are unaware of their own resonance, but it is possible to feel the vibrations in the mask of the face, the head and the chest. Those with very resonant voices need to balance sound with muscular diction to ensure they can be clearly understood.

Can You Feel Your Resonance?

- Gently tap on the 'mask' of the face (the front portion of the face, around the nose, cheek bones, sinuses, and facial bones) of the face while humming on /m/, /n/, /ng/, /v/ and /z/. Be aware of the vibrations around the nose, on the forehead, the skull and on the lips. Vibrations can also be felt on the back of the neck.

- Beat the chest with a fist, while sounding a long /mah/ sound and a long /maw/ sound as this will connect you to your chest resonance.

- Opening out from consonants /m/, /n/, /ng/, /v/ and /z/ to vowels /ah/, /aw/, /oh/ or /ay/ will transfer the resonance to the vowels. For example, /mah/, /naw/, /voh/, /zay/.

- Using the phrases 'many, many mumbling men', 'rumbling volcanoes', 'Zoe is a zebra at the zoo', emphasise the resonance in the /m/, /v/, /z/ and /ng/ sounds. Explore, exaggerate and enjoy the vibration from the resonance you create.

Practical Advice

When thinking about resonance, the following advice may be helpful.

–   Working on resonance will give your voice a full, round sound rather than a thin one.
–   Make sure that you investigate any possible medical reason for an imbalance of resonance.
–   Be aware of any residual tension or constriction you may be holding in the vocal tract as this will affect resonance. Try to make sure your tongue, jaw, neck and larynx are free from tension before attempting the exercises.
–   Keep free from tension during the exercises and think about your posture and how you are using your breath to support the sound. Remember, the quality of the laryngeal note is of critical importance when working on resonance.
–   Some accents make greater use of certain resonant qualities than others. For example, it is accepted that American English is more nasally resonant than British English. Be aware that different cultural or racial groups habitually prioritise different resonant qualities.
–   Listen to the resonance of different speakers to familiarise yourself with the difference that certain resonators bring to vocal quality; for example, listen to the change in the sound of your voice when you have a cold.

Tension and Resonance

'Vibrations are murdered by tension' (Kristin Linklater, 2006). When we feel anxious or under confident, or simply not connected to the message we are sharing at work, we tend to fall into a monotone and we may rely solely on volume to get our point across.

Tension is a significant factor that can greatly impact vocal quality and impede optimal vocal performance. When it comes to achieving 'best practice' in vocal technique, managing and minimising tension becomes crucial. Tension can manifest in various ways, and it can have adverse effects on both vocal production and resonance.

Tension in the jaw may be a result of tension in the shoulders and neck due to sitting at a desk all day, thereby restricting oral resonance. Excessive mobile phone use or unexpressed frustration can affect the quality, volume, pitch and resonance of the voice. When the body is free from excess tension and the skeletal framework can find its natural alignment, breathing improves and the voice functions without restriction.

Exercises for Oral Resonance

N.B. Before starting work on oral resonance, relax the pharynx by yawning, and release the tongue by stretching it outside the mouth and gently stroking the jaw downwards to release the temporomandibular joint around the jaw 'hinge'.

–   Imagine chewing gum or toffee which increases in size with each chew. As you do this you will be aware of the increased size and openness of the pharynx.
–   Try an 'inside' smile. In this exercise you relax the lips and 'smile' with the back of the mouth or where you feel the tonsils might be. The inside smile will increase your awareness of this area, this may make you yawn, embrace the yawn!
–   Deliberately create some tension and, with a tight jaw, tense tongue and restricted oral space, speak the line 'The five parked cars are mine'. Now repeat the line with a loose jaw, relaxed tongue and open oral space. Feel free to exaggerate! Notice the contrast in sound quality and the ease with which you articulate.

You can try this again with these sentences:

Now I see the fleecy clouds.	Not hot rolled gold, but cold rolled gold.	Mark Parker sent a letter to settle the bet.

Next, repeat this 'tension to relaxation' sequence using a short sentence you regularly say at work, for example, 'Great to see you again' or 'I'll put it in the diary', initially as if your teeth were stuck together and then as if you were slightly drunk or very sleepy. It is useful to observe the contrast between the sound and sensation produced by speaking in this manner with the sound and sensation produced when the sentence is spoken without tension. Which feels more familiar to you when under pressure? If you find yourself becoming tight and tense, can you introduce some softness?

Exercises for Pharyngeal Resonance

The pharynx is a large resonator and is linked to the smaller resonators of the oral and nasal resonators. It is a mobile and readily altered space. The pharynx is sensitive to changes in posture, tension and muscle configuration, and is responsive to emotional stress. Exercises to develop increased pharyngeal resonance are very useful, not only in enhancing the resonance of the voice by finding a connection with the chest but also, in releasing areas of tension in the jaw and tongue.

EXERCISE ONE

– Create an open and released oral cavity by moving into a yawn, feeling the increase in size of the oropharynx with a corresponding increase in the distance between the upper and lower molars. In this exercise it is most important to concentrate on the increased space at the back rather than the front of the mouth. Too much space at the front of the mouth will lead to tension in the jaw 'hinge' (temporomandibular joint).

– Relax the jaw and allow a limited opening at the front of the mouth.

– Produce an 'inside smile' at the back of the oral cavity. This might bring on a yawn; if so, allow it to develop and feel the expansion of the pharynx.

– Let the tongue protrude as much as is comfortably possible and attempt to speak a sentence clearly. It is the effort to achieve clarity that will open up the pharyngeal space. Obviously, the sound will not be natural, but that is not a requirement of this exercise. Relax and feel the space created. Monitor the effect by repeating the same sentence without protruding the tongue. Added resonance should have been achieved.

– From a yawn move into a sigh as you breathe out. Use /ah/ or /aw/for practice because this will encourage space in the mouth as well as in the pharynx. Your tongue tip should be touching the lower front teeth but should not be pressed against them.

– Once you have established the yawn, sigh out on /oh/ and then say the following sentences, keeping the pharynx as relaxed as possible.

'I own a golden opal,' said Owen.	Omar rose to the top of the organisation.	Only old goats wear home sewn overcoats.
Over and over and over again.	'Oh no, don't go,' cried Hope!	Woah, Jo, what a throw!

EXERCISE TWO

The vowel /ah/ or /aw/ is recommended in this exercise as this will encourage maximum oral and pharyngeal space. The tongue should be relaxed with the tip in contact with the lower front teeth.

Paul's car would not start as a sparkplug was worn.	Audrey and Aubrey almost always order four portions.	Farmer Martin in Dartmouth saw the larks soar at dawn.

EXERCISE THREE

Using the sentence 'Eve ate apples all afternoon', listen to the sound achieved when contrasting:

– Excessively loose cheek muscles vs. excessively tight cheek muscles.
– A retracted tongue vs. a forward, floppy tongue.
– Clenched teeth vs. an excessively open jaw.

Exercises for Nasal Resonance

The nasal resonators are the least adaptable in terms of their ability to change shape and size, but they are of considerable significance in the effect they have on voice quality. Extremes of disordered nasal resonance may occur because of certain oral and maxillofacial disorders. Habitual tongue and soft palate tension can produce a tight nasal sound. The goal for working on any single resonance quality is to achieve an overall balance between oral, pharyngeal and nasal resonators.

EXERCISE ONE

Produce the following sounds in sequence:

/m ah/m oh/m ee/	/n ah/n oh/n ee/	/ng ah/ng oh/ng ee/

As you repeat the exercise, notice the difference between the nasalised resonance of the /m/, /n/ and /ng/ and the denasalised oral resonance of the vowel. Try not to let nasalisation bleed into the vowel sound.

EXERCISE TWO

The following sentences are useful practice material for developing and feeling nasal resonance. Once again maintain the contrast between nasal consonants /m/ /n/ /ng/ and the non-nasal vowel.

Noel is missing singing soothing songs in Singapore.
Mary buys mouth-watering moussaka and mangoes from the market in Malvern.
November is not the month for munching many mince pies.
Noa the nice nurse never nurses noisy, naughty children.
In Nottingham nine hundred and ninety-nine nesting nightingales noisily sing and dance in the nearly night sky.
The morbid musicians mournfully murmur the mystical madrigal.
Such nonsensical sentences are nothing but a nuisance to the innocent onlooker.

There is room for improvisation here; feel free to make up your own sentences as well, and try regular phrases from your working day which feature nasal consonants.

Exercises for Chest Resonance

For professional voice users, it is important to identify the dominant resonator and to develop the underused resonators. Of particular importance for actors is the ability to switch selectively from one resonator to another; this can also be a useful skill for teachers who read to classes; narrators; those hoping to create varied and interesting speeches; those transitioning from large to small to one on one meetings throughout the day. It is a valuable skill for all communicators.

Chest resonance is often the easiest to feel and perceive physically, as it vibrates and resonates in the chest cavity, creating a sense of depth and fullness in the voice. Overuse of chest resonance makes the voice sound unbalanced and can be perceived as bombastic or inflexible.

EXERCISE ONE

- Sounding a sustained /m/ and opening to the vowel /ah/, gently beat the chest with both fists. /Mah/.

- Repeat the exercise using a sustained /v/ and opening to the vowels /ah/, /oh/, /aw/ and /oo/. For example, /vah/, /voh/, /vaw/, /voo/.

Do not push the voice below a comfortable note but try to experience chest resonance and feel the vibration of the sound in the front and middle and lower back.

EXERCISE TWO

- Start with the sound /vah/, /mah/ or /zah/.

- Glide from a comfortable note in the middle of your range down into the chest register, decreasing the energy or volume, and monitoring the sound very carefully to avoid a 'pushed' feeling.

- Feel the resonance as you 'sing' or 'chant' this sound.

To further this exercise, start at different points in your range and explore variety in pitch and the different types of resonance this creates.

EXERCISE THREE

Beat the chest with the fists while exploring the vowels – the quality and variety – in this poem:

> Had I the heavens' embroidered cloths,
> Enwrought with golden and silver light,
> The blue and the dim and the dark cloths
> Of night and light and the half-light,
> I would spread the cloths under your feet:
> But I, being poor, have only my dreams;
> I have spread my dreams under your feet;
> Tread softly because you tread on my dreams.
> 'Cloths of Heaven', William Butler Yeats (1839–1922)

Suggestions and Strategies

Mimicking voices from radio and television may provide a useful starting point from which to work on resonance, and there are many impressionists on social media revealing their process which can be fun and informative to watch. It is, however, extremely important at this early stage not to allow the voice to be pushed or forced down. Always remain as stress-free and playful as possible. As with any aspect of voice work, auditory, kinaesthetic and tactile feedback is important to develop awareness.

Recommendations for Further Developing Resonance

- Try reading poetry out loud. Attempt to explore the difference in sounds, physically and vocally: plosive (/p/, /t/, /k/, /b/, /d/, /g/) and sustained consonants (/m/, /n/, /ng/) or the shapes and resonance of vowels. A poetry collection such as 'Poem for the Day' is useful to build this practice; if you subscribe to the Poetry Foundation they will email you a poem every day. The Poetry Society is a great resource, and searching social media for 'slam poetry' or 'spoken word' will give you some vocal inspiration. Reading poetry aloud may be unfamiliar to you, but over time, many people discover a connection with emotion and a level of expression in their voice they never knew they had. Exploring the number of syllables in a word, which ones are stressed and which unstressed, the energy of different words and sounds, all release the music of the language.

- Try an acting class or join an amateur dramatics society.

- Listen to audiobooks and begin to recognise the techniques used by readers you enjoy.

- Join a debating society or speech-making group, such as Toastmasters™.

- Read aloud, don't mutter under your breath. Actively explore the energy, variety and resonance; feel the words in your mouth. Use poetry and prose, but also try non-fiction too – news bulletins, emails, presentations and articles. This will help you bring vocal expertise into your day-to-day conversations. The most effective way of gaining confidence in the ability to use words is to practise speaking aloud carefully. Read aloud from the verse and prose that make up the wealth of great literature. Carefully selected words

---

Continued

> trigger exciting and interesting sound patterns and images. The joy experienced when 'feeling and tasting' the vowels and consonants in the mouth is intensely rewarding. Choose passages that engender a passionate response and words that reflect your personal ideas and feelings. When there is commitment behind the word, the voice reflects it naturally.

Keeping Up Awareness

Consider a time when you felt 'unheard'; perhaps you felt you were not being listened to, or you thought your voice too quiet for the space. Resonance is an effective way to amplify your voice with ease and connect both with your message and with others. If you feel you aren't being 'heard', the following prompts might help you to feel more resonance and to connect more fully with your message and listener.

– Can you connect more with the vowels in your words? Vowels play a crucial role in shaping the quality and character of our voices. Each vowel has its unique sound, duration and resonance characteristics, influencing the emotional impact of our speech.

– Are you aware of your jaw? Are you carrying habitual tension there? Pay attention to your jaw as you sit at the computer, travel on the train or when looking at your phone; is it possible to find some release there?

– How open do you perceive your mouth to be when talking? Is there any reason why you are not opening your mouth? Are you concerned about how your teeth look or whether your breath smells? This may cause you to minimise the mouth-opening.

– How much of yourself are you putting into your message? Does your message resonate with you? Do you believe in what you are saying?

– Do you trust others? Do you feel that you are being scrutinised, and this is causing both tension and restraint?

– Think of a voice you love to listen to – how would you describe their voice? Can you identify the qualities that speak to you? Consider how you can bring more of those into your own speech.

Role-Specific Resonance

We have only looked at a few professions in this list, and just some of their specific resonance requirements; this is by no means an exhaustive list. The value here is to understand your audience, space and content and how that might require 'more' of you vocally, and specifically with resonance.

If your profession isn't listed, read the descriptions below and take some time to consider if there are connections to your needs as a professional voice user. For example, are you also working in a particularly large space, do you have to reach people at a distance, does the room you are in affect the way you sound? Could more time spent on the exercises in this chapter support you?

Law Enforcement/Security Guard

Practice diaphragmatic breathing and maintain good posture to ensure optimal vocal resonance. Focus on projecting and speaking with clarity and authority when addressing a crowd. Look at suggestions for eye levels and positioning yourself in Chapter 6 in order to make use of your environment to optimise resonance, for example finding a hard surface which your voice can bounce off, to prevent your voice from fading across distance.

Teachers/Trainers/Coaches

Pay attention to your projection and clarity. Use appropriate vocal dynamics and variety to engage students and maintain their attention. Incorporate short vocal warm-ups and breathing exercises into your day, and particularly before any difficult, rowdy classes. If you are teaching sports inside or outside, employ other aids such as flags, whistles or hand gestures.

Customer-Support Agents/Telephone Operators

Resonance matters in a call centre as it can help convey confidence and professionalism over the phone. Ensure you are working on breathing and be mindful of your posture; focus on muscular flexibility for clarity and employ modulation. Keep hydrated and take regular short vocal breaks to maintain vocal health and resonance. Maintain a relaxed and positive manner while speaking. Smiling can naturally enhance the resonance and warmth in your voice. Prepare for your shifts by checking that your environment is ergonomically sound, that you have a chair or seating that supports your back, allowing you to breathe 'properly' and utilise control over your voice.

Actors/Voiceover Artists/Broadcasters

Engage in a vocal and physical warm-up. Work on breath control, vocal range and vocal agility. As resonance shifting enables a performer to achieve vocal variety within a single performance, ensure you warm up each 'element' of your resonance for free and confident vocal dexterity. This is vital in audio-book work or if multi-roleing. Maintain vocal hydration throughout the day by drinking enough water, prior to and during performing.

Religious/Spiritual/Political Leaders

By tapping into their resonant voice, religious or spiritual leaders can create a powerful and sincere presence that resonates with their community, fostering a deeper connection and engagement. 'Bad' shouting, which, involves force-fully and loudly projecting the voice without necessarily utilising the natural resonators is often used to express intense emotion, convey urgency or grab attention. However, it typically involves increased tension in the vocal folds, resulting in a harsh, strained and less-controlled sound. Utilising the natural resonance chambers of the body to create a full, vibrant and well-projected sound, you can add depth, clarity and warmth to your voice, and help the voice to carry and be heard clearly without straining. Ensure you 'use' your space; in large spaces with high ceilings and hard surfaces sound has a longer reverberation time as the sound reflects and bounces off surfaces. This can enhance the natural resonance of the voice. Excessive reverb or echo in a space, however, can blur the clarity of the voice, making it harder for listeners to understand the individual words. It is important for such leaders to modify their vocal technique to ensure clear articulation and projection, balancing the benefits of the space's natural resonance with the need for intelligibility.

Sound Bite

The sound of your voice is adapted by resonance, which allows you to amplify and shape it in whatever way you want, from shrill and aggres-sive to warm and mellow.

---

7 Exploring Pitch

Introduction

When we consider the pitch of our voice, we are thinking in very simple terms about the perceived highness or lowness of the note produced by the vocal folds, dictating how high or how low our voice is. Our pitch range is, literally, the variety of pitch within the vocal repertoire of an individual, from the lowest to the highest note we can produce. But, of course, we don't often use all the notes in our range; we tend to keep to a particular set of habitual notes in our voice, which are easily accessible to us. In general, we have an average speaking range of two octaves, although we rarely use our full range when speaking. Contrast that with Mariah Carey who has a range of five octaves, while Beyonce has a range of three to four while singing. An adult woman's average range is from 165 to 300 Hz, while a man's is 60 to 180 Hz, giving a small crossover between male and female vocal ranges. Men's voices are generally deeper because the testosterone released during puberty causes their vocal folds to lengthen and thicken.

The exercises in this chapter may help you to extend your pitch or begin to feel comfortable using lower or higher sounds than you habitually do in day-to-day conversation. Physiology plays a part in pitch, and pitch modulation through exercises will not be a magic wand to give you the gift of pitch range like that of Alicia Keys, John Legend or Adele. However, becoming more accustomed to playing with pitch can allow you to employ pitch change to reflect meaning, highlight information or emphasise the feeling behind your words. A voice which uses a variety of pitches and explores its range sounds free and confident, adds expressivity to your speech and is one way to enhance an audience's engagement. The ability to move through pitches allows you to sound like 'you', even under stress, giving you the skills to make conscious changes when needed; for example, if you find yourself

DOI: 10.4324/9781003361114-8

'stuck' on one note or feeling as if your voice is much higher because you're anxious, understanding how to shift pitch will be extremely helpful.

We often express delight and surprise using the higher end of our pitch range. When we are making certain statements or being dismissive, we may, without thinking, use a lower pitch. When the question is asked 'How can I be a better storyteller', the unexpected answer may be pitch versatility (along with all of the other vocal elements we are exploring in this book!) because without incorporating variety in our pitch range, our storytelling becomes monotonous, lacking dynamic nuances that captivate listeners. A monotone delivery can be exhausting for the audience, as they are left deciphering meaning, struggling to determine the emotions conveyed and the intentions behind the words. The burden falls on them to transform the auditory information into a tangible narrative. Harnessing the power of pitch can breathe life into our delivery, infusing it with excitement, surprise or disinterest, guiding the listeners through a vivid and engaging experience where meaning is effortlessly conveyed.

The preferences we hold for the sound of another person's voice may have evolutionary roots, as supported by numerous scientific studies on voice attractiveness and the attributes associated with pitch, particularly in leaders. In a very general sense, lower-pitched voices are historically perceived as stronger and more competent, which may explain the preference. It goes without saying that pitch and competence are not intrinsically linked; however, your listener's biases may align them. Statements, dismissals and orders tend to be unconsciously delivered at the lower end of your range or by using a falling pitch pattern; meanwhile, questions, admiration and acquiescence are often instinctively voiced in your higher pitch range. It is important not to 'force' your voice into an unnaturally low pitch or use a continuous lower register because you believe it to be more desirable. Despite the UK *Equality Act 2010*, in practical terms, discrimination against women in the workplace remains, and may well be expressed covertly, if not overtly. One noted reaction to this is the way in which women have been encouraged, or felt pressured, to consciously adopt a lower pitch in the belief they will be taken more seriously. However, speaking only in the lowest few notes of your voice can be very limiting, potentially harming the voice and limiting its expressive range. This results in a lacklustre and constrained vocal quality with little possibility for vocal variety, and the voice becomes somewhat 'rigid' and inauthentic, and any 'gravitas' you may be seeking is subsequently lost. There are, no doubt, old-established linguistic 'codes' which have recognised pitch patterns, and despite changes to the accepted 'sound of power', the 'sound of certainty' is still represented by a lower pitch and the 'sound of doubt' represented by a higher pitch. When thinking about high and low, we mean *your* high and low, which are within your individual pitch range, and we are never suggesting that you force your voice to sound like someone else's. The exercises in this chapter will help you explore your particular pitch range, and the result may be that you discover notes you didn't know you had access to, giving your voice a natural energy and richness. The aim of this chapter is to provide you with pitch choice, offering you the option to use a variety of pitches when needed, vary your pitch more easily and align your intention with your sound.

Why Does Pitch Matter to Me?

Many professionals' first concern about their voice is that it is 'monotonous'. Perhaps they feel that they don't have access to pitch variation in their voice, or they find their pitch feels too 'high' when under pressure; often people are concerned that this makes them appear anxious or tense, or that anxiety and tension are leaking out behind the 'professional persona' and causing this pitch change.

The pitch of the voice will often carry the emotional content of speech. When an individual becomes excited or stressed, vocal pitch generally rises, and the voice becomes shrill. In the same way, when frightened or very angry, an individual may literally 'lose' their voice and be able only to whisper. Individuals tend to use a very low vocal pitch when they are attempting to maintain control or when they are in a situation in which they want to appear more authoritative.

We know that stress can make us feel out of control when it comes to pitch. The computer says, 'the meeting host will let you in soon' and suddenly your shoulders rise, you hold your breath, your heart starts racing and when you are finally let in to the 'room' your first words come out in a voice that doesn't seem to belong to you. An ability to modulate your pitch can give you the tools to adapt and alter your pitch even when under pressure. There are several familiar scenarios in which you may find that pitch is 'exposing' you and potentially affecting your communicative effectiveness.

Such situations include:

– When defending a belief or feeling under attack.
– When presenting an idea in which you are personally invested.
– Speaking to a large or rowdy crowd of people.
– Doing something meaningful, emotional or important such as delivering a wedding speech.

- When you have been kept waiting for a meeting to begin.
- Making a complaint or dealing with a grievance.
- Speaking with a recognised expert.
- In an interview situation.

The advantages for the individual candidate, best man, team leader, etc., who can employ a relaxed vocal quality regardless of nerves, and the disadvantages for another individual who cannot, are plain.

In summary, a lack of variety in vocal pitch – whether too high or too low – can result in monotony, reduced emotional expression, decreased impact and influence, and potential miscommunication in the workplace. Developing the ability to work with differing and varied vocal pitches can greatly enhance your communication skills. Excessive use of a singular pitch can potentially strain or damage the vocal folds. On the other hand, using a healthy and appropriate vocal pitch that is within your natural range can help maintain good vocal health. It allows your vocal folds to vibrate freely and efficiently without excessive strain or tension, which can help prevent vocal fold damage and maintain clear and smooth vocal production.

A lack of variety in vocal pitch may have several negative impacts in the workplace:

- If you consistently use the same pitch throughout your communication, it can become monotonous and dull, resulting in a lack of influence on, or engagement with, your audience, making your speech sound 'robotic' or uninteresting, less compelling, persuasive, authoritative or convincing, which may undermine your ability to influence others, whether you're giving a presentation, leading a team or negotiating with colleagues or clients.
- Vocal pitch is a key component of expressing emotions in speech. Limited pitch variation may result in you struggling to convey emotions effectively, such as enthusiasm, empathy or urgency.
- Lack of clarity in your message can be related to a lack of volume, but low volume is not always the culprit. It is likely that several contributing factors, including excessively high or excessively low pitch, are to blame.
- When told to 'speak up', many people simply raise their pitch and become strident, which is very stressful both for the speaker and the listeners. A voice that is shrill is likely to be alienating rather than engaging or inclusive. The effort involved in pushing the sound out is the very thing that limits it. If this style and pitch of delivery becomes habitual, the voice is likely to become damaged. For this reason, and for the sake of

effective communication, avoid responding when angry or frustrated. A voice that is perceived to be 'out of control' has low status and suggests desperation or intimidation. It is often much more effective to pause and take time to adjust your alignment and raise your status, before responding in a calm, controlled and 'grounded' manner.

What Is It, Exactly?

When we talked about pitch at the beginning of the chapter, we described it in simple terms as how high or how low the note is when produced by the vocal folds; we also mentioned that pitch changes occur naturally throughout life from childhood to adulthood to old age, with, in general, men's voices being lower in pitch than women's. In some instances, however, expected pitch changes do not occur and individuals do not have access to a pitch range that is appropriate to their age and gender. Pitch range refers to the variety of pitch which is within the vocal repertoire of an individual. Pitch movement, when it occurs within a word, is known as inflection, while pitch movement over a series of phrases or sentences is known as intonation. Someone who speaks in a monotone would be considered to have a narrow range, whereas someone who modulates their voice and encompasses a variety of pitches, both high and low, is deemed to employ a wide range.

Your Voice, Your Pitch, and Changes in Pitch

Your voice will change over the years due to ageing. Hormonal changes account for the voice breaks and uncertain pitch that occur in the male voice at puberty, where the vocal folds increase in length and thickness. For women, hormonal changes at puberty, during menstruation and during pregnancy cause an increase in fluid retention, resulting in an increase in vocal fold mass, or 'swelling' of the vocal folds. This, in turn, leads to a temporary lowering of the fundamental frequency of the voice, with a subsequent change in vocal quality. Females who are using their voices extensively with heavy vocal loading should be aware that their voices might be particularly vulnerable at these times.

The menopause signals a reduction in the production of oestrogen and progesterone hormones, and this decrease in oestrogen levels again leads to an increase in vocal fold mass, although instead of this effecting a temporary change in pitch, as in the premenstrual period, the change in postmenopausal pitch is permanent. In addition to perceptual voice quality changes, such as reduction in pitch and a narrower register (the range of the voice from high to low), other changes occur, such as:

- Lack of vocal intensity.
- Vocal fatigue.
- Decreased lubrication of the vocal folds, meaning that the vocal folds lose viscosity and the protective role of viscosity as a shock absorber is lost.
- Loss of lubrication both internally and externally brings about:
  - Increased rigidity.
  - Decreased flexibility.
  - An inability of the cricothyroid muscle to increase the tension of the vocal folds during phonation.

For some women, however, androgens – which contribute to a loss of secretion – become oestrogen in fat cells, thereby indirectly reversing some of the vocal effects of postmenopausal loss of oestrogen in those women with greater stores of fat cells. It should also be remembered that female hormonal changes do not occur in isolation; significant age-related changes will be occurring throughout the body at the same time, and the effect of these changes on voice quality should not be underestimated.

As with any musical instrument, if the free edges of the vocal folds are damaged, swollen, dry or lacking in tension, the resultant sound will be less than adequate. Typically, swollen vocal folds will give a husky, harsh, breathy quality; the free edges do not meet cleanly to vibrate easily together because of the increased mass or swelling, and often air escapes, leading to the breathy sound. It should, however, be noted that in many cases the changes are very subtle and may only be perceived by an experienced voice professional such as an elite singer or actor.

For some young men, despite normal laryngeal growth and the development of secondary sexual characteristics, the new adult male pitch fails to emerge, and they retain their prepubertal voice. For the individual who identifies as a different gender from that which they were assigned at birth, and is transitioning from male to female, experiencing a much lower pitch can be very distressing. It is important in terms of the transgender individual to anticipate likely vocal change, as this may not always be considered, and can be of great concern to the individual. Pharmacological solutions, which can be used to suppress pubertal change in prepubertal children until advice has been offered and counselling has been undertaken, will also serve to suppress pitch change.

For individuals who are transitioning at an older age, vocal change will have already taken place. In the case of female-to-male gender change, vocal change is usually managed satisfactorily with the use of hormones to achieve a lower pitch, but in the case of male-to-female gender change, achieving a higher pitch is more difficult. This may well need surgical intervention, known as voice feminisation surgery, where the focus is to raise the person's habitual speaking pitch and reduce their ability to produce a low-pitched voice. Intervention post-surgery is for specialist clinicians and multi-disciplinary teams. It is not within the scope of this publication to offer exercises for post-operative work on pitch, but for those unhappy with their vocal quality, referral to a speech and language therapist or speech pathologist is available. The exercises we've included are safe and do not infringe professional codes of practice.

Changes in pitch range are also noted as individuals enter 'middle' age. Again, differences between male and female voices are noted, specifically at the age at which these changes occur. Ageing changes in the male larynx tend to occur in the fourth decade; for women, as has already been noted, these changes occur at the time of the menopause, usually in the fifth decade. These changes are the result of specific tissue structural changes that occur within the folds, becoming less elastic and less well lubricated.

As the vocal folds become less elastic, bowing can occur; the vocal folds cannot therefore meet along their full length and, consequently, the lack of vibration along their full length leads to a weak breathy note. This seems to be particularly a problem with older men, leading to a thinner higher voice, whereas women, as has been noted, tend to have slightly thicker, more swollen, vocal folds in older age, limiting their range. In addition, there would appear to be a trend towards a decrease in range with increasing age. Laryngeal cartilages calcify, a process that begins quite early in adulthood, and starts sooner and is more complete in men than in women. The vocal folds of old people look very different from those of younger adults.

There are, therefore, changes in the sound of the voice and alterations to the larynx that accompany ageing, although it would be inappropriate to suggest that all the changes are the result of alterations to the laryngeal cartilages. Indeed, it may be that the loss of flexibility within the vocal folds means that glottal closure becomes less complete and less stable, and results in a sound that is perceived as being somewhat rough and perhaps breathy. This quality is one that is associated with older individuals.

As well as changes within the larynx, ageing brings about changes within the lungs, which deteriorate with increasing age, as noted below. Upper airway disorders may occur with age and sometimes older individuals will develop chronic obstructive pulmonary disease (COPD). Smoking will inevitably accelerate the deterioration of lung function in upper airway disease and indeed may, although not necessarily, have initiated it. Older individuals may also develop late onset asthma in middle to older age. Other changes because of ageing include:

– A reduction of the mobility of the thoracic cage.
– The ribs becoming less mobile.
– The lungs and bronchi shrinking and sinking to a lower position in the thorax, although the sensitivity of the airway is reduced, and coughing is less likely to occur.

By old age, the vocal changes are quite extensive in both sexes, although they are not inevitable, but certainly vocal deterioration needs to be seen in the light of other changes as a result of ageing such as:

– Limited mobility.
– Multiple medications.
– Lack of motivation or opportunity to communicate.
– Reduced hearing.
– Loss of teeth, which causes the upper and lower lips to lose support, and, because of the loss, the jaw decalcifies and erodes.

Paradoxically, the loss of teeth means the mouth is no longer able to open fully and the temporomandibular joint becomes less supple. Mouth opening is, of course, essential for articulatory precision and for adding oral resonance to the voice.

Physical activity will prevent noticeable deterioration in respiration, and it is important to avoid pollutants because these will affect the elastic recoil of the lungs. With declining respiratory function, voice quality is affected because of lack of breath support. It is likely that changes to the statutory retirement age which affects pension rights in the UK will contribute to older individuals remaining in professional roles, so it is important to be aware of vocal change. If, however, attention is paid to postural, respiratory and vocal health, it is possible to maintain a voice that sounds much younger than an individual's chronological age.

Environmental Awareness

In general (and obviously all manner of combinations exists and operate differently in different spaces), low ceilings, carpeted floors, covered walls and soft furnishings tend to 'dampen and deaden' sound and absorb the voice, making it more necessary to actively define consonants and pitch the voice appropriately, sometimes slightly higher. By contrast, hard surfaces, such as varnished timber or wooden tiles, steel-framed windows and doors, large expanses of glass and bare walls, tend to produce a bright, sharp and occasionally echoing sound. This acoustic may require a change in vocal pitch; because the reverberation of a sound can interfere with the next sound, making speech indistinct, a lower pitch and a slower pace may help.

Self-Assessment and Building Awareness

When speaking at work, particularly in situations that are important or when you feel under pressure, think about the quality of your voice. These questions will give you a picture of how your pitch behaves under pressure.

'Pitch Under Pressure' Checklist

Does your voice:	Yes	No
Remain the same?		
Remain flexible?		
Become increasingly strained?		
Become more breathy?		
Become increasingly husky?		
Become more harsh?		
Become lower in pitch?		
Become higher in pitch?		
Start to 'cut out' while you are speaking?		
Sometimes 'fade' away the longer you use it?		
Sometimes prove challenging to adjust in terms of volume?		
Sometimes feel resistant to changes in pitch?		
Sometimes disappear when you are speaking?		
Sometimes become unpredictable when you begin to speak?		
Sometimes need to be cleared when you are speaking?		

Find a private space where you can speak comfortably without any distractions. Use a voice recording app to record yourself as you go through the following prompts. After each prompt, take a moment to reflect on your vocal pitch and how you used it. Then, listen to the recording and answer the questions that follow.

Introduction	Start the recording by introducing yourself as if you are speaking in front of an audience. Use your natural speaking voice. When listening back to the recording observe your pitch. Were you speaking too high, too low or 'just right'? Consider whether you sounded relaxed, confident and engaging.
Pitch Variation	Paying attention to your pitch variation, try to vary your pitch to emphasise particular words or phrases. Listen to the recording and reflect on how effectively you used pitch variation to convey meaning and engage the listener. Is there room to do this more? Have a second attempt, this time increasing the variety of pitch, then try a third time with more extreme changes. You may notice you start to sound like a radio commercial or a sports commentator! Consider which of these three is most suitable for work.
Emotional Expression	Choose an emotion (such as excitement, surprise or pride) and express it in your voice while reading a sentence or two, you can read from any material. Pay attention to how your pitch reflects the emotion. Listen to the recording and assess whether your pitch effectively conveyed the intended emotion.
Pace and Pitch	Practice speaking at different paces, from slow to fast. Observe how your pitch changes accordingly. Reflect on whether you tend to speak faster or slower when you're nervous, excited or trying to emphasise a point. Listen to the recording and evaluate your pace and pitch in different speaking styles.
Tone and Mood	Experiment with different tones and moods such as serious, light-hearted or informative while delivering a short message. Notice how your pitch affects the tone and mood of your speech. Listen to the recording and analyse how well you were able to convey the desired tone and mood through your pitch.
Self-Assessment	Listen back to the entire recording of the above prompts and reflect on your vocal pitch throughout the exercise. Were you able to use pitch effectively to convey meaning, engage the listener and create the desired tone and mood? Were there any areas where you could improve your pitch or vocal variation? Take notes on your observations and set goals for improving your pitch in future public-speaking engagements.

Remember, becoming more aware of your vocal pitch and how you use it is an ongoing process. By regularly using this self-awareness test, reviewing your responses over time and actively working on improving your pitch with the exercises from this book you can introduce pitch flexibility to become a more dynamic and compelling speaker.

As you become more comfortable with manipulating your pitch, you might notice a shift in how you feel about your communication. This new-found control can boost your confidence, as you make intentional choices to align with your desired outcomes.

Practical Advice

Things to Consider

- Tiredness: Fatigue leads to loss of effective muscle function and a consequent reduction in the flexibility and easy movement of the vocal folds, reducing pitch range.
- Mental health: When the mind is under stress, the body is too, and the stress carries over into the voice. We know that low mood may affect posture and we therefore may have trouble with breathing; pitch can be affected and rise, or the voice becomes overly strident and possibly very low and monotonous. Changes in vocal quality and delivery can indeed be some of the early indicators of mental fragility, demonstrated by lack of engagement, reduced sentence length, limited pitch range, altered intonation patterns and, if mental health issues are related to drug or alcohol misuse, a hoarse or husky vocal quality.
- Changing the pitch range of your voice to match what you believe suits your age and gender may well feel uncomfortable initially. Family, friends and colleagues may take some time to accept/get used to the new pitch and, indeed, may well comment on it. Think about how you are going to deal with questions or comments. You may want to apply your new pitch gradually or only in certain situations initially until you feel comfortable.
- Most importantly, do not force your voice, do not try to speak at a higher or lower pitch until you have completed the exercises and if you feel any discomfort using your new pitch, stop!

Recommendations for Working on Altering the Pitch of Your Voice

- Any general tension should be eliminated before working on pitch as tension will limit your vocal range and flexibility by inhibiting the vertical movement of the larynx and the smooth approximation (coming together) of the vocal folds.

Continued

- If you find it difficult to achieve alteration to your pitch, feel the vertical movement of the larynx during pitch changes. You can identify the movement of your larynx by watching your throat in a mirror as you swallow, sensing the larynx move whilst swallowing, or by lightly placing your fingers across your throat (horizontally).

- Once you have achieved the new pitch, work on consolidating it, so it becomes habitual.

- Try to carefully monitor the new pitch by listening attentively as you use your voice and noting any periods where your voice returns to the previous pitch.

- Encourage flexibility and range within the pitch by allowing the vocal pitch to respond naturally to changes in thought and emotion.

Exercises for Exploring Pitch

Preliminary Exercises for Vocal Range

Exercises for range will have appeared in other chapters as part of developing volume and resonance. Range is more evident in relaxed voices, so endeavour to have fun with these exercises which for some may be daunting or exposing.

Use the whole body and move whenever possible during these exercises.

- Sirening: using the sound /n/ like at the beginning of 'night' or 'noon' or 'number' and (imitating the noise of a siren) allow a vocal circle of sound that you can imagine beginning between the shoulder blades, 'sliding' the sound over the top of the head and face. Keeping the sound moving and return to the starting point along an imaginary circular trajectory. This should be easy as long as you keep it playful and do not try to push. You will not hurt the voice in this way. The same can be done with the /ng/ sound (in song), /m/, /v/ and /z/.

- Sliding: stretching up with hands in the air, allow the spine to bend over, one vertebra at a time from the top of the spine down, until you are bent over at the waist. As you do so, make the sound of a vowel, such as /oo/, /ay/, /aw/ or /ah/. Make the vowel last as long as the journey from the extended stretch to the bent spine. This exercise can be done in reverse, starting the sound on the floor and sliding it upwards. Some people find this direction easier; others find it more difficult. Eventually, both will be possible. If you find the onset of the vowel difficult, precede it with an /m/.

- Bowling: using the arm to bowl, imagine the ball is the sound /m/ and as it leaves your hand lift the sound up and over the space almost in an arc. Open onto the vowel /ah/ halfway through the arc and sustain the sound until it 'lands' on the ground. Do this in slow motion so that it blends from the /m/ into the /ah/ smoothly as it arcs through the air – /mah/.

- Glide: make an /ah/ sound which will produce chest resonance. Feel the vibration by placing your hand on your upper chest. Make an /aw/, being aware of the resonance in the mouth. Notice how the lips form a megaphone shape. Now glide between the /ah/ and /aw/ sounds, from chest to mouth. With your hand on your chest you should feel the vibration shift from chest to mouth.

- Begin by patting the chest while sounding /mah/ and feel the vibrations. Glide the /ah/ vowel into an /aw/ in the mouth, slurring from one sound to another, e.g., /mah ... aw/.

- Repeat the exercise beginning with the /aw/ resonating in the mouth and then glide this sound upwards into an /ee/. The glide from the /aw/ to the /ee/ should be relaxed and effortless, and the overall balance of one sound moving from one space to another should be maintained. In all these exercises the smooth continuum of sound is worked for, and any feeling of pushed or strangulated sounds should be avoided. If a 'crack' in the flow of sound develops, just go slowly back over that area in the range. Using the hand or arm to describe the movement is often an effective aid to developing flexibility of the voice.

- Fire engine/ambulance siren: using /ng ... ah/, /ng ... ah/, /ng ... ah/, create movement between head and chest resonance. This exercise explores the vocal range and extends the extremes of pitch and resonance. The dual-pitch siren is used for different vehicles in different cities, so the title of this exercise may not be correct for everyone but can be adapted.

- Slurring and singing: using a piece of text or the lyrics of a song (just a few lines), slur the voice drunkenly and smoothly through the whole range. Try a line sung to a made-up tune. Then speak it to that tune. Finally omit the tune but keep the movement in the voice.

Exercises for Establishing Pitch Range

EXERCISE ONE

N.B. If 'movement' around the note is very limited initially, work on the exercises gently but regularly, extending pitch range little by little.

- Hum in a relaxed way, free of tension and feeling a buzz on your lips; /mmm/ up and down a few notes. Keep it playful and relaxed. Start exploring in a very small range. You can try extending this range as you continue to practice.

- Explore how low you can *easily* hum and how high you can *easily* hum; check that you are relaxed, and the sound is forward by placing your fingers on your lips and feeling the buzz. If you can't feel a buzz there may be unwanted tension, and it's worth revisiting the relaxation exercises.

EXERCISE TWO

Many words encourage the use of high or low pitch because of their meaning and associated sound.

The following word list is useful to encourage pitch change. Although this exercise may seem rather unnatural, using contrastive pairs of words is an excellent way in which to encourage variety of pitch. It should be approached in a playful, curious, manner, and if possible, find a variety of pitches within your higher and lower pitch ranges, so you don't become repetitive.

High Pitch	*Low Pitch*	*High Pitch*	*Low Pitch*	*High Pitch*	*Low Pitch*
ping	pong	ding	dong	treble	bass
high	low	hill	valley	air	ground
mountains	plains	holiday	school	smooth	rough
comedy	tragedy	delight	sorrow	slip	slide
soft	hard	light	dark	excited	bored

EXERCISE THREE

Explore the sound dynamic in the following word list to further encourage pitch change. Take these sound qualities beyond natural speech and focus on the qualities of the vowels and consonants.

High Pitch	Low Pitch	High Pitch	Low Pitch	High Pitch	Low Pitch
squeal	dungeon	screech	dump	hiss	dreary
creak	dark	joyful	snore	fly	sink
high	grim	hoity	moan	spring	musty
giddy	malice	shrill	deep	prick	stab
tingle	grumble	elegant	mangy	giggle	mangle

Once effective use of high and low pitch has been established in single words, move on to using them in sentences. Changes in tone will also be noted, particularly if the approach is playful and uninhibited.

EXERCISE FOUR

Sentences for exploring upper pitch range:

The sky was shining with the light of many twinkling stars.	The ball bounced up and up and into the net.	The baby chuckled and gurgled with delight.
The wind took the kite high up into the clear blue sky	The girl had never felt so happy and excited.	The cork flew high out of the champagne bottle.
The tiny kitten climbed to the top of the tree.	They laughed and laughed with happiness.	The birds cheeped and flew towards the trees.

EXERCISE FIVE

Sentences for exploring lower pitch range:

The fool watched his fireworks fail.	The news was full of gloom.	The boy trudged slowly home in the dark.
The man was slumped at the side of the road.	The shark swam around in the murky waters.	Deep in the forest the girl was lost.
The sun sank and there was darkness.	The man had a gruff and angry voice.	There was no way out of the tunnel.

EXERCISE SIX

Using sentences which are questions is a good way of exploring intonation. It is important that the intention is clear from the beginning of the sentence.

How did you do that?	Is your brother that man with the grey hair?	Have you any idea what time it is?
Where is the bottle of pills?	Who is going to open this gate?	Can you help me, please?
What is your opinion of this?	Which road should we take?	Is Melissa joining us?

EXERCISE SEVEN

Once vocal variety and modulation has been achieved, it is appropriate to combine their use in words and sentences.

–   Start with the months of the year. January can be said with a high pitch, February with a low pitch, March with a higher pitch, and so on.

–   Alter the pitch next time, starting with January on a low pitch.

Alternatively, use a sequence of numbers, gradually rising in pitch with each one. This exercise can also be reversed, so that the first number is on a high pitch and each successive number gets lower.

Short sentences can also be used, again with each successive word becoming higher and higher or lower and lower as appropriate or feels instinctive.

I can climb higher and higher.	I slipped, dropped the ball, and I fell down and down.	The kite climbed higher into the sky, swooped, dived and floated slowly down to earth.

EXERCISE EIGHT

Reading passages aloud may be incorporated into your work on pitch to ensure the voice rises or falls appropriately in relation to meaning. Sentences may be read out loud with successive words being emphasised on each reading. This will introduce pitch variation and illustrate well how it affects the meaning of the sentence. E.g.:

Three small cats.
Three **small** cats.
Three small **cats**.

Try these sentences several times and explore how the meaning changes if you shift the word emphasis:

Who did you say you knew at the school?	I thought you were going to bring the gift.	The bus was late, so I missed the show.
I never imagined the concert would be so long.	That boy insulted the old woman sitting beside me.	Charlotte throws great parties; they're relaxed and fun.

EXERCISE NINE

For movement up and down the scale, try the following exercise.

–   Use the hand to manipulate an imaginary yo-yo. Using the sound /ooo/ move the pitch up and down the scale following the movement of the yo-yo. When the yo-yo is high the pitch is high, when the yo-yo is low, the pitch is low. Allow the voice to glide effortlessly between the notes.

–   Then take the yo-yo to greater extremes of height and depth, letting the voice follow. Never push the sound; keep it relaxed and flowing.

–   This may be tried with other vowel sounds: /aw/, /ah/ and /ee/.

Now apply the yo-yo exercise to these lines of prose. Do not 'play safe'; allow the voice to sound uncontrolled and silly. Variety and movement in the pitch range should occur in individual words as well as in the sentence.

Why are you walking when the weather's wild?	Have you seen my sister Jean?	Silly Susan sleeps in solitary silence.
You and I are really running round and round in circles.	When the east wind howls and the waves are wild, you ought to hide inside.	Sarah is such a fantastic friend, we have such fun!

EXERCISE TEN

We often use the same limited pitch range habitually and do not realise the full variety of pitch that is open to us. When attempting to be heard over distance, for example, a common error is to keep the voice on one pitch.

Using the phrase 'Happy Birthday!', explore your vocal choices by:

- Laughing as you speak (if this is difficult and unnatural use a 'ho ho ho' mock laugh).
- Singing the phrase.
- Calling people towards you from a distance.
- Speaking each word on a different pitch.
- Slurring the line as if you were drunk.

Other phrases to try: 'Why don't we start?', 'I'll see you soon', 'Thanks for joining us'.

Playful Exercises for Range

EXERCISE ONE

It is important to play and not to strive for perfection because this usually results in creating tension rather than releasing it.

- Draw a wavy line and trace this pattern with your finger as you sound /oo/, moving up and down your range.
- 'Sing' phrases or sentences in an 'operatic' voice. The verse in the following exercise can be used for this. Keep the exercise playful.
- Using these words deliberately move (or preferably slur) the voice from your lowest notes to your highest. A secondary exercise with this piece of text is to make a decision about which words 'feel' higher pitched to you and which 'lower', and repeat the poem with indulgence. Enjoy these pitch extremes!

Since there's no help, come let us kiss and part.
Nay, I have done, you get no more of me;
And I am glad, yea, glad with all my heart,
That thus so cleanly I myself can free.

From Michael Drayton's 'Loves Farewell' (circa 1619)

EXERCISE TWO

- Begin with saying 'bubble' in a low pitch, imagining you are describing a large 'gloopy' bubble.

- Raise the pitch as you repeat the word 'bubble' over and over and the imagined bubbles get smaller and lighter.

- Use the body to help create the image and repeat the word bubble as many times as you like to move through your pitch, from very large bubbles to very small bubbles.

EXERCISE THREE

- Imagine you are outdoors on a mountain, on a beach or in a field: call to an imaginary friend to 'Come this way', gesturing with your hand as you call.

- Notice how the voice needs more breath support and range as the distance between you widens.

Suggestions and Strategies

Recommendations for Further Exploration of Pitch

Strategic Pitch Pattern Variation

Varying your pitch can aid in the clarity and comprehension of your message. By colouring certain words or phrases with higher or lower pitches, you can highlight key points, clarify important information and guide the listener's understanding. Make sure that you avoid becoming too 'enthusiastic' in terms of pitch variety, as that can become irritating and predictable, and the audience can begin to 'tune out'. It's a fine balance achieving variety with sincerity and without falling into a more 'theatrical' or 'contrived' pitch pattern. The brain is able to extract statistical regularity from surrounding sounds and it is this ability to analyse our acoustic environment that allows the brain to capture predictable patterns in sound sequences. However, natural sound environments are rarely predictable and often contain some level of randomness, and therefore so should you. The audience can detect

Continued

changes in the randomness in the pitch and so if the pitch pattern becomes too predictable the audience may 'switch off' or become distracted by identifying and predicting the pitch patterns.

Join a Choir!

The value of singing goes beyond exploring vocabulary, memory training and technical aspects of breath, pitch, communication and precision of sounds because, as with all language, its delivery is a gestalt, involving body, breath, mind, intention, rhythm, musicality and interpretation. Singing develops not only musicality but also the interpersonal and ensemble skills of group timing, anticipation and co-operation. For many people, the act of group speaking or singing allows them a great deal of freedom to explore their own creative powers and imagination. It is inclusive and brings a sense of companionship, and it provides the opportunity to be in a team and to perform safely without exposure.

Sing in the Shower!

As with singing as part of a group, singing alone in the shower allows great freedom to perform without the restraint of those around listening to you. That freedom encourages a relaxed approach, encourages you to avoid tension and the sound of the shower tends to supersede the noise of your voice, so you can be free of feedback. The steam will have the added benefit of lubricating your vocal tract, particularly if you breathe through your mouth.

Read Aloud!

There are significant differences between fluent personal reading and the art and skill of reading aloud to an audience. The reader has the book in front of them and can follow the printed word whereas an audience cannot, so they must rely on the voice they hear. The audience is therefore at a considerable disadvantage and must be helped to 'enter the world of the story' through dynamic and expressive interpretation and intelligent phrasing.

The art of the teacher, for example, who reads to the class is that of the storyteller, an art which, sadly for many children, is being eroded and replaced by technology. In the lives of many children, the primary school teacher is the only adult who ever reads to them. Whenever you have the opportunity, try to read aloud to the best of your ability; imagine

Continued

an excited audience waiting to be stimulated and excited by words and language, and to be inspired in turn to read for themselves. Imagining a receptive audience is a useful technique when recording yourself for professional purposes as it can add warmth and colour into your voice.

Strive to engage your listener's imagination by vocally formulating images of the language. The story is not only contained in the words but in the soundscape: vowels and consonants add to the music and energy of the language as do alliteration, repetition, pace, inflection, emphasis and pause. Connecting with, and honouring, the rhythm gives an added dimension to the story. Most stories offer the reader the opportunity to explore vocal tone and to move away from habitual pitch through characterisation. While some may find this challenging, the story is bound to be improved and the characters brought to life more vividly.

Suggestions for Improving Sight-reading

– Ensure your posture is comfortable and aligned so that breathing is free and easy.

– Actively release the shoulders, neck and jaw so that the voice is not constricted.

– Sit or stand with a well-aligned and open posture with head, neck and shoulders relaxed and free so that the voice is capable of effortless projection.

– Eye contact allows you to include your audience and share the story, and to read 'to them' not 'at them'. If you are not a confident reader, mark your script so that you work out in advance when you can comfortably make eye contact; in a pause or at the end of a sentence.

– Explore the soundscape and rhythm of the story.

– Employ the aspects of vocal modulation such as pace, pitch, pause, inflection, emphasis, and use the dynamic qualities of vowels and consonants.

As well as reading prose aloud, poetry is a wonderful vehicle for encouraging pitch changes within a limited passage of time and material. Have a look at poems that are playful and interesting. The works of Lemn Sissay, Roger McGough, Maya Angelou, Michael Rosen, Pam Ayres, Mary Oliver and Wendy Cope are some suggestions for you to try. They are usually fun to read, albeit with a strong message, and the language is uncomplicated, with a strong guiding rhythm.

Pitch in Presentation, Performance and Pitches!

Day-to-Day

In the workplace, individuals can incorporate these activities to improve their overall vocal resonance and pitch variety.

- Warm up: dedicate a few minutes each day to vocal warm-ups and exercises. This practice helps maintain vocal health and flexibility, leading to better pitch control.

- Seek feedback: ask for feedback from colleagues or supervisors on your vocal delivery. Consider seeking professional coaching or training to further develop your vocal skills, including pitch variation.

- Experiment: When on phone calls, experiment with modulating your pitch to convey different emotions or emphasise important points. This can add expressiveness and engagement to your voice without the other person necessarily realising you're consciously working on pitch variation.

- Storytell: Incorporate storytelling techniques in your conversations or presentations. Use changes in pitch to differentiate 'characters' or emphasise key moments in the narrative. This allows for natural variations in pitch without it being too obvious.

On the Day

In the five minutes before presenting, you can do the following quick activities to warm up your voice and ensure pitch variety:

- Take a few gentle deep breaths. Sigh the breath out.

- Stretch and loosen up: perform a few gentle neck, shoulder and jaw stretches to release any tension or constriction. Run your tongue over your teeth and chew an imaginary toffee. Relaxation in these areas can contribute to better pitch control.

- Hum gently, sensing vibration on the lips and explore different pitches. Start from a comfortable range and gradually expand to higher and lower pitches.

- Tongue-twisters: practice tongue-twisters or difficult phrases in your material that might trip you up, or vocal exercises that involve rapid articulation. This helps improve vocal agility and can indirectly contribute to pitch variation.

Sound Bite

Effective use of pitch and variety allows you to share ideas and emotions in a dynamic way. It allows you to engage, encourage, persuade and influence your listeners at every level.

8 | Muscular Flexibility

Introduction

Rather than use the term articulation, which we feel limits the expanse of this chapter, since its focus is more on the formation of clear and distinct sounds in speech, we are using the term 'muscular flexibility' for the title of this chapter. Flexibility is the ability to move muscles and joints through a full normal range of motion. Flexibility helps promote efficient movement, preventing incorrect body alignment, which we have already emphasised in relation to vocal quality, and flexibility also maintains appropriate muscle length and balance.

If you ask someone in what ways they might like to improve their communication and speech, one of the most common answers is 'I want to be clearer' or 'I hate being asked to repeat myself' or 'I don't feel heard'. There is a shared, and important, desire for clarity amongst most professional voice users. Clarity may mean, among other things, the clarity of your thought structure, sharing your thoughts clearly with others or the audible quality of 'clarity' in speech. For many people, the latter is interpreted as clear diction, precise articulation, alongside suitable volume, expression and intention, all rely on muscular flexibility. We co-ordinate over 100 muscles when we speak and for our speech to be easy to produce, and easy to comprehend, becoming more flexible and freer of tension is extremely useful.

Why Does Muscular Flexibility Matter to Me?

As we've already mentioned, the majority of professional voice users cite clarity as an important feature of their speech. Clarity is seen as demonstrating professionalism and expertise. One of the reasons for this is the link between lack of clarity and slurred or indistinct speech which is, along

136

DOI: 10.4324/9781003361114-9

with physical instability, demonstrably a common feature of intoxication or 'sloshed', 'wrecked', 'blotto' or, in effect, drunk and disorderly. Making a link with lack of clarity and being drunk is the assumption that you are not 'in control', and, of course, that is the opposite of being professional and composed. The image of being out of control is a powerful one and that impression can so easily be transferred to the audience through stumbling, mumbling or nothing more than a lack of vocal clarity. Regrettably, an audience who knows little of your personal circumstances can jump to conclusions, as has often been recounted by those who have a medical disorder that affects clarity of speech such as Parkinson's disease, cerebral palsy or motor neurone disease. Fortunately, more public information and recognition is now available, so these incidents are hopefully becoming less. The issue is that often unclear speech is not only seen as being linked to a lack of control but also to a lack of clarity of thought; the designation of rambling applies not only to a speech but also to the speaker.

While disability discrimination is reducing, it would be naive to suggest that it has disappeared completely and, in many occupations, muscular flexibility and vocal clarity are critical in order not to compromise the message. There are certainly some occupational roles in which sounding articulate and energetic, alongside clear diction or muscular flexibility, is advantageous, such as marketing, information delivery, spoken language interpreting, educating and performing, to name a few. The ability to be understood and ensure effective communication with one's audience holds immense value in all professional and social environments.

In this chapter we're going to look at how you can become more agile, efficient and muscular in your speech, ensuring your message is clear and understood the first time round.

There are many benefits to muscular flexibility. Knowing your speech is clear, and being able to make adjustments if you are misunderstood, can make you feel more confident, reduce frustration and convey competence or professionalism which, in turn, positions you as a dynamic, efficient and capable individual in your field. Muscular flexibility is important for clear and effective communication because it also allows us to produce a wide range of speech sounds, and extends our range of volume, pitch and tone. Without muscular flexibility, our speech would be limited in terms of the sounds we could produce, which could lead to difficulty in being understood. Think about trying to communicate when you have your mouth full or you are brushing your teeth: the tongue can't move, the jaw is held in one position – whether open or shut, there is no easy movement of any of the articulators and the message goes unheard. Additional muscularity not only increases clarity and volume but also connects words with their inherent meaning and power. When there is commitment behind the spoken word, including articulatory precision, the voice reflects it naturally and the listener is clear about the message.

What Is It, Exactly?

The primary purpose of the articulators, lips, teeth, gums, jaws, tongue and hard and soft palates, is, in fact, for use in the process of chewing and swallowing. They are very successfully adapted to the special purposes of speech, all working together in the articulation of consonants and vowels. The juxtaposition of these articulators and their flexibility in moving and changing within the oral cavity contributes to the clarity of the sound, both in isolation and in continuous speech or song.

Developing muscular flexibility involves a combination of targeted exercises and techniques that focus on creating agility and dexterity in the muscles and articulators involved in speech production, increasing their range of motion and reducing tension, and improving control and coordination, allowing for greater precision and responsiveness in vocal articulation.

For some of us, the ability to use our articulators at speed and with muscularity, is compromised.

– Are there, perhaps, auditory problems? Can we hear the sound we are trying to create, the 'target' sound, correctly?
– Is there, as we've mentioned above, a specific disorder that prevents the full range of tongue movements?
– Is there perhaps a problem with dentition which may make it difficult for the tongue to make the required fine movements needed to make contact with the teeth?
– Is there perhaps a problem with the hard or soft palate as a consequence of an injury or a genetic disorder?

Kinaesthetic and Tactile Feedback

If an individual's muscular or physical ability, or both, are compromised, it can affect their ability to make the required contact with other articulators to produce consonant sounds, or for the tongue to make the required shape within the oral cavity to produce a vowel sound. As a result, the clarity of their speech is in jeopardy. Speech, which is imprecise and difficult to understand, because of inefficient use of the articulators, will detract as much as poor vocal quality from your communication, resulting in a loss of meaning.

It is for this reason that it is essential that your lips, tongue, soft palate and pharynx are as mobile as possible. It is also crucial that there is an awareness of the position and movement of the lips, tongue, soft palate and pharynx. This awareness is also known as 'kinaesthetic' feedback. Tactile feedback (learning through the sense of touch) in these areas, and from the teeth, hard palate and jaw, is also necessary. Tactile feedback refers to the use of your sense of touch to provide information and awareness about your voice work. You can develop a greater sense of control, coordination and awareness, which allows you to adjust and enhance your overall speech production and clarity, although making changes in speech habits takes time.

Tension

Considering how the lips, teeth, gums, jaws, tongue and hard and soft palates may be used in order to articulate sound, we can imagine how easy it is for tension to build up without you being aware of it. By working through the exercises in this chapter you will gain more insight into your habitual places of tension and increase your flexibility, speed and precision in producing speech.

Environment and Tension

Feeling you are being overheard in a work setting, whether large or small, can be an intimidating experience, and may induce tension. Try to ignore this very understandable reponse. Having awareness around situations that make you self conscious can prompt you to focus on strategies that will allow you to monitor and manage tension levels. This is important because over time, tension can gradually build up in your jaw, tongue, lips and soft palate without you realising it, until it's too late.

Yawning and stretching are very useful ways to unwind and release tension. The yawn opens the oral space, lifts the soft palate and then releases the jaw. It is also one of the most effective ways to release tension in the pharynx. It provides extra oxygen and, in that way, energises, so never try to stifle or supress a yawn.

Emotional Tension and the Articulators

As with work on breathing exercises, work on the jaw, lips and tongue can produce unexpected and uncomfortable emotional responses. Be aware that emotional tension can be held in these areas. For example, one hears, 'keep a stiff upper lip', 'grit your teeth', 'bite your lip to stop crying'. Emotional responses are quite normal and unless it brings back distressing memories or revives emotions that you cannot deal with, there is no need to be concerned. Do acknowledge any anxiety you feel, or if you are working with a voice coach/clinician/voice specialist, and are feeling in any way distressed, discuss how you are feeling with them.

When we feel nervous or anxious, our bodies often respond with increased muscle tension as a result of the 'fight-or-flight' response. In the context of speech, this tension can affect the muscles involved in speech production. The increased tension in these muscles can lead to a strange sensation in your mouth, slurring, stumbling or difficulty articulating words smoothly. The tension can disrupt the coordination and fluidity required for clear speech; this is a common physiological response to stress or nervousness. Anxiety may also affect your breathing patterns, leading to shallower or irregular breaths. Inadequate breath control can impact speech clarity, causing words to be 'fluffy' or unclear.

To address this issue, it can be helpful to practice relaxation techniques before speaking or engaging in situations that make you nervous and work on the exercises in this chapter.

Self-Assessment and Building Awareness

N.B. These tasks should be performed again after doing the exercises later in this chapter to assess the increase in range of motion or clarity.

Tongue: assess your range of motion. Using a mirror, stick out your tongue, try and touch your chin with your tongue, point your tongue towards your left ear then your right ear, and finally attempt to touch your nose. Observe any tension or strain in your muscles and note any limitations in your range of motion.

Record: record yourself speaking a passage of any text and listen back to assess the clarity, intelligibility and ease of your speech production.

Self-reflection: are there any situations in which you are regularly asked to repeat yourself? Take a moment to reflect on that situation. What kind of environment are you in? How confident do you feel in that scenario? Is there anything you can do to make yourself clearer or more audible? Is it because you are speaking too quickly and losing clarity to speed?

Tongue-twister: record a tongue-twister which requires a lot of dexterity and flexibility; remember to re-record following the exercises

Continued

in this chapter and make a note of the difference – particularly in flow of speech, clarity of speech, ease of speech. You can try this one:

I want a proper cup of coffee from a proper coffee shop,
A 'venti', half-caf, macchiato, quad-shot,
Latte, double strength, sugar free, cocoa topped,
Half fat, dairy free, extra-large, single shot,
Keep cup, paper cup, cup and saucer, thermos,
I want a proper cup of coffee from a proper coffee shop.

Below are some questions to help you reflect on your muscular flexibility and clarity. The answers to these questions may point to more than muscular flexibility alone, but also help you to view your 'clarity' as a whole, including where you are with breath, pace, pronunciation and volume.

It is important to note that self-assessment can have its limits and may not provide a complete picture of your muscular flexibility in terms of speech. Working with a voice coach can provide more personalised and accurate assessment, as well as targeted exercises and techniques to improve your speech production abilities.

These questions are prompts you can return to, to assess your progress and target your practice, make a note of your answers and revisit at a later date.

Muscular Flexibility Awareness Prompts

Do you often get asked to repeat yourself?	– Consider which environments you are in at the time. Are they particularly noisy? Do you feel you could increase your clarity? – Consider what types of situations you are in. Work, social or at home? – Consider whether you are holding emotional tension. Is anything holding you back in these situations such as uncertainty, nervousness or feeling unheard? – Consider your level of calmness in these situations. Are you feeling either particularly relaxed or particularly tense?
Are you aware of any specific consonant combinations or words that are difficult to say?	– Consider making a list of words and incorporating these into your warm-up. – Consider focusing your warm-up on the sounds in these words, to 'loosen' up and target your flexibility towards those 'tricky' sounds.

141

Are you concerned about mumbling?	– Is there a reason for mumbling? Perhaps a lack of conviction in what you are saying, or possibly purely habitual? Perhaps you are extremely relaxed and at ease with the company you are in? – Can you use any reminders to alert yourself to the need not to mumble, for example, sticky notes or small stickers on your PC or mobile? – Are you feeling hesitant or unsure about expressing yourself, or concerned about the reaction, so that mumbling is a form of protection? – Are you speaking too quickly, rushing through sentences or thoughts, causing words to be unclear? – Are you feeling shy and avoiding drawing attention to yourself? Can you prioritise your message and focus on sharing information so that you feel less 'in the spotlight' and your message becomes clearer? – Are you speaking with objects in the mouth (e.g., chewing gum, retainers, pens, hair!) that can hinder clear speech? – How are you feeling? When feeling anxious or nervous, sometimes we may mumble unconsciously as a result of increased muscle tension, shallow breathing or a heightened self-consciousness.
Do you feel the energy of your speech matches your enthusiasm or how committed you are to your ideas?	– Muscular flexibility boosts clarity, which amplifies your message. Can you do a little more work on identifying your key points that will help you navigate your way through your speech, and help your audience to hear the key moments of your speech? – Can you give your speech more bite? Can you spend some more time practising your speech or the kind of content your regularly deliver, and enjoy finding the words that you can be muscular with, using the consonants in a curious and playful way? – Can you find time to work on a piece of script or text and play with different levels of 'engagement' on a sliding scale from 'couldn't care less' to 'ridiculously excited' (or something similar) and notice how much muscular energy is required from you to represent these different energies and levels of dedication to sharing your idea?
Do you feel the way you sound doesn't reflect your expertise?	– How crisp and energetic our speech is can be perceived by others as a signifier of our level of expertise. Can you approach a phrase you use regularly at work such as 'This is the best product on the market' or 'I'd like to thank you all for your hard work' and play with different levels of 'expertise', starting off very low on the scale, as if you are a complete imposter – someone who has walked into the wrong meeting room perhaps! – and then gradually move up that scale, to world expert. Notice how this changes your energy and the muscularity in your speech. – Observe how experts, with limited time, such as news and weathercasters, share their message using the skills of pitch, pause, pace and precision.

142

Practical Advice

- Tension causes muscular inflexibility, so before beginning any work on increasing muscular flexibility, start with a yawn and a stretch, which not only releases tension but also stimulates energy and can be used throughout a session.
- Check that there is no accompanying head and shoulder tension when doing the exercises.
- Muscular flexibility exercises should be done at a moderate speed initially. Do not try to rush through the exercises – speed is not a criterion of success. Precision is more important than speed.
- Make sure you are not holding your breath when completing the exercises.
- When working on muscular flexibility, always use a mirror to give you visual and kinaesthetic feedback.
- Try to think of each movement separately and build up the sequence gradually.
- Do you code-switch? If you are in a younger age group, where limited muscularity is often the norm, recognise that peer pressure and comment may be an issue. Do you think that clarity would distance you from your peers? Are you already aware that you code-switch from your speech at work to that of at home, from your speech with old friends to that of colleagues in professional settings? Have a think about how you change your speech in a number of different situations or indeed in different languages.
- Use your 'new', more precise, articulation when talking on your mobile/landline phone initially, until you feel more comfortable with what may sound (to you) like a very over-exaggerated way of speaking.
- In certain languages, only a moderate amount of jaw opening is used when speaking, and in certain cultures, female speakers protect the lower half of their face in public, so if you feel that work on your jaw, lips and tongue does not sit comfortably with your cultural considerations, then please ignore this advice.
- Making changes to articulatory movements may feel uncomfortable and strange, initially. In fact, they can seem exaggerated and unacceptable.

N.B. It is always important to be aware that poor/limited flexibility can be the result of impairment and if so, practice will not make perfect. If you are in any way concerned about your ability to carry out the following exercises, do not hesitate to discuss this further with your GP, voice coach/clinician/voice specialist. This is something that would be discussed in a clinical setting but if you are working on your own, you may not have been aware of any problem until you started the exercises. Never assume it is nothing – it's always worth checking it out by making an appointment to see your GP.

Exercises for Muscular Flexibility

Exercises to Release Tension and Stimulate Energy

Before we start, it's important to release tension. Yawning and stretching are useful ways in which to counter tension and to stimulate energy and should be encouraged at points throughout a practice session.

EXERCISE ONE

We love a yawn! Yawning opens up the oral space, exercises the facial muscles, lifts the soft palate and then releases the jaw. It is one of the best ways to release tension in the pharynx. In providing extra oxygen, it also energises. The yawn should be enjoyed, not stifled or suppressed.

Any oral activity, particularly that involving the tongue, can stimulate the yawning process. This should be explained, as individuals are often embarrassed by their desire to yawn in voice sessions, feeling that a yawn indicates boredom.

–   The yawn may also be taken into a body stretch. Lift the arms above the head and then stretch to extend to the very tips of the fingers. Let the head tilt back and feel the pharynx enlarging and opening. The stretch should be felt in the spine, back and abdominal muscles. For those stretching while sitting, allow the stretch to extend to the legs and toes.

–   Floor stretches such as the 'cat stretch' may be tried. Start from a position on all fours with weight evenly balanced, then sit back on the heels and take the arms forward with the fingers on the floor so that the stretch is felt along the back through the arms to the fingertips. If you are working with a partner, they can apply gentle pressure to the back with the flat of the hands. This pressure will aid and extend the stretch.

N.B. It should always be remembered that individuals with a history of back or neck problems should only attempt this type of stretch with the permission of their general practitioner.

If you prefer an exercise which doesn't involve anyone else applying pressure to your back, you could try the following exercise. Only try this if you are reasonably mobile and your balance is not in question.

EXERCISE TWO

– The Cat-Cow pose, also known as Marjaryasana-Bitilasana, is a gentle yoga exercise that helps to stretch and strengthen the spine, improve flexibility and promote body awareness. Remember, the intention is to gently release tension, calm the mind and relieve stress.

– Starting from a hands-and-knees tabletop position, ensure that your knees are positioned directly under your hips and your hands are aligned with your shoulders. This alignment provides stability.

– In the first half of the pose, marjaryasana (cat pose), as you exhale, gently round your back, tuck your chin towards your chest, and draw your belly button towards your spine and release your head towards the ground. Take this movement slowly and mindfully, focusing on the stretch and release in your spine.

– Moving into the second half, bitilasana (cow pose), inhale gently and allow your belly to sink toward the ground, creating a gentle arch in your back. Gently lift your gaze upward without straining your neck. Focus on lengthening the back of your neck while keeping it in line with your spine as if you are reaching the crown of your head towards the ceiling. Continue to move between Cow and the Cat poses with each breath, synchronising your movements with your breath. Inhale as you transition to Cow, and exhale as you transition to Cat.

– Repeat for several rounds, gradually increasing the range of motion and exploring the full stretch of your spine. You can also add variations, such as circling your hips or incorporating gentle side-to-side movements. Flow smoothly and gradually through the poses, feeling the gentle stretch and movement along your spine. Pay attention to the sensations in your body and focus on maintaining a smooth and fluid breath.

– After completing the desired number of rounds, come back to a neutral tabletop position, with your spine in a neutral position and your head aligned with your spine.

N.B. If you feel any discomfort or tension, modify the pose by keeping your head in line with your spine without lifting your gaze too high. For those with knee or wrist sensitivity, you can modify the pose by practising it while seated upright in a chair.

Another exercise which is gentle and impact free, regardless of your level of fitness, is the one below.

EXERCISE THREE

–   Sit comfortably in a chair or stand with your feet hip-width apart, making close contact with the floor. Close your eyes if it feels comfortable for you. Begin by gently shaking your arms, allowing them to loosen and relax. Then, move on to shaking your legs, feeling the muscles and joints releasing any tension. Let your torso and shoulders join in the shaking, allowing the movement to flow through your entire body. Visualise any stress or tension being shaken off with each movement. Continue shaking for a few minutes or until you sense a feeling of release and renewal. Take a few deep breaths and notice how your body feels afterwards.

Remember to adjust the intensity of the shaking according to your comfort level and any physical limitations you may have. The goal is to create a sense of release and renewal by stimulating the body's energy flow and releasing tension, regardless of whether you're standing or sitting.

Exercises for Releasing the Jaw

N.B. These exercises are also useful for deconstriction work. It is important when exercising the jaw to keep the tongue relaxed, with the tip touching the lower front teeth. Remember that the extension must come at the temporomandibular or 'hinge' level.

–   Clench the jaw with teeth pressed tightly together. Now relax and allow the lower teeth to move away from the top teeth. Feel the difference between the tension and release states.
–   Imagine that the jaw is a vice. Slowly and gently 'unwind' the vice. This should be at the 'hinge' (temporomandibular joint), not the front of

the mouth, and should feel as though the gap between the upper and lower back molars is increasing. When trying the exercise allow the 'vice mechanism' to become more relaxed.

–   Using the fingers, stroke the jaw downwards; start at the level of the 'hinge' and ease the jaw down bit by bit. Feel the upper and lower teeth separating while keeping the lips together with light contact.

–   Imagine that there are springs between the upper and lower back molars which prevent the teeth from meeting. Encourage the molars to spring away from each other, creating a bigger and bigger space. Maintain a fluidity of movement and avoid tension.

A relaxed but open yawn is also a very good way of increasing jaw muscularity and is a very effective way of releasing tension.

Exercises for Opening the Pharynx

Exercises for opening the pharynx are often similar to jaw exercises and should be done in conjunction with them.

–   Keeping the lips together with light contact, try to produce a full yawn and then a half or attempted yawn. Feel the increased space at the back of your mouth.

–   With lips lightly together, breathe in through the nose. Ensure the jaw is not clenched and there is space between your upper and lower teeth. Begin to softly smile, and feel the apples of your cheeks rising. With that, you will feel the space increasing and widening at the back of the mouth, almost as if you are smiling from that place. This is known as the 'inside smile'. This increases awareness of this area and encourages a more open setting.

–   Extend the tongue out of the mouth as far as possible and then try to speak clearly. This is extremely difficult to do but a certain degree of clarity can be achieved. This exercise needs to be approached with an attitude of fun as the individual both looks and sounds ridiculous. Once you put your tongue back into your mouth you will notice how much clearer your speech is and the freedom and space in your mouth.

–   Deliberately create tension in the jaw, tongue and pharynx and speak a sentence in this manner. Next, contrast the sound heard and the sensation felt with the same sentence spoken without tension.

Exercises for the Lips

- Purse the lips, maintaining quite tight contact, and rotate them in a clockwise direction. Repeat this several times, then stop and release contact before beginning again in the opposite direction. Once this has been practised several times, continue the exercise but without stopping in the middle. Change direction fairly frequently.

- Curl the upper lip towards the nose – try balancing a pencil on the lip to check the degree of curl. Now curl the lower lip down towards the chin.

- With closed lips, keep the air pressure within the mouth and blow the cheeks up. Once that occurs, use the fingers to press against the cheeks and 'pop' them, allowing the air to escape.

- Maintaining light contact between the lips, purse and then spread them in a smile. It is important to feel the contrasting muscle activity in the lips and cheeks.

- Suck the lips in over the teeth so that there is little of the lips showing. Maintain that position and then release by smacking the lips apart.

Exercises for the Tongue

What is a 'strong tongue'? In these exercises we are looking to create dexterity and flexibility to allow you to speak swiftly, clearly and in a muscular manner, and feel more in control and consequently more confident when speaking. Some of these exercises may make you laugh, or yawn. Both are fine!

N.B. It will be necessary at first to practise tongue exercises using a mirror, until becoming more adept.

- Tuck the tongue tip behind the lower front teeth and flatten the blade of the tongue in the mouth. Alter the mass of the tongue by bunching it forward and out of the mouth while maintaining contact with the lower front teeth with the tongue tip.

- Stick the tongue out of the mouth with the sides folded upward so that the tongue forms a funnel shape. Next flatten the sides so that the tongue is wide and flat. Repeat this exercise, alternately funnelling and flattening the tongue.

- Extending the tongue with its tip pointed, use it like a pen to draw your signature.

– Roll the tip and body of the tongue backward into the mouth towards the soft palate and then quickly flick it out again, rather as a lizard or chameleon does when it catches a fly.

– Extend the tongue and try to touch the nose with the tip of it.

Exercises for Increasing Precision in the Use of the Articulators

Once control and increased kinaesthetic and tactile awareness of the articulators have been achieved, it is important to move towards increased precision in the use of the articulators in continuous speech. Using consonant cluster word lists and tongue-twisters is an appropriate starting point.

Working with tongue-twisters can become very mechanical and boring unless approached imaginatively. It is important to find the meaning and sense in the tongue-twister so that individuals are not simply repeating them parrot fashion. It is often useful to work on tongue-twisters using gross body movement, for example, clapping or stamping out the rhythm. Once the rhythm is found, many individuals find that the articulatory process becomes easier. The following tongue-twisters may be used.

Both Lips (Sounds /p/, /b/, /m/, /w/)

A white witch watched a woebegone walrus winding white wool.	A big beetle bit a body in a big black bag.	Wise wives whistle whilst weaving woollen waistcoats.
A pale pink proud peacock pompously preened its pretty plumage.	A monk's monkey mounted a monastery wall and munched melon and macaroni.	Blake's back brake block broke, Peter's pedal went kaput.

Tongue Tip and Alveolar Ridge (Sounds /d/, /t/, /s/, /z/)

N.B. For voiceless /s/ and voiced /z/: the exact position in which /s/ and /z/ are made can vary from the alveolar ridge for some individuals and behind the lower front teeth for others. Both positions use a groove or funnel in the tongue.

149

A tutor who tooted the flute, tried to tutor two tutors to toot.	A sick sparrow sang six sad spring songs sheltering under a squat shrub.	A single solid silver sifter sifts sifted sugar.
Particularly tactile, particular tactility.	A dozen double damask dinner napkins.	Tim tentatively took two tablets at a time.

Lower Lip and Upper Teeth (Sounds /f/, /v/)

A crow flew over the river with a lump of raw liver.	Five French friars fanning a fainted flea.	Three fluffy feathers fell from Vera's feeble fan.
To fight 'flu and fever fast, flee from fog and veer away from vibrant functions.	Fancy Nancy didn't fancy doing fancy work but Fancy Nancy's fancy aunty did fancy Fancy Nancy doing fancy work.	Five flashy flappers flitting forth fleetingly found four very flighty flappers flirting vigorously.

Tongue Blade and Front of Hard Palate (Sounds /tsh/, /dzh/, /sh/, /zh/)

The Chief Sheikh's sheep section.	Joan joyously joined jaunty John in jingling jigs.	Cheerful children chant charming tunes.
If a dog chews shoes, what shoes should he choose to chew?	Shall Sarah Silling share her silver shilling?	Sixty-six shy schoolmasters sail a ship serenely on a shining sea.

Tongue Tip and Upper Teeth (Sounds Voiceless /th/ and Voiced /th/)

Three thousand thrushes.	The Leith police dismisseth us.	Whistle for the thistle sifter.
The sixth sick sheikh's sixth sheep's sick.	Through six thick swamps stumbled Sammy.	Sometimes I like the thick smoothie, but the thin smoothie is silky and sweet.

Back of Tongue and Soft Palate (Sounds /k/, /g/, /ng/)

A king carried crates of cabbages across a crooked court.	Kingfishers quickly catch colourful crabs and crayfish.	The kangaroo sang a song about a box of frogs singing in the sand.
Can you recall and recount the capitals of countries such as Canada, Kuwait, Croatia and Cuba?	A skunk sat on a stump. The skunk thunk the stump stunk and the stump thunk the skunk stunk.	Sinking funds set aside crucial cash in case of encountering ghastly calamities.

Tongue Tip Raised to Mid Palate for /r/

A roving raven on the roofing, raving.	A rural ruler should be truly rural and recognise rural rivalry.	Running regularly is really great for your heart rate.
A rhinoceros ordered ribs of beef, rabbit, rolls, raspberries, radishes, rhubarb crumble and rice.	Requesting a raise is risky, but Rachel risked it and requested a raise.	Robin redbreasts are rarely seen in pairs, they are solitary birds often seen at Christmas.

Tongue Pressed Against Alveolar Ridge for /n/

A nightingale knew no night was nicer than a nice night to sing nocturnally.	Ninety-nine indigo dinner invitations.	No more nice nutmeg for the nutty nougat.
Newspapers often interview enthusiastic novices.	Never knowingly neglect geraniums in November.	Nora never needed a nap in Naples.

Final Consonants

N.B. In connected speech, final consonants are often dropped altogether. For the professional voice user, particularly when addressing a large crowd, they are important because meaning can be compromised if the final consonant is not articulated.

If you work in an emergency environment where articulatory precision is particularly important – such as emergency medicine, in an operating theatre, as an emergency call handler, in hospitality, in air-traffic control or in transport industries such as a pilot in command or a ship's captain – then you need superior articulatory skills; without the benefit of additional visual cues like the ability to lip-read, there is the possibility that words might be misheard especially if, as in the case of the official language of the air – English – pilots may not have English as their first language. In other pressurised environments such as hospitality or policing or security there is an equal need for articulatory clarity as the consequences for auditory confusion could be very serious.

The following texts are useful to increase attention to the precision required for final consonants.

As I was going to St Ives, I met a man with seven wives,
Each wife had seven sacks, each sack had seven cats,
Each cat had seven kits:

Kits, cats, sacks and wives,
How many were there going to St Ives?

Minimal Pairs Final Consonant Practice Where the Final Consonant Changes the Meaning of the Word

wind winged	clothe close	rink ring	teethe tease	breathe breeze
stage stays	wage ways	rage raise	change chains	barge bars
ford forge	purred purge	rice rise	coffee copy	cuff cup
sift sipped	dock dog	duck dug	frock frog	muck mug
got god	hat had	write ride	loose lose	bat bad
heart hard	pace pays	eight aid	cart card	bought bored

Difficult Consonant Clusters

In the following exercises we are including consonant clusters that are often difficult to pronounce. While they may fit the received pronunciation (RP) model, we are not in any way suggesting that your accent needs to change, but they are sounds that are important for professional voice users, who need dexterity and precision for clarity. Actors need to be able to produce the full spectrum of sounds, depending on what is required for a specific role. They need to be flexible and capable of executing any articulatory demands and it can therefore be useful to master them, so you have them in your repertoire when needed.

Words Beginning with /str/ – straddle

In words beginning with /str/ (straddle) the sound is a complicated consonant cluster where all the sounds are formed in a very limited space. Work through them slowly at first – 'sss-t-rrr', feel the tongue move from the /s/ towards the /t/ and up and slightly back for the /r/. Due to the complexity of this sound it can be easier to say 'shhtr', e.g., 'shhtreet' or 'shhtrike'. Although this alternative to /str/ is unlikely to confuse your listener or have them thinking you are saying another word instead, it can be useful to work on /str/ precision for the sake of muscularity, dexterity and clarity.

stride	strain	strong	struck
strict	stray	strip	straight
straddle	stroke	streamer	strict

Words with /st/ at the End

thirst	ghost	worst	rest
first	just	wrist	must
post	bust	pest	hoist

Words with /sts/ at the End

pests	posts	roasts	thrusts
hosts	masts	priests	boasts
firsts	chests	lists	toasts

Amidst the mists and fiercest frosts,
with barest wrists and stoutest boasts,
he thrusts his fists against the posts,
and still insists he sees the ghosts.

Exercises to Help Increase Precision of Rapid Articulatory Change

N.B. Repeat each exercise several times slowly before building up speed. Accuracy first, speed second.

Moving from /s/ (alveolar ridge and tongue tip) to /sh/ (blade of tongue with wider funnel):

Where she sits, she shines and where she shines, she sits.	Sam's sock shop stocks short spotted sheer silk socks.	Miss Smith's fish-sauce shop seldom sells shellfish.

Moving from /f/ (lower lip and upper teeth) to /s/ (tongue tip and alveolar ridge):

Fresh fish flash, shimmer and flit then flounder in filthy shifting shallows.	Fran feeds fish fresh fish food.	Friendly fleas and fireflies, friendly fleas and fireflies, friendly fleas and fireflies.

Moving from /k/ (back of the tongue and soft palate) to /t/ (alveolar ridge and tongue tip):

"Kitty, kitty, kitty" (repeat five times, increasing the pace gradually).	"Psst! Psst! Psst!" "Kitty, kitty, kitty" (repeat five times).	Now alternate from calling the cat with a Pssst! to telling it to Shhhh! "Psst! Shhhh! Psst! Shhhh! Psst! Shhhh! Psst! Shhhh!'

Moving from /d/ (alveolar ridge and tongue tip – voiced) to /t/ (alveolar ridge and tongue tip – voiceless). (It can help to clap the rhythm for this tongue-twister, and don't forget to try and make sense of it; finding the logic will make speaking it easier!):

> What a to-do, to die today, at a minute or two 'til two.
> A thing distinctly hard to say, but harder still to do.
> For they'll beat a tattoo at a twenty to two,
> A RatataTatataTatataToo,
> And the dragon will come when he hears the drum,
> At a minute or two 'til two today, at a minute or two 'til two.

Sounds move from /d/ to /dzh/ (alveolar ridge + tongue tip (voiced) for /d/ – duel, duke, due). To form the sound /dzh/, the tongue moves from the position for /d/ and then the tip releases into the position for /zh/ – jewel, James, George, etc.:

> A duel was fought on account of the jewel
> The duke would not give to the jeweller.
> The jeweller told the duke, with a note of rebuke
> A duel would surely ensue.
> The jewel was fought for and ended the duel
> The jeweller took the jewel as his due.

Tongue tip and alveolar ridge (/d/, /s/, /z/):

> Denise sees the fleece. Denise sees the fleas.
> At least Denise could sneeze, then feed and freeze the fleas.

Voiced /dzh/ (hedge) and voiceless /tsh/ (church). These sounds are a combination of /d+zh/ and /t+sh/:

> Hedge sparrows hatch eggs in church hedgerows.
> Jumping jellybeans are enjoyed by cheerful gentlemen.
> Jade, Chelsea, John and Chester took the challenge to judge the Chiltern high jump.

Tongue tip and alveolar ridge for /z/ and lips for /w/ (sounds move between /z/ to /w/):

> Fuzzy Wuzzy was a bear,
> Fuzzy Wuzzy had no hair,
> Fuzzy Wuzzy wasn't very fuzzy,
> was he?

/w/ (lips) and /th/ (tongue and teeth):

> Whether the weather be fine, or whether the weather be not,
> Whether the weather be cold, or whether the weather be hot,
> We'll weather the weather, whatever the weather, whether we like it or not.

Finding the Energy in the Word

EXERCISE ONE

With the following words, notice how the word sounds like the action they describe and how the consonant energy creates the dynamic. It may be helpful for you to match the word with a physical action when saying it aloud to really feel the energetic quality.

bounce box burst batter bash blunder	goad gash garrotte gag	nag nip nod nurse noose nick	twist turn tweak throw tickle troop trim
crash crumple charge choke clap chop cut kill kiss kick	hit help harm hash hop hang	pull prod push plunge point	vex vomit vanquish vilify
dig dash ditch dive dodge douse duel	jog jump jiggle jive jitter juggle jumble	quiet quell queue	wedge wail weep whisk wallow
explode exhaust embattle entice	light lift lob ladle lag lap latch lash	rush rake raid rage ram rattle	yell yearn yawn
flog free fight fritter	muddle malign maroon master melt mince	struggle stagger scratch slice stumble slide shrink	zip zoom zap zigzag

EXERCISE TWO

Moving on from imparting energy to one- and two-syllable words, try the following exercise using multisyllabic words, where the consonants may be used to break them up.

This is a very good exercise to use when an individual habitually fails to pay sufficient attention to the articulatory features of words causing them to run into one another; as a result, the spoken word lacks clarity and becomes monotonous to the listener.

N.B. Remember that in British English not all syllables take strong stress. Allow both weak and strong syllables to release the energy and rhythm of the word.

The key stress, where you will place most energy, and speak higher or louder, is in bold. For example, **a**-gi-tate. Some words have more than one stress.

a-gi-tate	claus-tro-**pho**-bic	per-pen-**dic**-u-lar
in-**teg**-ri-ty	the-**a**-tri-cal	De-**men**-tia
ec-cen-**tri**-ci-ty	mus-cu-**la**-ri-ty	in-**ter**-pre-tive
al-pha-**bet**-i-cal	Shos-ta-**ko**-vich	ac-**cel**-er-ate
a-**gree**-ment	his-tri-**on**-ics	de-**ve**-lop-ment

EXERCISE THREE

A slightly more advanced exercise involves selecting single words and, with the image of a dart board, using the words as darts to be propelled at the board. The impetus of the plosive consonant /t/, /d/, /k/, /g/, /p/, /b/ either 'propels' the word or 'lands it'. This exercise needs very careful monitoring, as it is important that control and support of breathing are achieved so that there is no likelihood of hard attack or tension. Gaze ahead and 'throw the dart' whilst speaking the word. Use your arm as you speak. The following words are very successful for sound and image:

hit	pierce	jab	strike
hug	tap	herd	sink
swift	glide	cuddle	press
attack	dart	bob	guide
dappled	peppered	tingled	fizzed
crackle	shuddered	bubbled	plotted

Exercises for /r/

Before working on /r/, stretch the tongue by gently holding the relaxed jaw and lifting the tongue to the teeth ridge. Make sure there is space between the teeth. Then move the tongue from behind the top front teeth backward towards the soft palate.

– Initial smooth /r/

Run rabbit, run rabbit, run, run, run.	Red roses, rusty rings and Russian roulette.	Rusty the restless rooster roams around the ranch.

– Medial /r/

Direct me in the direction of Durham.	Eric and Irina are terrible worriers.	Hurry Larry carry Barry to the lorry.
Flora and Myra requested marigolds and orange blossom.	Rory rarely wears their furry orange trousers.	Row, row, row your boat, Gently down the stream. Merrily, merrily, merrily, merrily, Life is but a dream.

– Blended /r/

When /r/ follows a plosive phoneme, such as /p/ /b/ /t/ /d/ /k/ /g/, it requires rapid release of the tongue tip. The two sounds should blend into one rather than be heard as two separate sounds:

pr			
Proud Prunella preens.	Prince prefers primroses, probably.	Practically prank-proof.	Priests produce prize prawns.
br			
Brainy British broadcasters.	Bring broad beans and bread rolls.	Bright brilliant brushes.	Brash brass bridles.
tr			
Triple train tracks.	Tremendous, trusted tribes.	Trendy trailing trellises.	Try treating Trudy to the truth.
dr			
Dreyfus drizzles drops of drink on drunkards.	The dressmaker drew up dresses made from drapes.	Drago the drowsy dragon dreads drought.	Dramatic Drake dreams of dreadful drumming.
kr			
Craig cracks crafty criminal cases.	Crates of cream crash, creating a clamour!	Crowds crawl creatively in crimpled creased creations.	Crime writers cruise across Croatia.

gr			
Good gracious! Great green gremlins.	Grant begrudges Graham's grand greenhouse.	Grumbling grandfathers grant grandchildren grace.	Grumpy greengrocers growing grapes.

Articulation Warm-Up Games

For exercising the articulators, the following activity is very useful. This is a vocal game, not to be taken too seriously, but allowing you freedom to explore your vocal range without the association that words often bring.

> − Try to create the sounds heard in an office: keyboards, telephones, photocopying machines, cash registers. Sounds from building sites, city streets, train stations and the countryside all provide suitable opportunities for similar exercises.
>
> − 'Play' a well-known song by creating the sound of any of the following musical instruments with your voice: double bass, flute, piano, guitar, saxophone, violin, oboe, drums. Some suggestions for songs are: 'Happy Birthday', 'Twinkle Twinkle, Little Star', 'Yellow Submarine', 'Nessun Dorma'.
>
> − This exercise can be taken a stage further by attempting to play two contrasting instruments. It is an excellent way to introduce vocal range and flexibility and particularly successful when working with a small group of people who are comfortable together and feel able to experiment vocally without being self-conscious.

Once precision of articulation is achieved, it is useful to continue working on flexibility by finding the energy in words. This is an important stage in voice work, particularly useful in encouraging a more lively and dynamic delivery.

Suggestions and Strategies

Tailor-Made Tongue-Twisters

To enhance your ability to effectively share information in meetings, whether face-to-face or online, consider these preparation tips. Identify phrases you frequently use and examine if any contain challenging vocabulary, such as medical or scientific terms, place names or unfamiliar words. Create a list of these words on your phone or sticky notes placed around the house, and practice! Record yourself, turn them into custom-made tongue-twisters, and repeat them until you master them. Familiarity with these words will boost your competence and confidence, alleviating concerns about stumbling during your presentation.

Prior to your meeting, do a general warm-up and then practise these words with positive energy. If you're unsure about pronouncing a word correctly, consult a dictionary pronunciation website and listen to the pronunciation, then repeat it. Youglish.com is a valuable resource where you can hear multiple people pronouncing the word you've searched for.

Recommendations for Incorporating Muscular Flexibility into Your Daily Life

– Actors warm up for stage performances to prepare their 'equipment' and warm up their performance 'engine' It is interesting to note that even actors with just a few lines need to be equally warmed up as those with many lines. The actor who comes on to say 'The queen, my lord, is dead'– one of their only five lines in the play – needs to be just as warmed up before their performance as Macbeth does with over 700 lines, particularly as they are delivering such a crucial piece of information. When we have limited time to make an impression, such as when introducing ourselves in a meeting, it becomes crucial to make the most of the few words we use. Pressure and tension can arise in these situations, especially in the morning, when dehydration, fatigue or tension when you haven't yet 'warmed up' into your working day may contribute to mumbling and stumbling. Staying hydrated and taking a moment for relaxing and breathing, followed by a quick tongue and lip warm-up, can be extremely beneficial.

– With online communication, factors like amplified voices through computer microphones and relaxed postures on sofas or perching on uncomfortable chairs can contribute to the loss of clarity. Distracting ambient noise or the need to remain quiet in public places further hinder our ability to communicate clearly. If you are somewhere where you need to be quiet, clarity will help you be understood, and reduce the need for repetition. Despite the potential feeling of being overly expressive or flamboyant, speaking with agility, muscularity and clarity offers significant advantages. It ensures immediate understanding, conveys confidence and

Continued

animation, and brings energy to the meeting. These qualities can lead to numerous rewards and even expedite the meeting process.

- Incorporating practices such as yoga, Pilates or Tai Chi can promote overall body flexibility and alignment, which indirectly supports vocal flexibility. Consistency and regular practice are key to developing and maintaining muscular flexibility, as it is a gradual process that requires ongoing commitment.

- Think about walking quickly to work and generating energy before you begin – use up any excess tension that way.

- Try and use all of the tongue-twisters in this chapter but vary them – don't fall into a predictable pattern of using the same small selection on each occasion. The internet is a great resource for many more.

- Muscularity and its result, clarity, means that you will be better understood by your listeners and so the need to achieve a higher volume will be reduced.

- At events, whether professional or personal, pay attention to others' speech. Evaluate the clarity and identify factors contributing to ease or difficulty. Focus on their speech skills alongside the content. What are they using to make their speech clear? Are they slowing the rate down fractionally? Are there certain vocal elements that they habitually use, for example, focusing on the final syllable of a word? Do you notice they are, where appropriate, using more lip-rounding, for example? When you do speak to someone with clear speech, occasionally look away from them, to test whether you are able to hear them with the same clarity but without any visual cues.

- Try to develop an awareness of the soundscape and dynamics of words so that language becomes alive rather than simply printed symbols. A great way to work on this is to look at advertising slogans and onomatopoeic words in comics and children's books such as 'splash, swoosh, gurgle, Kapow! Zap!'. This playful use of the articulatory organs helps to develop vocal and verbal muscle and imbue sound with energy. Practice can help to maintain the imaginative use of words. Explore your use of language through prose and verse.

- Explore pieces of text you find fun to say: limericks; song lyrics; jokes; rap lyrics. Use YouTube as a resource; it has a lot of speech material and is great for tongue-twisters.

Continued

- Challenge yourself to try a tongue-twister at different times in the day, e.g., first thing, mid-morning, afternoon, evening and bed-time. Do you notice any difference – does practice make perfect by the end of the day or are you better fresh from a night's sleep?
- Use the voice diary at the back of this book to make a written record of how much you've spoken, what you've eaten/drunk, how calm you are, etc. on a daily basis. Alternatively, you could record on your mobile or simply have a numerical legend that you use – for example 5 = talked a lot, 1 = talked very little – but along-side, make a note of how you were feeling and how it changed your muscularity and speech in general.

Sound Bite

Muscular flexibility allows you to change negative established patterns of speech and encourage new and more effective patterns, encourages increased mobility of the articulators, and limits the need for increased volume when trying to be heard.

When an uninhibited desire to communicate is connected to easy energised flexibility and a free breath stream, clarity and articulation is seldom a problem.

9 | Working for Variety

Introduction

Vocal quality is a critical factor in the immediate connection established between speaker and listener, a link which is often dependent on emotional warmth, fluency and use of language.

It is one of the many ways in which you can influence the outcome of all speech, from negotiation to establishing team values to building relationships, vocal variety allows you to develop a connection between the mind, emotion and language, and bring your language alive.

Think back to a time when you were part of a town hall meeting, or any other live event, and the influence this spoken communication had on you, as opposed to a long email in which you simply read a set of instructions. The information may be the same, but the effect is different.

It is inevitable that there will be some element of value judgement from you, the listener, relating to your individual preference for a particular vocal quality, and how you then interpret or remember the information you've been given. Vocal quality, with its diverse features – encompassing voice, tone and delivery – can be a divisive aspect, as discussed in previous chapters, and may affect your perception of someone, or theirs of you. For example, you may have memories of a difficult conversation which involved a speaker with a specific accent; have been given painful news or had an emotional encounter which deeply affected you with someone with a specific vocal tone; or you may instead just find a specific vocal quality unpleasant to listen to. What is not in question is the fact that vocal variety is an important aspect of communicative effectiveness and so for the professional voice user, information, meaning and feelings are shared through your words and your voice, and 'how' you share your message can have a major effect on how your audience processes your message, their willingness to keep listening or be potentially turned off.

DOI: 10.4324/9781003361114-10

For every individual whose job relies on their ability to communicate effectively with others, through the medium of voice, that ability is tested day in and day out in the work environment. For anyone whose 'label' or 'title' comes under the umbrella term of occupational voice user or professional voice user, their success is dependent on forging a link with their 'audience', through effective voice use. The communication process is, by its very nature, transactional – what takes place when two or more people interact in a work environment is underpinned by a plethora of factors, perceptual, cognitive, affective and performative.

Working for variety is a sometimes-forgotten soft skill which can cultivate that connection with your audience, establish a link and allow the relationship to thrive.

Most of us have sat through an informative speech on a potentially interesting topic, only to be met with a monotonous tone, the whole presentation delivered with the same vocal 'colour', volume and pace. Ultimately, we walk away dissatisfied, perhaps feeling as if the speaker is holding back, or not confident in their idea, or simply doesn't want to be there. As a speaker, we may even have kicked ourselves at the end of an event, aware that we have stayed in a narrow zone of vocal expression whether due to nerves, fatigue, uncertainty, lack of breath, feeling overwhelmed or even disconnected.

In this chapter, we will be addressing not only vocal quality but communicative effectiveness. While it is possible to assess vocal quality by looking at vocal parameters such as pitch, onset of note, clarity and resonance – the list is extensive – it is just as important to consider how effectively the voice can be used to communicate: to persuade, enlighten, inform, amuse, empower, collaborate, connect.

Why Does Working for Variety Matter to Me?

As a professional voice user you may possess a naturally pleasant voice or strong technical skills; however, vocal variety goes beyond mere aesthetics – it holds the key to unlocking the full potential of your communication and connecting deeply with your audience.

Vocal variety enables you to infuse your voice with a rich array of tones, rhythms and inflections that captivate and inspire. By varying your pitch, pace, volume and emphasis you can express a wide range of emotions, enhance storytelling and evoke profound responses in your audience.

Moreover, vocal variety ensures that your message remains dynamic and engaging, preventing monotony or disinterest. It allows you to emphasise key points, create suspense and highlight nuances, effectively guiding your listeners' attention and understanding. By grasping vocal variety, you can become a masterful communicator who leaves a lasting impact on every interaction, be it on stage, in the recording studio or during public speaking engagements.

Think about how you might tell an exciting story to friends, how you set the scene vocally, spontaneously employing different tactics for suspense and humour, or how your vocal quality changes when responding sympathetically or cheering someone on. These instinctive adjustments, and your ability to employ variety, texture and vocal colour can get lost at work. One of several reasons for this may be that you are trying 'too hard' to control the impression you are making; another cause could be that the environment doesn't feel safe enough for you to be 'yourself', and a particular problem may be that tension and anxiety has, in the moment, overridden your natural voice and expression. Thinking back to Chapter 3, 'Relaxation and Release of Tension', where we looked in depth at the effect of tension on the voice, we need to remember that tension restricts and suppresses the pitch range and may leach energy from the voice.

If, however, you are relaxed and can sound like yourself, you are speaking with authority about a topic you know well, you are able to connect with the words. You can pause where you want your audience to process, speed up when you hope to create momentum, highlight your key ideas with pitch change, and you slow down on the big ideas. In this way, you will be in a position to share your knowledge, be more inspiring, enthusiastic and convincing, as well as appearing relaxed and in control of how you are formulating your message, whilst being more authentic in the way in which you share this idea. Phew! Wouldn't that be nice! These ideal scenarios are attainable, and an exciting prospect. Vocal variety is the key, and the key to variety is tension release and thoughtful consideration of your audience.

In this way, working on variety in your speech can be the answer to many questions, such as:

- How can I bring more warmth into my leadership?
- How can I be more convincing?
- How can I sound more relaxed?
- How can I inspire my team?
- How can I pitch this idea, and show how proud of it I am?
- How can I sound more knowledgeable?
- How can I sound more like myself at work?
- How do I sound less formal/stiff?

- How do I sound more professional and prepared?
- How can I sound more interesting or interested?
- How can I tell a joke better?
- How do I sound more authentic?

For most listeners, a voice which is lively, interesting and varied will be more appealing than one which is not, irrespective of vocal quality. It should be possible to use the voice effectively to successfully convey a full range of thoughts and emotions that others can relate to, such as warmth, conviction, ease, certainty, pride, enthusiasm, intrigue, earnestness, amusement, excitement. When there is commitment, purpose and intention to engage and inform your audience using variety to enhance the sound of your message, it can be powerful, for both listener and speaker. Stretching slightly out of your comfort zone with variety can be the step you need to take to emulate your communication heroes, build confidence and allow you to express your message fully.

Variety can be achieved by increasing and varying pace, using pause effectively, monitoring the prosodic elements of the voice and encouraging an awareness of the paralinguistic features of communication. Paralanguage refers to any feature of verbal language that does not involve words but adds emphasis or meaning to utterances; not *what* you say, but *how* you say it. Loudness, rate, pitch, tone of voice, speed, breathing, pauses and punctuation, accent, fluency and modulation are a few examples of paralinguistic communication. It is a component of 'meta communication' that may modify meaning, give nuance or convey emotion; throat-clearing, groaning, 'mmm's, 'hmm's, sighs and gasps. In text-only communication, these paralinguistic elements are displayed by emoticons, emojis, font and colour choices, capitalisation and the use of abstract characters. There is evidence that this increased and increasing use of digital communication is changing our spoken communication and reducing our emotional vocabulary as we increasingly mirror the digital with shorter and more direct communication. We are potentially sacrificing some of the expressive elements that can be conveyed through longer, more elaborate verbal exchanges and leaning towards abbreviations and acronyms, which may impact the overall level of expressiveness and emotional connection.

What Do We Mean by Variety?

Imagine sitting down to play the piano in front of a crowd, only to discover that you can only use a single key. Your ability to create a beautiful melody that resonates with the audience is severely limited. The lack of variety makes the piano performance monotonous and fails to engage the listeners, causing their interest to wane rapidly. Similarly, in the realm of spoken communication, the power of vocal variety becomes paramount. By skilfully adjusting your pitch, pace and volume, you can keep your audience captivated, emphasise important points and deliver your message with clarity and impact. Embracing vocal variety allows you to infuse life into your words, captivating your listeners and leaving a lasting impression. During a single working day, you may find yourself addressing diverse audiences. Whether you're seeking to motivate your team, generate excitement for a project, negotiate a pay raise, deliver a persuasive closing statement or an inspirational speech, the need for vocal variety becomes even more apparent. Just as different songs require various tones, rhythms and emotions, each professional scenario demands the adept use of different 'notes' and 'styles' in your voice. By harnessing the power of vocal variety, you can adapt to the unique demands of each situation, connect with your audience and effectively convey your message.

Vocal variety suggests enthusiasm, confidence and credibility, and allows you to appear more passionate, knowledgeable and authentic, which in turn helps build rapport, establish trust and make a lasting impression.

What Is It, Exactly?

To create variety, to keep things interesting, we are looking predominantly at using a variety of tone, varied pitch, useful and diverse pause, a range of speeds, a choice of volumes and an awareness of the paralinguistic features of communication. We can learn to be alert to any habitual vocal patterns or repetitive features of our speech which might not be serving our message. The aim is for all these elements to represent how we feel, not to create a false performance or 'mask'. The exercises in this book will help you to develop these skills.

The level of vocal variety used conversationally can vary across different languages and is influenced by various factors such as phonetic features, intonation patterns and cultural norms. The English language, for example, is known for its stress-timed rhythm, which can provide opportunities for vocal variation and dynamism in delivery; other languages, like Spanish, Italian and Arabic, for example, are known for their melodic intonation patterns, which offer an alternative facet of vocal expression. Tonal languages such as Mandarin Chinese, Thai and Yoruba utilise pitch variations to convey different meanings. The rising and falling tones in these languages create a melodic intonation that adds a unique dimension to vocal communication.

We have previously discussed paralinguistic features of speech, many of which provide opportunities for variety: volume, pace, pitch, pause, flow.

However some paralinguistic features such as fillers, or discourse markers such as 'umm, err, ah, so, well, like, you know …', can sometimes do the opposite, particularly if they are unconscious, repetitive and habitual. Fillers can contribute to a monotonous tone if they are used excessively and become a habitual pattern in speech and can disrupt the natural rhythm and flow of speech, leading to a lack of variation in pitch, pace and overall vocal expression. The 'umm', 'err', 'ah' sounds are generally a natural hesitation sound, and often made on one consistent note; if used very regularly it is going to be hard to find variety, and your speech may sound as if it were 'flatlining' as you are constantly returning to the same pitch in between your words and this lends a 'samey' quality to your voice. Various other factors such as lack of awareness, limited vocal range or a habit of speaking in a particular tone can also contribute to a monotonous voice. It is important to note that vocal variety encompasses more than just the absence of fillers. It involves conscious control and exploration of pitch, pace, volume, emphasis and other vocal elements to create a dynamic and engaging voice.

Self-Assessment and Building Awareness.

Thinking about your own verbal communication style. How many, if any, of the following statements apply to you/can you identify with?

Vocal Variety Personal Inventory

My voice sounds boring to me.	
When I'm talking to others, I find it difficult to vary my voice.	
I sometimes feel people switch off as they listen to me.	
My voice makes me sound disinterested.	
I sometimes think people take me at my word; they don't realise when I am making a joke.	
I'm sometimes told I sound aggressive, even though I am only trying to make a point.	
I often run out of air when I am talking.	
My voice can sound very loud and uncontrolled if I get upset.	
I try to sound confident, but I feel that my voice can let me down and I sound hesitant instead.	
I'm aware of a significant difference between my written and spoken communication in terms of the responses I get.	
I feel I use fillers too regularly.	
I want to vary my voice but don't know how.	

If you answered yes to any, or all, of the above questions it is possible that there are several elements, which have been discussed in previous sections, that combine to reduce your communicative effectiveness. You may be experiencing a level of tension and anxiety which, as was mentioned above and in the chapter on release of tension, reduce the amount of air that you have to support your voice. That can have the effect of making your voice appear unsteady and hesitant; it can also reduce the pitch variety and energy in the voice. You may feel that you have not got proper 'control' over a situation – maybe you were suddenly asked to take over the briefing or give staff bad news. Did your voice properly reflect what you were required to do and how did you manage the situation? At the end of this section several self-help strategies are explored that will allow you to maintain effective voice under stress, during periods of anxiety and in situations which you feel are threatening in terms of your self-esteem.

If you have to make an important presentation – either to persuade a jury, talk to pupils or parents, hold a town hall meeting, an AGM, lead a political rally, interact with members of the general public, politicians, staff members, colleagues, other team leaders and so forth – it is important to avoid the worst effects of tension and stress.

Following the shift to online meetings during the pandemic, although people are beginning to return to in-person meetings a substantial percentage of communication remains online. Despite access to constantly improving software and digital effects, the human voice remains our most potent communication tool. The exercises in this chapter are designed to help you harness its full potential.

Here are some other ways in which you can assess your vocal variety:

Record: One way to assess your vocal variety is to record yourself speaking in everyday situations, such as during a conversation with a friend or family member, or during an online meeting. Listen to the recording and take note of any patterns or habits you notice in your speech. For example, do you tend to use the same tone of voice throughout the conversation, do you vary your pitch and volume?

Feedback: Another way to assess your vocal variety is to ask for feedback from someone you trust, such as a friend or family member. Ask them to listen to you speak in different situations and provide feedback on your use of vocal variety. Be open to their feedback and take note of any suggestions they offer. It can be useful to give them a guide of what they should be listening for – maybe they can note down the words they notice you extending or changing pitch on, when they felt particularly

Continued

connected to you, words they couldn't hear or were rushed, or whether they noticed excessive use of fillers, monotone, mono volume, mono speed. Let them know your specific goals so they can provide useful and focused feedback.

Style: The aim of a task like this is to ensure the appropriate amount of vocal variety is used for different audiences and different intentions. Record yourself speaking in three ways:

1. A weather report taken from the internet.
2. A children's story.
3. An inspiring speech – the internet is an amazing resource, alongside many books that are anthologies of great speeches, and also you can view the transcripts for all TED Talks on their website.

Listen back to these recordings and assess yourself on the following points:

1. How much vocal variety did you notice? Did you feel it was an appropriate amount of variety for the text, for your desired audience? Where did you notice most variety – in pace, pitch, pausing or volume?
2. Could you have improved the experience for your imagined listener by doing anything differently?
3. If you were the listener, would you want more or less vocal variety?
4. How much more vocal variety did you notice in Recording 2? Is there room for more, or did you feel it was style over substance?

To facilitate personal growth and development, it is essential not only to engage in self-assessment but also to consider practical strategies for implementing change. This can be achieved through gradual adjustments or by prioritising one change at a time, based on your capacity to adapt. The following advice aims to assist you in this process.

Practical Advice

– Check on your level of tension throughout the day. Be aware of sites of tension and deal with them? Think about the exercises in Chapter 3, 'Release of Tension', and use those before a big meeting. If you find it difficult to monitor tension throughout the day, start with just two 'checkpoints' during the day: on arriving at work and on leaving work. Once these have become habitual increase the number throughout the day.

– Select a familiar topic or material you often deliver and challenge yourself to infuse it with vivid imagery and atmosphere. Begin by mastering your content and clarifying your core message. Identify elements within the subject matter that can be brought to life with descriptive language, metaphors, and storytelling techniques. Rehearse your material aloud several times, emphasising images and atmosphere. Well-placed pauses can create suspense or reflection, shifts in tone can signify mood changes or emotion within your speech. Highlight key points and interesting words with pitch changes, energetic consonants and elongated vowels, which all add to the atmosphere. Recording your practice sessions enables self-assessment and fine-tuning. With consistent practice and constructive feedback, however challenging it is to listen to yourself in an objective way, a seemingly mundane topic can be transformed into an imagery rich, memorable presentation.

– If you need to give a talk or presentation always practise saying it out loud and try to move, stamp, clap or dance while practising, to release tension and inject rhythm and dynamism into the talk/presentation. You will need to say the presentation out loud to develop the muscle memory. Build up from an easy walk around the room, speaking the presentation out loud, to a much more energetic stamp or clap around the room, and finally a state where you can move easily and continuously as you speak out loud.

– Strive to develop a link between the language you use and the way in which you are using your voice. Listeners quickly pick up on discrepancies between your words and their emotional delivery. While this may be perceived by others as insincerity, it could simply reflect a challenge in aligning your spoken words with the emotional essence of the content. As a helpful exercise, select 5 words that evoke a 'happy' feeling for you and infuse them with that emotion as you say the word aloud. Choose a handful of words from the word lists in Chapter 7 and assign emotions such as 'regret', 'confusion', 'gratitude' or 'love' to each of them. Speak them aloud focusing on experiencing, and conveying, the prescribed emotion. If necessary, feel free to adjust the assigned emotion. For the more confident, experienced speaker, locate a passage of text in a news or magazine article that elicits a particular emotion in you, whether it's anger, sadness, compassion, awe or joy. Read the passage aloud, focusing on experiencing the predominant emotion. Take your time progressing to this exercise, and if it is emotionally challenging return to the single word lists and gradually adjust the emotional intensity. In a speech, we aspire to convey a wide range of emotions to the listener, but it's valuable to start with this foundational exercise. As you progress, you can delve into more specific emotions and elicit a wide array of responses.

– Draw from a variety of sources, such as poetry, memoir, fiction and drama; all are rich in expressive content. As you speak the material out loud, aim to adjust your delivery to authentically convey the spectrum of emotional content within the words. Take your time to feel the mood and energy of the piece. Over time, you'll move beyond simply infusing individual words with emotion or applying a single attitude or emotion to the entire piece. Instead, you'll be able to identify and express a broader range of emotions that flow throughout the entire text. This approach will lead to a more nuanced, emotionally rich delivery and enhance your ability to deeply connect with the words, enabling you to eloquently convey their nuanced sentiments.

– Role play is a very valuable strategy to move away from habitual vocal patterns. Assume a 'character' and 'speak in the character of ...', for example you could choose the role of a judge, a curious child, a navy commander, a politician, a nurturing grandparent etc. Allow yourself to indulge in stereotypical or even caricature voices to really explore your vocal range. Use text or improvisation to explore these different vocal characteristics.

Practical Preparation

Vocal variety is inhibited if tension is present and it is necessary to avoid other features that damage, reduce or affect the voice quality. There are several practical ways in which you can prepare for important presentations and here are some that relate to physical and mental preparations, some in terms of the run up to the presentation and some on the day itself.

– Remember the importance of preparation and rehearsal.
– Harness excess tension and use it productively – move purposefully and use gesture.
– Use visualisation, mentally rehearsing and envisioning yourself delivering a successful and engaging presentation.

- Take the time to acknowledge your audience, and consciously begin at a slower pace to guard against your delivery accelerating to the point where your 'message' becomes unclear due to the audience not having enough time to process the content.

- Use breathing to reduce your heart rate and support your voice.

- Dissipate excess adrenaline beforehand by, for example, going for a walk or walking upstairs rather than taking a lift.

- Increase your fluid intake. Do this by planning to drink at fixed times throughout the day. Use 'reminders' to achieve this.

- Steam your vocal folds before the presentation.

- Clothing and footwear should be comfortable but at the same time they should give you confidence. Remember the need to keep your body well balanced so that you maximise the breath capacity to support your voice.

- Smoking and alcohol are dehydrating and will irritate your vocal folds, making the sound and quality of your voice less predictable. There is limited data on the long-term effects of vaping, but the particles inhaled while vaping can cause inflammation and irritation in your lungs, which can lead to lung damage like scarring and narrowing of the tubes that bring air in and out of your lungs. E-liquid, also called e-juice or vape juice, usually contains flavouring, nicotine propylene glycol and glycerine and a number of other harmful ingredients.

- Drug use, such as inhalation of marijuana, has the same effect as smoking, but it heats to a much higher temperature and has more of an effect on the vulnerable surface of the vocal folds.

- Cannabis has a complex effect on the cardiovascular system, including raising the resting heart rate, dilating blood vessels and making the heart pump harder. Dilation of the small blood vessels in the vocal folds means that as the vulnerable surfaces of the vocal folds meet together at speed and with some force to produce sound, they become more prone to damage, with the potential for the vocal folds to haemorrhage and distort the vocal quality.

- Try to avoid heavy/large meals before a presentation.

- Do not allow a previous bad experience to affect your performance. Acknowledge your concerns and work on your mindset leading up to the event, and practice calming breath and relaxation techniques just beforehand to ensure you are feeling present and focused.

Exercises to Encourage Vocal Variety
Through Varying Intonation

EXERCISE ONE

Using one word to convey some very different responses.
Answer the question, 'Is your favourite colour blue?' Respond with a
'no' to convey:

Doubt – 'I'm not sure'.

Certainty – 'Certainly not'.

Amusement – 'I can't take this question seriously'.

Boredom – 'What a silly question'.

Irritation – 'Why are you asking?'

Questioning – 'Why, should it be?'

Observe how the voice modulates in pitch and varies in pace with
these different responses. Pay attention to the natural vocal variety you
instinctively employ to convey distinct narratives.

EXERCISE TWO

Answer the question, 'Are you sure you know what to do?'
Respond with a 'yes' to convey:

Excited – 'Yes and I can't wait to start'.	Annoyed – 'Are you suggesting I don't?'
Uncertainty – 'No, not really'.	Sarcasm – 'Why, don't you?'
Long-suffering – 'I'll go crazy if I'm asked again'.	Anxious – 'I'm not actually sure, but hoping for the best'.
Definite – 'Yes and now I must go'.	Disdain – 'Of course I do'.

To extend this exercise, you can experiment with different questions
and with adjusting your 'yes' or 'no' on a scale from 1 to 10. For
instance, a 'disgusted' response at level 1 might be mildly so, while a
'disgusted' response at level 10 could convey being utterly appalled.

EXERCISE THREE

Speak the following phrases aloud, try and find how many different ways or tones you can use to say them.

'Oh, really, honestly!', 'I don't believe it', 'That's amazing'.

With all these exercises its important to have a clear intention of the message you are trying to convey and to use gesture freely, as it will free up your variety. If your intention is clear, and urgent, your voice will follow suit.

When working on variety, it is advisable to record the exercises to assess and monitor progress and change over time. Use your mobile phone to record yourself and then ask yourself: Did I notice anything different about my voice? Did it sound more interesting? Was it achievable to modulate my voice using Exercise One, Two and Three? Did I manage to convey several meanings with the same word or phrase?

Always remember the power of the breath in supporting the voice; take time and think about your breathing but do not push your voice; your breath will support it and allow it to make changes without undue effort.

EXERCISE FOUR

A melodramatic scenario will offer the freedom to play and to go 'over the top' vocally, developing and extending range, intonation, pause and pace and experiencing a variety of volume. Gradually the exaggerated vocal range can be toned down and a more natural quality achieved, but the experience of variety is retained. Using the scripts below, work with a willing partner, or read both roles yourself. Perhaps start at a level 7 on the 'melodrama-meter', then move to an energetic 10, then gradually bring it down to something very minimal and naturalistic, and finally return to an energetic performance level of between 6 and 8, probably the most useful and frequently used 'level' for professional voice users. Scene B is written in a less melodramatic tone, which can be heightened to a melodramatic performance level and then returned to a naturalistic state. Enjoy observing how your voice has the ability to match the energy required by the scenario.

A.
A: Where has he gone?
B: That way, I think.
A: Do you know why?
B: He would not say.
A: Oh, this is terrible!
B: I think he is vile.
A: Oh, please don't say that!
B: I am sorry to say it but the man's a rogue!

B.
A: Did you drink the milk?
B: Yes, I did.
A: All the milk?
B: I left a tiny bit.
A: Oh, that's a shame!
B: What's the problem?
A: I need a cup of tea.
B: Oh dear, I'm so sorry.

With melodrama, words may be accompanied by physical gesture, bringing an additional dimension and vocal and physical energy to the exercise.

EXERCISE FIVE

Try to find a physical action/gesture to express the dynamics of words such as:

thump	thrust	rumble	quake	pull
push	press	cuddle	clutch	grab
climb	shake	dash	dig	wobble

Make gestures as expansive as possible, matching the energy of the word.

EXERCISE SIX

Try singing or chanting the melodrama scripts as if in an operetta. Think of it as a continuous utterance.

> Where has he gone? That way, I think. Do you know why? He would not say. Oh, this is terrible! I think he is vile. Oh, please don't say that! I am sorry to say it but the man's a rogue!

Notice how the vowels lengthen, speech becomes more melodious and range increases dramatically. It is always important to monitor breath support and capacity with song and to avoid areas of tension or forcing of the voice.

Take the above exercise from song/chant into speech, trying to find a similarly melodious quality. Incorporate gesture and use this to aid vocalisation. Try this exercise in three distinct stages:

1. Song/chant.
2. Melodramatic speech with a song- or chant-like quality.
3. Speech with more melody than usual.

N.B. In all these exercises control and capacity of breath is vital but the temptation to 'push' vocally must be resisted. Always maintain easy voicing. Some exercises may not appeal to you, if you feel too self-conscious you don't have to do them, but as you become more familiar with this work you may want to stretch yourself out of your comfort zone.

A Note on Exploring Vocal Variety

Some readers may have been concerned that introducing too much variety may make them sound like a hyperactive children's TV presenter. This is not the aim, we promise. At first, it may feel strange to utilise a wider range of variety in a work setting; people may even comment on the change in your communication style or vocal quality, but in our experience the comments are likely to be positive; you might just get some great feedback, you might find a more attentive audience. It is worth having a go at the exercises in this chapter, even if they feel a little silly. There is growth in stepping outside familiar territory, particularly if you feel that the comfort zone isn't working for you. Remember, what you do in the safety of your own private space isn't what you have to bring to the world. These are exercises, not necessarily models for what to do in the office; just like a warmup, or as with muscular flexibility, the aim is not to perform tongue-twisters for a crowd in the boardroom; you may not be using these exercises as your medium for updating stakeholders. Try the exercises alone at a commitment level of 8 to 10, but as you initially employ this new vocal freedom in your communication start introducing it into your day-to-day delivery at a performance level of 4 to 6 and see what happens. This can be fun, and *if* it's fun, you're much more likely to be relaxed. This relaxation, combined with a commitment to your ideas and an expression of your emotional connection to the subject, can invite some genuine spontaneity into the voice and a more genuinely 'live' relationship with your listeners.

All that we've looked at already in the previous chapters – posture, release of tension, breath support, deconstruction, onset of the note, resonance, pitch, muscular flexibility and volume – provide the scaffolding that is needed to bring us logically to working with vocal variety. As professional voice users, we need to optimise all those aspects of voice to achieve the level of vocal flexibility and responsiveness required by the role.

Working with variety, however, is not solely reserved for elevated prose, presentations, or professional settings. It is a valuable skill to apply in everyday interactions, whether at social gatherings with friends, family events, or situations where employing variety aids in navigating potentially challenging circumstances, such as medical, legal or financial matters, by increasing the clarity of your message and listener engagement.

Two non-vocal elements that add variety to speech are pause and pace. They generate anticipation and movement within communication. Pauses are valuable in creating atmosphere and building anticipation and when you want to emphasise important facts and phrases. Pauses, however, if used in the wrong place can break the sense in a phrase and confuse your listeners. A change to a faster pace in an exciting passage will add to the experience of your listener; slowing down the pace can suggest a conclusion, while a pace that is too regular becomes monotonous and causes your listener/audience to disengage or lose interest. As always, the advice is to be guided by the meaning. The more you read aloud, the more skilful you will become.

Recommendations for Preparation and Delivery of a Speech or Presentation

- Prepare well so that you feel confident.
- Research your audience and formulate your speech accordingly.
- Familiarise yourself with the space and lectern if you are using one.
- Assess the height and width of the room, the texture of the curtains and carpets etc., as these will affect the acoustic.
- Rehearse your speech in the space so that you can hear how the acoustic works before you give your presentation.
- Ask for feedback on vocal levels.
- Insist on a levels check if you are using a microphone.
- Welcome adrenaline. Don't be afraid of it; it is natural, and you can use it positively.
- Avoid over-breathing as this can add to your nervousness. Breathing out is vital as we tend to 'hold breath' in stressful situations.
- Make a positive entrance and hold your space before beginning.

Continued

- Connect with the audience by looking at all of them, making eye contact with some and smile before you begin.
- Speak more slowly than you would in conversation as your audience needs time to hear, decode, understand and respond.
- Move confidently and deliberately in a relaxed manner, rather than shuffling the feet or fidgeting.
- If something goes wrong, acknowledge it, correct it and move on. Audiences do not mind vulnerability. In fact, it can win them over and allow them to concentrate on what you are saying now, and not the mistake.
- Consider the way posture or body language might be perceived.
- Finish your speech on a definite note so that the audience knows when to clap; avoid 'fizzling or fading out' as it confuses the audience.
- Answer questions in a firm and friendly way and if you do not know the answer, say so.
- Remain physically and vocally confident until you have exited the room.
- If you find your mouth is very dry and is impacting your ability to create variety, try, with lips together, to gently bite the end of your tongue – it will immediately cause increased saliva in your mouth, which you can swallow inconspicuously. The swallow mechanism has the effect of repositioning your larynx within the vocal tract. This 'repositioning' will affect your voice, making it sound much less tense.

Vocal Flexibility and Tension Release

As we've already noted, making a speech is extremely stressful for all but the most experienced and well-trained speaker. Reduction of stress and anxiety, through relaxation, allows mobility and flexibility to enter your voice. Changing the focus from yourself to your audience is often a positive way of reducing self-consciousness and fear and helping you to relax. Think about pivoting from fear as the speaker to focusing on the listener or audience.

Outward Focus

Use some of these 'outward focus' suggestions; some, if not all of them, will help.

- Focus on the message and your audience rather than your situation, and the situation will become less intimidating.
- Make eye contact with members of your audience; don't look over their heads or at the floor.
- Remember your desire to share your information is paramount.
- Remember your audience wants to hear what you have to say.
- Remember your audience wants you to succeed.
- Looking after the audience's needs will shift the focus from your own.
- Put the audience at ease by being physically confident.
- Be loud enough for your audience to hear you.
- Be slow enough for your audience to understand you.
- Allow the voice to be varied and interesting so that the audience is engaged.
- Smiling not only breaks down barriers and helps the audience and the speaker to relax but 'brightens' the vocal quality and opens the vocal range.
- Emphasise the important information and the details they need to remember.
- Avoid emphasising with stress only; use pause, inflection and pitch to make words stand out.
- Attempt to make the formal occasion relaxed and conversational, although your speech will be formulated in a non-conversational way.

Suggestions and Strategies

Observe

Listen to news or current affairs and make a note of influencers or leaders or those on social media. Can you identify those who you feel have energised, enthusiastic and appropriate presentation styles? Try and identify how they achieved this. Did they signpost the most important elements of their presentation by using pause before important points? Did their pitch rise before an exciting or informative section of their presentation, or did they speed up? Did they use a downward inflection to signal an important and/or a disconcerting piece of news?

Try to make a note of their individual styles but also find points of commonality – pitch rises, use of pause, change in speed. Record yourself using your own material, like a fictitious work meeting or an interview script; listen, and then try it again using some of the techniques you've identified in speakers you admire. You can also use some less personal material, like a weather report or a paragraph from a newspaper.

N.B. Use text to begin with to practice your vocal variety. Think of it as a template from which we can learn how to employ vocal variety and then move these new-found skills into impromptu speech.

Preparation

When preparing a presentation/meeting script/speech with the intention of using vocal variety, there are several techniques you can employ to enhance your delivery. Here's a step-by-step approach to help you incorporate pauses, emphasis and appropriate pitch variation.

Understand the Content

Read and analyse your script, or a favourite passage from a book, to grasp its overall message, key ideas and emotional tone. Identify ideas that require emphasis, moments where pauses could enhance impact and areas where pitch changes can reinforce meaning.

Mark Significant Points

Highlight or underline words, phrases or sentences that carry weight or convey essential information. These are the areas where you may want to apply emphasis or pauses.

Experiment with Emphasis

Consider the intention behind each emphasised word or phrase. Ask: What am I trying to convey? Excitement, importance, surprise or contrast etc? Attempt increased volume, stress or intensity to make them stand out.

Utilise Pauses Strategically

Look for natural breaks in the script, such as at the end of a sentence, before or after key points, or opportunities to build suspense. Pause briefly to allow the audience to absorb the information or to emphasise a particular word or phrase.

Apply Congruent Pitch Changes

Identify words or phrases that evoke specific emotions or require different tonal qualities. Experiment with raising or lowering your pitch to match the emotional intent. For example, you might use a higher pitch for excitement or enthusiasm and a lower pitch for seriousness or contemplation.

Rehearse and Refine

Practice reading the script aloud, incorporating pauses, emphasis and pitch changes. Record yourself and listen back to assess the effectiveness of your vocal variety. Adjust as needed, ensuring that the variations feel natural and serve the purpose of enhancing the script's meaning.

Seek Feedback

Share your performance with others, such as trusted colleagues, friends or a communication coach. Ask for their input on the clarity and impact of your vocal variety. Consider their suggestions and make refinements accordingly.

Revisit and Refine

Continuously review and refine your script, paying attention to areas where vocal variety can be further enhanced. Experiment with different approaches and techniques to find the most compelling delivery.

Remember, vocal variety should align with the content and purpose of the script. By strategically incorporating pauses, emphasis and congruent pitch changes, you can bring depth, interest and engagement to your performance.

Visual Cues for Vocal Variety

When preparing a speech for delivery, incorporating visual cues can be a powerful technique to stimulate vocal variety and prevent a monotonous, predictable performance. By highlighting your script in multiple different colours, utilising underlines or arrows to indicate length or emphasis and adding emoticons to represent mood, you can effectively break free from a stagnant, evenly paced delivery. There's no right or wrong way of doing this, and it's a great way to familiarise yourself with your message and shifts in the script's energy. Here's how you can leverage visual cues to enhance your script and trigger your brain to activate variety:

–   Highlighters: use different coloured markers or highlighters on paper or on your computer to distinguish key sections, important points or emotional cues within your script. Assign specific colours to different types of emphasis, such as excitement, urgency or contemplation. This visual differentiation will prompt your brain to adapt your delivery, accordingly, ensuring a varied and engaging performance.

- Annotation: underline, circle or star words or phrases that require added weight or emphasis in your delivery. This visual cue serves as a reminder to highlight those sections, allowing them to stand out and grab the audience's attention. Similarly, use arrows to indicate rising or falling intonation, guiding you to vary your pitch and inflection for added expressiveness.

- Emoticons: it sounds simple, but incorporating doodles strategically throughout your script to represent different moods and energies can be effective. These visual symbols act as cues to align your vocal delivery with the intended emotional tone. Encountering a smiley face might prompt you to inject enthusiasm or positivity into your voice, while a sad, angry or confused face will lead to a distinct shift in tone and energy.

Through the use of visual cues, you actively stimulate your brain to employ vocal variety during your speech, aiding in memory retention. These cues, with their vibrant colours, underlines, arrows, and mood indicators, act as reminders for dynamic shifts in pace, emphasis, and mood, captivating your audience and enhancing your message's impact. Ensure the cues complement your natural style and align with your script's content and purpose. Experiment with combinations, practice with them, and adapt as necessary to fit your unique communication style.

Sound Bite

Vocal variety gives your voice energy; it allows you to match the dynamic of the spoken word to the emotional content of the language.

Development and Control of Volume

Introduction

We have established that effective communication is a fundamental aspect of any workplace, and volume plays an important role in how your message is received and interpreted by your listener. At this point in the book we hope that what might have initially seemed a multiplicity of diverse factors that influence vocal quality have come together to shape not only your confidence in your own voice but also to give the listener an impression of expertise, authority and confidence in you and your ideas. Volume is another crucial element, not only in terms of audibility, but also in how your audience interprets your communication, knowledge and personality. An audience may interpret extremes of volume as signs of arrogance, aggression, bullishness or dominance when excessively loud, or as indications of uncertainty, timidity, fear, neediness, confusion or disinterest when excessively quiet. These are just a few examples of potential assumptions. It is valuable for you to be aware of your habitual volume, be aware of how that may be interpreted or how it could impact your effectiveness as a communicator, and to make adjustments if needed.

Later in the chapter we have included a section on projection, which is often a concern of the professional voice user. Projection is frequently misunderstood by the speaker as the sole factor affecting their volume, clarity or muscular flexibility. In reality, projection is the harmonious synchronisation of all these elements.

Why Does Volume Matter to Me?

There are (dated) stereotypes about confidence, presence and authority being 'loud' and nervousness, doubt and insecurity being 'quiet'. This is by

DOI: 10.4324/9781003361114-11

no means a blanket truth; however, it is worth being aware of this cliché, and having the ability to work against it if you choose. We do need to be heard, but we don't need to be 'loud' in general terms. Think of some someone you know who you would describe as having 'quiet confidence' and how they display this attribute without excessive volume or garrulousness whilst remaining audible.

We see clients who come to us with the statement, 'My voice is simply quieter than other people's'. Biologically there may be some difference in the volume you can achieve due to genetics, or possibly if you have a voice disorder, affecting the movement or pathology of the vocal folds. However, there is far more evidence to support volume being culturally or personality based. Many clients will self-identify as shy or introverted but feel a social pressure to be louder or feel it necessary to increase their habitual volume to meet the demands of their particular work culture. Many will recognise that their family or cultural background has influenced the volume at which they speak, and find they are quieter than others in their workplace and, perhaps, in social situations. Equally, some cultural backgrounds naturally communicate at higher volumes than others. This is a fascinating area of study which we cannot fully explore in this book, but it is worth acknowledging, and perhaps you can take a moment to think about the volume levels you experienced in your childhood home, school, social group and, now, in your workplace. If you communicate at work in a second language, it is worth contemplating whether you notice volume differences between speakers of your first language and those with whom you work.

We cannot forget that different professional environments require different levels of volume. Where you are using your voice in large or open spaces, and often against background noise, communication is particularly taxing. For those whose work requires a certain level of loudness, it is important to avoid excessive effort to be heard as it can lead to vocal abuse, stridency and tension. In other circumstances you may be required to use significant volume for long periods of time, which creates the potential for vocal fatigue or, in extreme examples, lasting damage.

For a significant number of professional voice users, audibility and clarity is a problem. Being audible means that you can be heard, but 'being heard' is more than just about being audible.

Clarity is a complex issue, but low volume is not always the culprit. Several contributing factors, which we've already outlined – such as tension, low morale, poor breath support, a lack of balanced resonance, too high or too low a pitch, limited muscular flexibility and lack of variety – are also part of the equation. In addition, we need to remember that most of us don't work in 'extreme' conditions, but need to master making smaller, appropriate, adjustments and being aware of volume requirements for the task in hand. As we move through the day we may need to employ a slightly higher volume to address our team, lower our voices to have a discreet conversation, or adjust our volume at a work dinner as we contend with background noise; we skilfully, and generally subconsciously, alter our vocal volume and quality throughout the day as we move from a video call to maybe addressing the board room, then on to a small evening event. Granted, we may be assisted by technology in some of these instances, but we still need to be able to make these adjustments cogniscently, confidently and with ease. When it comes to volume, flexibility is key.

For many occupational voice users, poor control of volume may in part be related to age; a reduction in hearing as part of ageing is not inevitable, but it is a common consequence. Age-related hearing loss may be coupled with a variety of factors, many of which have occurred over years, such as an inherited condition, noise exposure, injury, disease or illness, the use of certain ototoxic medications, such as:

– Aspirin, when large doses (8 to 12 pills a day) are taken.
– Non-steroidal anti-inflammatory drugs (NSAIDs).
– Certain antibiotics.
– Loop diuretics, used to treat high blood pressure and heart failure.
– Certain medicines used to treat cancer.

Those with hearing loss may have difficulty accurately perceiving their own speech volume. It can be difficult to self-monitor and they may be speaking too loudly or shouting because they are not able to gauge their own volume. Age-related hearing loss can begin as early as a person's thirties or forties and worsen gradually over time. Speaking loudly can be a way for individuals with hearing loss to compensate for their reduced ability to hear, believing that in raising their own voice they will increase the chance of being heard, understood and included in the conversation. Noisy environments can be very isolating, and shouting may be an attempt to overcome the communication challenges. Not everyone recognises that they are experiencing hearing loss, and their colleagues are unlikely to be aware, and we can see how shouting or speaking at high volume could easily be misconstrued.

The exercises in this chapter are to help you find movement with your use of volume – they are not about shouting or causing damage; this is something to be very conscious of. Begin with incremental adjustments and monitor how your voice feels. In order to feel comfortable with making changes in the workplace, it is best to start with a playful approach and practice in a safe, private space where there is nothing at stake so you don't feel overly exposed or vulnerable. We are not advocating volume for volume's sake; rather we emphasise that your volume should match your need. For instance, in a noisy coffee shop, the craving for caffeine might instinctively lead a speaker to employ a higher volume, clearer articulation and stronger eye contact to ensure their order is correct and their caffeine fix is guaranteed! Children are particularly instinctive with their volume, yelling at a friend across the park so they can attract their attention, and whispering as they play hide-and-seek to avoid being found. Keep this playfulness in mind as you approach the exercises, and consider how to apply the idea of using the appropriate volume for what you *need* or want to achieve.

What Is It, Exactly?

Vocal volume refers to how loud or how quiet your voice is. For the professional voice user, use of range and clarity for emphasis is as important as volume in terms of making your voice heard and will, indeed, cause much less damage to your voice.

The volume of sound is principally a result of the pressure of the air that is blown past the vocal folds; the more forcefully the air is expelled from the lungs, the more the pressure is raised and volume increases. Similarly, decreasing the air pressure results in a decrease in volume. Of course, the vocal folds must increase their internal tension as they vibrate as, if they do not, the increased air pressure will simply blow them apart and interrupt vibration. The tensing of the vocal folds usually happens instinctively without conscious effort. For those with vocal fold paralysis or other types of vocal fold weakness, as a result of, for example, a degenerative neurological condition, increasing tension is often very difficult if not impossible and, as a result, increasing the volume of their voice is extremely hard to achieve without medical intervention. If you are finding it very difficult to increase volume after working on the exercises in this chapter, please do speak to your GP.

Self-Assessment and Building Awareness

Thinking about the volume of your voice, how many, if any, of the following statements apply to you? How many can you identify with?

My voice sounds quite loud to me.	
I have been told by other people that I am speaking too loudly.	
I have been told that my voice is too quiet.	
I've been told to speak up, on occasion/quite often/all the time.	
I find it difficult to judge how loud my voice is when I start to speak.	
I have noticed that after a meeting or a presentation or when speaking to a group of people in a noisy room I had to 'push/force' my voice out, to be heard.	
When I speak loudly my voice feels strained.	
I feel that my voice is too quiet to allow me to make an impression when meeting new people.	
I sometimes/often/regularly feel that if I had a louder voice, it would give me more confidence.	
I feel that I am regularly overlooked by colleagues and people in authority because I am too quiet.	
I don't feel that my voice reflects my personality.	
No one has told me I'm too quiet, but I think I am and believe that's why people don't listen to me.	

If you agreed with one or more of the statements above, you may indeed want to work on your volume, whether that is increasing or reducing it, or generally being more textured in your use of volume or being able to adjust it more quickly. Perhaps you want to feel more confident when you use a less habitual volume level; perhaps you want to tailor your volume more appropriately to the occasion or you want to match your volume to that of your peers and adjust swiftly between communication mediums. You may feel you need to know how to approach volume safely or with more ease. The exercises in this chapter will help you to build stamina, skill and awareness. Volume perception is complex, and perhaps your own assessment is coloured by some long-held personal beliefs, so asking a few trusted friends or peers for feedback is useful.

Record and Reflect

Consider recording some of your meetings to effectively monitor your volume in online discussions. Audio recording the entire session or using screen recording features can be helpful. By reviewing the recordings, you can listen to the voices, including your own, as they may be perceived by your colleagues. It's worth noting that if you're using a

Continued

phone to record, your voice may appear louder compared to computer audio due to the phone's proximity to your voice. Remember your voice will not sound quite like it does in your head, as discussed in Chapter 9, 'Working for Variety'.

Additionally, you can request recordings of any public presentations you deliver. If these options are not feasible, you can record yourself conversing with a group of friends and assess how your volume compares to theirs. This self-assessment can aid in identifying any necessary adjustments to ensure effective communication.

An excessively loud voice on a telephone or video call can cause distortion and disrupt the audio quality for other participants. This distortion can make it challenging for others to understand what is being said and can lead to discomfort or annoyance. It can make it difficult for others to contribute or express their thoughts effectively, leading to imbalances in the communication dynamics. An overly loud voice can create an unintended perception and interpretation of the speaker's emotions, intentions or assertiveness. Others may perceive the loudness as aggressiveness, dominance or even anger, which can affect the overall atmosphere and collaboration in the video call. A continuously loud voice can be fatiguing and distracting, not only for yourself but also for the other participants. It can make it harder for them to concentrate on the discussion or absorb the information you are sharing, reducing overall engagement.

If you speak too quietly, it may lead to misunderstandings, missed information and a breakdown in communication. You may give the impression that you're disinterested or not actively engaged in the conversation. This can affect how others perceive your involvement and willingness to contribute, potentially leading to decreased participation or exclusion from the discussion. A quiet voice may make it challenging to share your ideas effectively and assertively. If volume is consistently low, others may overlook or undervalue your input, diminishing your influence. In group discussions, it's important for everyone to have an equal opportunity to express their thoughts and opinions. When you speak too quietly, you may unintentionally contribute less, allowing dominant voices to overshadow yours and potentially hindering a balanced exchange of ideas. Depending on the quality of the audio equipment or internet connection, being too quiet might exacerbate difficulties in hearing you clearly. It is important to consider the quality of your microphone and internet connection to mitigate such technical limitations.

Practical Advice

–   When working on volume, start with checking your posture – remember to keep it open and confident, monitor your levels of tension and think about relaxing any area of your body that feels tight. Try some of the exercises in Chapter 3, dealing with release of tension, before working on volume.

–   Relax your back to maximise lung expansion.

–   Aim for an open, not rounded or hunched shoulder position.

–   Check on your breathing; modify your breathing pattern; if it is too fast, make sure you slow down and have enough breath to support your voice.

–   Release and sustain your breath when you speak; do not force the words out. If you have a naturally quiet voice, you can find yourself not necessarily shouting but pushing and squeezing your voice out which results in a thin, hard tone which can be 'misread' by the audience as unfriendly, fearful or tentative.

–   Think about the relationship between energy and breath. Energy should not lead to restrictive tension – it should come from a relaxed open vocal tract and good breath support.

–   Make sure to take the focus away from the larynx and rely on using breath and energy to achieve increased volume.

–   Increase the use of vocal range and variety plus clarity/muscular flexibility for emphasis rather than relying on volume alone.

–   Give full value to vowel sounds – they carry the emotion of the message.

–   Avoid using too much stress and not enough inflection to emphasise and deliver your message, otherwise it can come across to the listener as aggressive and intimidating.

–   Consider using a slower pace than you would if having a face-to-face conversation and make effective use of pause to get your message across; this gives the speaker status and gravitas and allows the audience time to decode and digest what you are saying.

Exercises for Volume Control

With all the following exercises, it is essential to monitor breath capacity, control and support. A common fault is the tendency to let too much air escape initially, causing a sudden, rather than a gradual, decrease in the size of the ribcage.

The following exercises require a playful approach. Try all these exercises and find the ones that are you find most useful, and use these regularly.

EXERCISE ONE

- Using the sound /sh/, imitate the sound of the sea ebbing and flowing. As the wave breaks on the seashore, increase the volume, and reduce it as the sea ebbs away: sh ... SH ... sh ... SH ... sh
- Using the sounds /v/ or /ng/, imitate the sound of a car or an aircraft approaching you, passing by and receding into the distance: /vvvVVVvvv/
- Using the sound /z/, imitate the noise of a mosquito, approaching, passing, receding and returning: /zzzzZZZZzzzzZZZZ/. Similar exercises, such as approaching and departing chugging trains, and soft and loud ringing or tolling bells, may be tried using sung or chanted, rather than spoken, sounds.

EXERCISE TWO

Imagine playing with the volume control on a radio and try to imitate the variety of sound. Work with the sounds /woo/, /wee/, /wow/, either on their own or as a blend, moving from one to the other. As you move the imaginary volume control your volume responds accordingly, if *just* audible is at 1, and very loud (but not shouting) is at 10, try moving the control from 1 to 10, and 10 to 1, moving smoothly through all the levels in between. Play around with the volume, moving randomly through the volumes. Use different pitches.

EXERCISE THREE

Determine the point of focus for a sound some distance away but not too far for easy delivery.

Imagine rolling a light ball of sound across the floor to the target. Use an underarm bowling movement to follow the sound through. Use /moh/, /mah/ and /may/, sustaining the /m/ and then increasing the volume as the sound rolls to its destination.

Now roll these sentences 'across the floor' in a similar way. Initially increase volume gradually on each word, then increase volume phrase by phrase.

Over every ocean, over every hill.	Hour after hour after hour.
Again and again and again.	Many men are merry.

Extend this exercise by altering the volume spontaneously with the 'radio volume control'. Avoid excessive loudness, but do encourage a subtle range of sound.

EXERCISE FOUR

Making sure posture is maintained, imagine a line of sound that is some short distance away, say 2 metres. Try to pull in this line, smoothly increasing volume as the line draws closer. This concept of drawing the sound towards you prevents the common problem of head thrust in an attempt to increase volume. Use the sound /hah/ initially to avoid hard vocal attack. The sentences in Exercise 3 can be used to develop this exercise.

EXERCISE FIVE

Stand in the middle of a room and select five focal points at varying distances. These need not be on any one level and can be on the ceiling, floor or at different points on a wall. A phrase should be spoken at a volume appropriate to the distance of each point. It is important to concentrate mental as well as vocal energy on the point of focus. It is also important to vary levels of intensity as well as volume. The following short phrases from Shakespeare plays may be helpful.

When we are born, we cry that we are come
To this great stage of fools.

(*King Lear*, William Shakespeare)

Reputation, reputation, I have lost my reputation!

(*Othello*, William Shakespeare)

Tomorrow, and tomorrow and tomorrow
Creeps in this petty pace from day to day,
To the last syllable of recorded time;

(*Macbeth*, William Shakespeare)

EXERCISE SIX

Using the following text, speak as if laughing joyously, increasing the volume line by line. If unable to laugh, speak the passage with energy and enjoyment. This will keep the breath supply buoyant and encourage an easy, tension-free delivery. Monitor breath economically.

> All the world's a stage,
> And all the men and women merely players,
> They have their exits and their entrances;
> And each man in his time plays many parts.
>
> (*As You Like It*, William Shakespeare)

The same exercise may be done with other material, increasing volume phrase by phrase, and playing with intensity. Newsstand or market calls encourage sustained volume without tension. You can use a newspaper headline and repeat the line at varying pitches, using your full range while calling, not shouting, the phrase. Try, for example, 'Read all about it', 'Roll up, roll up', 'Apples, apples, five for a pound!', 'Hero saves family!'

Projection

Introduction

Projection of the voice allows a speaker to be heard in large spaces without amplification. Projection requires range, clear articulation and a desire to take command of the space and share information with the audience. Projection is dependent on the ability to provide an adequate, unrestricted breath supply to fully support vocal fold movement that is without tension or constriction. A well-supported, free and unrestricted note will allow specific resonators to give warmth, energy and volume to the voice. A common fault is to lock the neck, thrust the head forward and force out the sound, which can cause vocal strain. If the audience has to strain to hear what is being said due to lack of vocal projection, its ability to assimilate information is impeded.

Public speaking, even to small groups, is a situation of fear for many people, so posture, relaxation and coping with nerves are important aspects to consider. Developing a confident and generous attitude to communication and focusing on the audience's needs is critical as, if the speaker looks 'uncomfortable', with posture that is defensive or anxious, this will be perceived by the audience as a sign of lack of confidence and commitment. If possible, becoming familiar with the space and rehearsing in it in advance is ideal.

Practical Advice

–   Show confidence through an open and relaxed stance, with your weight well distributed over both feet. Be aware of any forward thrust of your head and neck.

–   Monitor your posture, check how you are standing, try not to lock your knees, stand with your weight on one leg or slump in the middle, 'collapsing' your midriff.

–   Think about your eye levels; try to position yourself to take in the whole audience.

–   Remember that your name is on the guest list, the audience has come to see you, not to intimidate you. Keep a sense of ownership of the space.

–   Retain a positive attitude to the audience and an enjoyment in communicating.

–   Prepare your material, whether this is a speech, a lecture or a religious service.

–   Make sure it is well-written and well-rehearsed.

–   Don't disconnect with the material, as this will lead to an automatic delivery and could lead to a monotonous sound lacking in range.

–   Prepare your breathing mechanism and vocal muscles.

–   Release your tongue, jaw and shoulders.

–   Maintain an upward eye contact, particularly towards the ends of thoughts or sentences.

Acoustic Influences on Projection and Control of Volume

The influence of the acoustic properties of a space should not be underestimated. If speaking for the first time in a new space, it is important to assess the space and modify the voice accordingly. The following should be observed: the height and shape of the ceiling; the quality of the floor covering, furnishings and curtaining; structure and composition of the wall surfaces; the size and number of windows; the dimensions of the room; the number of people in the audience; outside influences such as traffic and air-conditioning units which might create additional environmental noise.

Every space is different but, generally, rooms with high ceilings and hard surfaces (such as wood-block flooring) in, for example, halls and gyms, will generally produce additional vibrations and can produce an echo, while thick carpeting, low ceilings and soft furnishings tend to dampen and absorb sound.

If possible, speakers should rehearse in the space and ask for feedback on the acoustics to assess the required level of volume before beginning the speech. Should this not be possible, a hand clap will give a good indication of the degree of reverberation. In certain circumstances it is necessary to change pitch slightly to redress the acoustic balance.

Working in the open air can be challenging as sound diminishes over distance and without surfaces for sound to 'bounce off'; projection is compromised and leads to significant demands on the voice. Bringing groups or your audience closer to yourself or standing near a wall or on a platform can be helpful.

In such cases, whistles and megaphones can be useful to teachers and sports coaches. Public speakers should always use public address systems when available but should investigate ways to use them correctly and effectively; if you are using a microphone in such circumstances request to familiarise yourself with it before the event.

Projection Exercises

N.B. These exercises are also useful for developing volume.

EXERCISE ONE

- Using a ball (or an imaginary ball), stand and bounce the ball onto the floor while saying /bah/.
- 'bah, bah, bah, bah, bah, bah, bah'
- Repeat, using the word 'bounce'.
- Play with alternating small physical and vocal bounces with bigger ones.
- Engage the whole body as this is done, not just the voice and the hands.
- Co-ordinate the sound with the bounce. As the bounce gets bigger, increase the volume.

EXERCISE TWO

Using a large ball, stand a short distance from a wall and throw the ball at the wall saying 'Now' with a sustained /n/. Start at a low volume, but not whispering.

- Step further back from the wall and repeat the exercise. This time throw the ball harder and say 'Now' louder.

- Repeat, increasing the distance from the wall, the energy of the throw and the volume of the voice on each coordinated action, but do not shout.

EXERCISE THREE

Speak a line such as 'Row, row, row your boat', while standing at one end of the room.

- Take a step into the room and repeat, increasing the volume slightly.

- Repeat this exercise, getting gradually louder with each step. It is important not to go from very soft to very loud too quickly.

- Repeat the same exercise while singing/chanting 'Row, row, row your boat'.

EXERCISE FOUR

- Facing a wall, identify a spot and project the sound /oo/ on to the spot.

- Slowly walk away from the wall (making sure not to fall over anything!) and increase volume at the same time.

- At the end of the breath, take time to breathe, maintain focus on the spot on the wall, and then begin on the same volume and gradually decrease the volume while returning to the wall.

- When confident with /oo/, explore other sounds and pitches.

- Notice that the breath control varies depending on the sound and pitch.

EXERCISE FIVE

– Imagine creating a circular motion with your hand in the air as you make a continuous 'siren' sound using the /n/ consonant sound. Use the hand to draw small circles at the same time as voicing. Allow the voice to stay 'connected' to the physical action.

– Increase the size of the circles and allow the voice to increase its range with the size of the circle.

Extreme Volume: Shouting

Shouting Safely

All of the exercises for volume and projection can be used as preparation for shouting. It is particularly important to use the exercises for breathing, jaw release and opening the pharynx before attempting projection exercises. The shout should only be attempted by an accomplished voice user – it is not suitable for someone whose voice is in any way vulnerable. Any pain or discomfort indicates that the exercises should be discontinued until more skill in the basic volume exercises is acquired.

It is possible to increase volume to a considerable degree without damaging the vocal folds, providing control and support are present and undue tension is eradicated. For some professional voice users, it is necessary to produce 'The Shout!'. This should be possible if you pay careful attention to all the elements of voice production that have already been mentioned in the book, in particular, secure breath support and freedom from laryngeal tension.

Shouting safely requires considerable practice and if possible, unless you are suddenly in a state of emergency or trying to alert someone in an emergency, try to work from a call in the first instance. A call is less associated with tension and is a much healthier option.

Working on projection alongside volume will be much more efficient than shouting and will certainly allow you to gain attention over a distance without losing the warmth, energy and volume to your voice.

Practical Advice (in Addition to That Given for Volume and Projection)

- Avoid shouting without preparing the body and the breath first.
- Avoid poking the head and neck forward.
- Avoid thrusting upwards and/or forwards of the chin.
- Avoid clenching the jaw and teeth.
- Avoid shortening the neck.
- Avoid a collapse of the upper chest.
- Avoid a collapse in the centre of the body and shortening of the spine.
- Avoid hard/harsh onset of the shout.
- Avoid forcing sound out with insufficient breath support.
- Focus on creating a grounded open stance with weight on both feet and a sense of being connected to the floor.
- Connect with a fully supported breath.
- Maintain relaxed shoulders.
- Release occipital point and neck muscles.
- Ensure mobility of the larynx during vocalisation.
- Engage an exercised soft palate.
- Ensure the tongue is released with the tip forward so that the tongue does not 'bunch'.
- Aim for pharyngeal release, creating a free open throat (a sense of space behind the tongue and lifted soft palate).

Sports coaches, referees, security personnel, emergency workers and DJs are all people for whom shouting may need to be an occasional option. Actors may also need to shout professionally, but they are often in receipt of training. Certainly, if you find that you are having to 'shout' more frequently than you anticipated when you were appointed to your role, then we would strongly recommend that you seek professional work with a voice coach; shouting without training can leave your vocal folds in a vulnerable condition.

We've included some suggestions for those using their voice outside, in a field, a stadium or a large outside space. Adapt these ideas in line with the space in which you are working and your specific role.

- If possible, use a megaphone. This may be quickly made with a piece of cardboard. If this is not possible, the hand should be cupped around the mouth and the speaker should try to 'call' rather than shout.

- Remember, keeping a healthy voice is much more likely if a sense of humour is retained. In laughter the voice is wonderfully free; the joyous 'Yes!' produced by a supporter after their team suddenly makes a brilliant move after playing abysmally is very different from the exasperated 'Come on!' before the successful event.

- Set out clear boundaries about behaviour, and enforce them. This will avoid the need to shout while attempting to maintain order.

- Make sure players keep in sight and ask them to respond to visual commands such as hand or flag signals.

- Wear warm clothing, scarves and gloves; warm up if necessary, by exercising. Take a team near to a wall or keep them close in order to use a more conversational voice level when coaching.

- Do not battle against the wind; if the wind is blowing it is unlikely that the speaker will be easily audible. Players are more likely to understand a speaker who is clearly mouthing the words. The use of a control, such as a whistle or flags or a signalling system that is understood by players, is recommended in order to preserve vocal health in difficult sporting situations.

The swimming coach has the least enviable job! The acoustics in indoor pools are invariably poor, because of the abundance of hard surfaces and high ceilings. Often, they are echo chambers and the space becomes incredibly noisy, particularly if the classes take place while public or shared sessions are occurring simultaneously.

In testing vocal situations:

- Apply your knowledge of posture, breath and voice production.
- Be aware of head–neck alignment, particularly when cold or when shouting at a group or cheering on your team.
- If you suffer from allergies, keep an antihistamine spray or tablets on hand.
- Carry drinking water.
- Avoid 'competing' with extraneous noise.
- Use a megaphone or other 'control' such as a flag or whistle.

- Encourage visual forms of communication.
- Set clear boundaries about discipline in swimming pools, gym halls or sports fields.
- Monitor posture.
- Maintain relaxed posture while using volume.
- Avoid shouting, where possible gather groups around you in a sheltered position.
- Develop your ability to use high volume and 'shout safely'.
- In extreme situations, such as in an emergency or where safety is paramount, the use of a control to minimise voice use is important; whistles can be high-pitched enough to pierce the noisy acoustic. Using a flag to gain attention can be effective, but often a sound signal will be needed as well.

Suggestions and Strategies

Recommendations for Day-to-Day Tactics to Explore Habitual Volume

- When you approach a group of people, do so with a wave as you say 'Hello'. Raising your hand opens your ribs and back (see posture exercises) and alerts your audience before you speak so you already have their attention and will be less inclined to shout or not say 'Hello' at all. Using this tactic on a regular basis will make you more comfortable and more confident when approaching, or bidding farewell to, a group of people.
- As discussed earlier in this chapter, familiarising yourself with 'braver' volume choices can be done in low-stake situations and with people you may never meet again, for example, when ordering food in a restaurant, speaking to a delivery driver, waiting in a queue or perhaps when chatting to children by playfully matching their volume dynamics.
- Explore your quieter volume levels; do so by increasing muscular flexibility, precision and energetic articulation whilst making more eye contact and giving your conversation partner or audience more attention. Experiment with different lengths of pauses, emphasising specific words and employing vocal nuances to maintain interest and captivate your listeners. Observe if this works for you and

Continued

whether your message still gets across; it is likely that you will be able to draw your audience towards you, and not need to use high volume. Clarity, sincerity and connection may do the work for you.

Being Heard in Group Situations

If you want to 'speak up' in unfamiliar or uncomfortable situations, try these tactics:

- Collate your thoughts and prepare key points or questions you want to contribute prior to your call or presentation. Having a clear idea of what you want to say can boost your confidence and make it easier to speak up.

- Actively engage in the conversation by listening attentively; this will help you stay connected and identify opportunities to interject. Nodding and using gestures can show your interest and make you feel more involved in the conversation, so that when you do speak you don't feel like you're contributing for the first time.

- Start by contributing in small increments. Begin with brief comments, questions or observations, gradually increasing your level of participation as you become more comfortable.

- Developing relationships and trust with the individuals you communicate with regularly can create a supportive environment that encourages your participation. As you become more familiar and comfortable with the group, speaking up may feel less daunting.

- Remember that your insights and unique perspective are valuable. If you have something to contribute, your input can enrich the discussion and provide fresh insights that others may not have considered.

- Engage in active dialogue by asking questions, seeking clarification and offering constructive feedback. Actively participating in the discussion demonstrates your interest and involvement while fostering a sense of collaboration within the group.

- If the main group conversation feels overwhelming, try breaking off into smaller subgroups or finding individuals who are engaged in more intimate conversations. This can create a more conducive environment for sharing your thoughts and actively participating.

- Join discussion groups outside of the work setting, where stakes are lower.

Calling, Not Shouting

In the privacy of your car, try experimenting with 'greeting' other drivers at differing distances, in order to feel the volume variations needed to 'reach' people. Alternatively, if you are walking in the countryside or by the sea, experiment with 'calling' at longer distances than you normally have the opportunity to do in the office or at home, without embarrassment. If you have a dog, you may already be used to this 'game'; always remember to 'call' the dog towards you rather than 'shout at' the dog. You can also apply this idea when watching live sports.

Awareness of Danger Zones

Consider whether responding immediately is necessary in the face of extreme noise or background noise. You can use gesture to indicate that you are waiting to speak until the noise passes. An example of this might be, when going through a tunnel on the Tube, to wait until you get to the next station before making your point and thereby limit the chances of trying to shout over noise.

Speaking with Headphones

Using headphones while speaking can sometimes lead to straining your voice and causing discomfort. When wearing headphones, there is a tendency to increase your vocal volume to compensate for the perceived noise isolation, particularly if you are also speaking above noise on transport or a noisy street. You may unintentionally speak louder than necessary, which can lead to vocal strain and fatigue. Some headphones may cover or partially block the ears which can cause a sensation of pressure or discomfort when speaking, alongside creating a sense of isolation for some, which can make it difficult to gauge your own voice's volume and quality. Without proper feedback, you may unknowingly strain your voice or speak in an unnatural manner, leading to vocal fatigue. If you wear over-ear headphones for an extended period, the weight and continuous pressure on your ears and the surrounding muscles can contribute to tension and strain, which can eventually impact your voice.

– Remind yourself to use your natural speaking voice without overcompensating.

- Consider using open-back or semi-open headphones that allow for better airflow and provide a more natural sound experience. These headphones allow some external sound to be heard, providing better feedback for vocal control.

- It is recommended to only cover one ear with over-ear headphones, in order to get some feedback from your own voice, and to hear your natural voice as it resonates in your own head to ensure a more accurate perception of how you sound and maintain a natural delivery style.

- Pay attention to your posture, breathing and vocal technique when speaking with headphones.

Remember to Warm Up!

This might seem obvious; however, working on tension release, posture, breath, muscular flexibility, range, resonance and volume exercises before you rehearse or deliver your speech or presentation will 'free' your sound. As you rehearse, move! 'Dance' your speech, use large arm movements, expanding your body in size; combined with light-hearted and easy voicing, try chanting your speech or singing it. The aim here is not perfection, but playful, uninhibited exploration. Going into your speech with this energy means you are less likely to shut down and revert to 'tightness' and restricted volume.

> ### Sound Bite
>
> Projection is the ability to use your voice effectively with power and clarity, to reach your audience without damaging your vocal folds. It is not about yelling!

Communication in the Workplace

Introduction

Effective communication goes beyond the mere words we speak. It encompasses the way we deliver those words, the emotional impact we create and the connections we foster with our audience. By embracing the full potential of our voice, we can leave a lasting impression, make others feel valued and build meaningful relationships.

In this chapter, we delve into the broader skills of communication. Communication is not solely about the mechanics of the voice; it encompasses the integration of mind, body and voice, as they intertwine to shape your overall communication experience. We explore how you can cultivate your vocal skills to effectively serve your purpose, while prioritising your vocal health.

By shifting your focus towards your audience, acknowledging their needs as listeners and understanding the impact you have on them, you can establish a stronger connection and engagement. This holistic approach allows you to communicate with authenticity, confidence and resonance. Through practical techniques, self-reflection exercises and daily-life tasks, we aim to empower you to become a more effective and engaging communicator.

The 'Spotlight Effect' and Outward Focus

The 'spotlight effect', coined by Thomas Gilovich, Victoria Husted Medvec and Kenneth Savitsky, refers to the tendency of individuals to feel as if they are in the 'spotlight' – literal or metaphorical – and overestimate the extent to which others are scrutinising their appearance, behaviour, voice and performance, closely observing, evaluating or judging their every move.

DOI: 10.4324/9781003361114-12

In public speaking and communication, the 'spotlight effect' is common and can have various negative effects on the presenter. It can increase self-consciousness, anxiety and self-doubt, leading to a fear of judgement and negative evaluation and, potentially, a fear of speaking. The presenter may become overly focused on their own performance, appearance, mistakes or their voice, which can make them forget their purpose of connection, ignore the audience experience and hinder their ability to communicate effectively.

> N.B. When you feel the heat of the 'spotlight' on you, try turning that light onto your audience, shine your metaphorical light on them, or imagine that light is glowing from within you.

Throughout this chapter, we will explore how to tailor our communication specifically for the benefit of the audience, with a particular emphasis on utilising the power of our voice as the medium. We will look at the essential elements of effective communication that prioritise the audience and their needs and enable you to do your best, even amidst the adrenaline rush of public speaking. By emphasising preparation, practice, authenticity, story-telling, variety and clear communication, professional voice users can turn their light onto the audience, creating a more significant impact.

As with the exercises in the earlier chapters, we encourage you to play with these ideas, try them on for size, practice and find pleasure in working on and enhancing your spoken communication. None of us are born 'great speakers', but over time and with focused effort we observe, experiment, make mistakes, try again, find what works for us, practise and gain confidence.

The Business of Communication

Professional voice users are in the 'business of communication', with the goal of conveying messages, influencing opinions and building relationships through speech. Effective communication is crucial across sectors like business, politics, media, education, healthcare and entertainment. This emphasises the need to develop your communication skills, adapt to diverse environments, use appropriate styles and methods and foster successful interactions. Successful professionals who excel in the business of communication recognise the power of effective verbal and nonverbal communication, empathy, clarity and persuasion, to achieve their goals and positively impact others.

What Makes a Great Communicator?

Think of the teachers who left a lasting impression during your school days. It's likely that their enthusiasm, not just the content they taught, made them memorable. Similarly, recall a recent conference, event or TED Talk. The speakers who stood out to you were likely those who effectively communicated their passion and genuine interest in the topic. They captured your attention and left a lasting impact. For many of us, the skills of 'getting the message across' have either never been formally learned or else have been given a low priority in our professional training. Not all professional voice users have had any formal voice training or the opportunities to develop communication skills before being faced with work-place expectations and challenges, and acquiring and honing these skills becomes vital for career growth.

The Communication Model

This model can apply to other forms of communication, such as sign language or written communication, but we are focusing on voice and speech.

The Communicators	The senders and receivers of messages. The speaker and the audience.
The Message	Sender's thoughts, information or ideas which are encoded into a physical form (speech) which can then be decoded by the receiver (audience), who then attaches meaning. Structure, choice of words and communication style. Think of two people throwing and catching a ball; the ball is the message!
The Medium	The way of conveying the message. We are looking at the medium of voice and body language, and the way we share messages through our posture and physical expression.
The Channel	In verbal exchanges communicators use the vocal-auditory channel, which carries speech, and the body.
The Noise	'Noise' refers to any interference with the success of the communication or distortion of the message so that the meaning is not understood. Voice disorders, voice quality issues, technological issues, misperceptions, nerves, environmental factors such as unhelpful acoustics, inaudibility, incongruent gesture or inappropriate delivery style.

The Feedback	Judging the extent to which the message has been successfully received and the impact it has had on the listener is through feedback we receive from the listener and the way we listen to others. Body language, level of engagement, retention of information, feedback are all types of feedback we may receive.
The Context	All communication takes place within a specific context and the context impacts our communication style and is important for the success or otherwise of the communication. The time, place and particular relationship of the exchange exerts considerable influence on its success or otherwise!

Vocal health and voice quality, as explored thus far, play a significant role for professional voice users, as they enhance the effectiveness of spoken communication. This encompasses various elements, including the message, medium, channel, noise, feedback and context. Consider a situation where you attempted to be humorous or sarcastic in a text or email, but the absence of 'voice' led to misinterpretation of the intended tone. Having a voice disorder or lacking effective voice usage can further distract from your message. In such cases, listeners exert extra effort to overcome 'the noise' – the confusion, distraction or inaudibility – and consequently this reduces their processing capacity for understanding the information. In this chapter we will look at the various elements through the lens of the communication model to help you integrate your whole voice – your tension-free, aligned, breath supported, deconstricted, resonant, variably pitched, well-articulated, aurally interesting and easily audible voice! – into successful communication.

Self-Assessment and Building Awareness

Asking yourself these questions and keeping a note of your answers, which you can refer to at a later date, can be a great way to observe your progress, define your goals and target areas of your communication that you want to pay more attention to.

Am I clearly articulating my thoughts and ideas? Is my structure and approach working for me? If not, what is getting in the way? Do I need more preparation, or a different approach for this audience? Is something else standing in the way of clarity?
Am I able to convey empathy and understanding when needed? Am I conscious of the relationship I have with the listener and what they need from me in this situation? Am I able to show them that?
Am I adapting my communication style to different audiences or situations? Am I able to use different tones, volumes and energy levels? Am I able to tailor my message to different groups, and adapt my delivery to suit the room/mode/listeners?
Am I effectively using nonverbal cues, such as eye contact and body language, to enhance my message? Thinking back to a recent presentation or speech, did I consciously use any? Were they supporting the message, or distracting?
Am I able to convey my message with confidence and assertiveness?
How well do I provide constructive feedback and actively receive feedback from others?
Am I consciously employing active listening, am I genuinely paying attention to others? Are there ways I might improve?
How well do I handle conflict or difficult conversations? Can I notice any patterns in how these conversations go? Is there anything I would like to change?
Do I use appropriate and engaging storytelling techniques to connect with others? Do I match my vocal energy to these techniques?
How well do I use vocal variety, such as pitch, tone and volume, to convey different emotions and emphasise key points?
Am I mindful of my pace of speech? Is there anything I'd like to change? If so, why?
Am I conscious of my body language? Am I using open and engaged postures to convey attentiveness and approachability? Are there times my body language is closed?
Am I aware of any unconscious habits in my body language or voice that may distract or detract from my communication?
How well do I use gestures and facial expressions to enhance my message and convey emotions or emphasis? If I were to use more, what would be the effect?

THE COMMUNICATORS

As a professional voice user who has picked up this book, you already understand the value of effective communication in your work and personal life. By conveying your thoughts, ideas and feedback effectively, you can establish strong connections, influence others and nurture supportive working relationships. Effective communication is also vital for teamwork, enabling clear understanding of roles, efficient information-sharing, problem-solving, decision-making and conflict resolution.

In the communication model, both the speaker (sender) and the audience (receiver) play important roles in the process of effective communication. As the speaker, your responsibility is to encode your thoughts into a form that can be understood by the audience, via your choice of words, tone, gestures and nonverbal cues. A tailored message to meet the needs of your audience, alongside your authentic presence and confident delivery, can create rapport, capturing the attention of your audience throughout your delivery.

As the receiver of the message, the audience is responsible for actively engaging with the speaker's communication. Their role involves attentively listening, observing and interpreting the message being conveyed, ideally in a receptive, open-minded and focused way. They play an active role in decoding and interpreting the message, extracting meaning and making sense of the information presented. As professional voice users, we aim to lay the groundwork for that to happen.

What Can Hinder Audience Decoding?

- The audience's personal biases or preconceived notions can affect how the audience interprets the message.
- The complexity or density of the information presented can overwhelm the audience's cognitive capacity, limiting their ability to process and decode the message effectively.
- Speakers who struggle to articulate their thoughts coherently or fail to organise their speech in a logical manner can confuse the audience and hinder their decoding process.
- Excessive jargon, technical terms or specialised vocabulary without providing sufficient explanations or context may not help the audience grasp the meaning of the message.
- Speakers who lack clarity, speak too quickly or softly, mumble or have a monotonous tone can make it challenging for the audience to understand and decode the message accurately.
- If a speaker lacks appropriate nonverbal cues or displays conflicting body language, it can create distractions and make it harder for the audience to decode the intended message.
- Speakers who fail to engage the audience through interactive elements, storytelling or audience participation may struggle to maintain the audience's attention and interest, making it more difficult for them to decode the message.

- While visual aids can enhance understanding, relying too heavily on them without proper explanation or integration can divert the audience's attention and hinder their ability to decode the message. Excessive text on visual aids can be distracting and the listener will end up reading them.

- Difficult environments, whether because they are acoustically challenging or because there are technical difficulties.

- The listener may be dealing with something personal which is causing a distraction.

We will look at these obstacles in greater depth in this chapter and discover strategies to avoid them. As mentioned, the audience might make certain assumptions or have biases that will distort your message, and these are discussed below. These assumptions could equally be discussed in 'The Noise' section of this chapter as they can become 'noise' for the audience and interrupt their decoding or attention.

Vocal Perceptions

Your voice is an incredible tool that can greatly influence how others perceive you. It's not just about *what* you say but, also, *how* you say it. The quality of your voice, including factors like pitch, tone and resonance, along with your accent and the way you deliver your words, all play a role in shaping the impressions you make.

When we hear an unfamiliar voice, we automatically form assumptions about the person behind the voice. Quick, unconscious conclusions are made about age, physical appearance, educational background, family background, social class, status, where you live, your political beliefs, how assertive you are and even your level of intelligence. Reflect on this the next time you speak to someone on the phone for the first time before meeting them. What assumptions do you make? While our voices do play a significant role in shaping first impressions, they are, of course, just one piece of the puzzle and may not provide an accurate representation of who a person truly is. There's a lot more to an individual than what meets the ear. However, it is fascinating that, if we choose, we can influence, vocally, how others perceive us and make choices to shape those impressions.

It is not only your voice that gives a first impression. Factors ranging from clothing style to posture play a role in how impressions are formed. Something as small as a 'too-gentle' handshake (Bernieri and Petty, 2011) may influence personal judgements as it may make one appear overly passive, just as someone with a louder voice may be perceived as overly confident.

A major component of first impressions is visual, what is seen: the person's appearance, posture, body language, facial expression, eye contact. What is heard, namely the voice quality, the pitch of the voice, the pace and use of pause, the clarity of speech and the accent that the person has, determines the auditory component of an initial impression, whereas the words that are said are initially very low on the list. It may seem almost unbelievable that, through what appears to be a rather arbitrary set of criteria, decisions are made which will affect future relationships, but that in fact is what appears to happen. The validity of this form of judgement lies in the fact that most people when asked how often they have altered their first impression of someone will respond 'rarely'. A major barrier to interpersonal communication lies in an individual's natural tendency to judge – to approve or disapprove of – the statements of the other person. Statements do not need to be verbal; as has been said earlier, statements are made by an individual's choice of clothes, hairstyle, facial expression and body language.

When forming an impression of other people, individuals are influenced by a set of beliefs and values known in psychology as the false-consensus effect or false-consensus bias (Fabrigar and Krosnick, 1995), by which they overestimate the extent to which their opinions, beliefs, preferences, values and habits are normal and typical of those of others, and their belief that other people have similar beliefs. The false-consensus effect is significant in communication because it can influence how individuals perceive the reception and understanding of their messages. People may assume that others interpret and agree with their viewpoints to a greater extent than they truly do, and that their message is therefore clear. This bias can lead to a lack of accurate understanding of the audience's actual perspectives, potentially hindering effective communication. Being aware of the false-consensus effect can help individuals avoid assumptions about how their material might be understood or received, and better understand the diverse perspectives and needs of their audience. By actively seeking input, listening attentively and promoting an inclusive environment for dialogue, communicators can overcome this bias and foster more effective and empathetic communication.

Within the workplace, it is important to realise that colleagues, clients, customers and industry peers make instinctive judgements at the beginning of every new relationship. An incorrect assumption early on in a relationship can determine the quality of ongoing communication, often with critical results. Given the need to maximise the opportunity to communicate effectively, how can this best first impression be achieved?

Making a good first impression with your communication style can be challenging due to all of the factors mentioned above. However, in the professional world certain universally acknowledged principles govern first impressions, in addition to workplace expectations that encompass qualities such as punctuality, preparedness, proactiveness and reliability.

Recommendations for First Impressions

- Start with good posture, make eye contact and offer a friendly greeting. Positive body language signals openness, approachability and confidence. Avoid crossing your arms or displaying closed-off gestures, as they may give the impression of disinterest or defensiveness. More information on body language is included in 'The Message' later in this chapter.

- Introduce yourself, in a way that makes it easy for people to hear, and remember, your name. This may mean adjusting pace, volume or clarity.

- Give your full attention to the person you're communicating with. Show genuine interest in their thoughts and ideas. Practice active listening (see the section on 'The Feedback') by paraphrasing and asking clarifying questions. This demonstrates respect and helps build rapport.

- Build initial connections based on shared values or experiences, creating a positive and memorable first impression and a strong foundation for effective communication. Approach interactions with a positive mindset. Enthusiasm is contagious and can leave a lasting impression.

- Treat everyone in the workplace, regardless of their position or role, with respect, courtesy, kindness and empathy to encourage an open dialogue.

- Show professionalism in your interactions, maintain appropriate boundaries (including your own), and be mindful of cultural sensitivities.

- Communicate in a clear and concise manner. Avoid jargon or technical terms that may be unfamiliar to others. Tailor your communication style to the needs and preferences of your audience.

- Communicate with authenticity. People appreciate sincerity and are more likely to trust and connect with someone who is genuine in their approach. Focus on the purpose of your communication and meeting your audience's needs, rather than attempting to impress.

Continued

- Adapt to different communication styles and preferences. Pay attention to nonverbal cues, match the pace and tone of the conversation and be responsive to the needs of the other person. Flexibility promotes effective communication and rapport.
- Come prepared to engage in meaningful conversations. Research the topic, or the person you'll be interacting with, to have some background knowledge and feel more confident.

The moment you enter a room you bring with you a persona. Assumptions are made by your audience immediately on that first impression. No matter how dedicated you are, your success as a communicator will depend upon more than commitment, passion and knowledge. It will require the ability to project a persona that engages, inspires or commands authority and respect.

Posture, status and confidence, clothing, general attitude, manner, the way in which you use and structure language and, above all, your vocal delivery, provoke a response in the listener from which they form a perception of you, the speaker. These perceptions may be incorrect, as we have previously discussed; nevertheless, if the voice used is shrill, it might indicate a confrontational quality and you may be thought of as aggressive or stressed; if posture is slouched, it might suggest a lack of assertiveness or enthusiasm, you may be thought of as distant or reluctant; and if eye contact is avoided, it might imply hesitance or disinterest in the conversation, and your listener may brand you as lacking commitment. While it is clear these perceptions can be inaccurate, once established they can be difficult to change, and being aware of this can help us navigate it and, if desired, reshape initial impressions.

Take note of the initial impressions you form when meeting others and take a moment to reflect on the factors that triggered a strong response within you. It's possible that these reactions stem from an alignment or misalignment of values. Consider what you would like people to perceive during their first encounter with you. It can be beneficial to identify your own personal values, as they can serve as a guiding compass for your interactions. Online resources, such as Brené Brown's 'Living into our Values' exercise (www.brenebrown.com), can provide valuable insights and assistance in uncovering and understanding your values.

The Professional 'Mask' and Authenticity

Do you have a 'phone voice' or feel like you are wearing a mask to create a good first impression? It's common to have a certain level of adaptation or 'work manner', or professional persona, that helps us navigate professional environments and make positive first impressions; this is likely to be different from our 'sitting at home on the sofa watching TV' manner; just as you wouldn't wear your suit to swim in, or your swimmers at a conference! It is, of course, natural, and useful, to have different modes of operating for different situations. 'Masking' or adopting a persona in the workplace is a protective strategy, or habit, that some professionals employ to showcase their passion for their work while maintaining personal integrity and privacy, or when they are struggling to find the energy to 'show up'. While masking can help navigate social and professional interactions, it can have negative effects, such as increased stress, burnout and a sense of disconnection from one's authentic self.

This can be relevant for neurodivergent individuals who may feel the need to camouflage behaviour and thought processes to conform to neurotypical environments.

In a world that increasingly values 'authenticity', it's important to understand what it truly means and how we can achieve it while still meeting the requirements of the workplace.

– Are you aware of masking or adopting an altered persona at work?
– What effect do you think it has on you and your energy?
– Have you found a balance between feeling professional and authentic?

There is a positive, growing call for professionals to be 'authentic', and professional voice users ideally should be able to bring their whole selves to work without fear of judgement or prejudice. We are in no way suggesting you need an alter ego or 'mask' to perform well; however, it is crucial for all professionals to be mindful of how their body language and vocal tone can be interpreted. Observing others and gaining awareness of one's own habitual voice and body language is key. Identifying personal physical patterns and vocal idiosyncrasies may require external feedback, such as video recordings or input from objective colleagues or a voice and communication coach, to gain valuable insights. By promoting self-awareness and providing an inclusive environment, professionals can navigate the balance between authenticity and effective professional communication.

Authenticity, in this context, refers to the act of staying true to oneself and ensuring that our actions and communication align with our thoughts, beliefs and values. It involves cultivating a sense of congruence between our inner selves and the way we present ourselves to others, maintaining a delicate balance between expressing our true selves and meeting professional expectations.

Take time to understand your own values, passions and strengths. Reflect on how these align with your work and find ways to incorporate them into your professional life and communication.

- Identify your personal and professional values.

- Embrace openness and authenticity when interacting with others, sharing your ideas, concerns and aspirations. This vulnerability can foster deeper connections and trust with colleagues.

- If it is safe to do so be honest and transparent in your communication, avoiding excessive embellishments or sugar-coating. Authenticity is about being genuine and sincere in your interactions.

- Boundaries support authenticity by helping individuals align their actions and communication with their true selves and communicate honestly and transparently. Nedra Glover Tawwab (2021), a therapist and expert on boundaries, and Henry Cloud (2017), provide valuable insights and guidance on setting and maintaining boundaries and communicating them clearly to foster honest, open communication. Boundaries help us establish healthy relationships, reduce stress, ward off burn out, communicate assertively, protect our emotional and mental health and create a sense of balance in our lives. By setting and respecting boundaries, individuals can navigate the demands of the workplace while staying true to themselves and fostering a culture of authenticity.

Authenticity doesn't mean discarding professionalism or disregarding workplace norms. It's about being true to yourself while still meeting the expectations and requirements of your professional environment. It is important to have some awareness of how your body language and vocal tone can be interpreted and whether they align with the message you intend to convey. Being mindful of these nonverbal cues helps ensure that the message people receive corresponds with your true feelings and intentions. By paying attention to your body language and vocal tone, you can make adjustments as needed to ensure effective and congruent communication.

Human beings are inherently complex and multifaceted, and our responses vary depending on the context and individuals involved. We naturally employ different body language and vocabulary based on the person we are addressing and the level of formality in a given situation. This adaptability is not a sign of insincerity or falseness, but rather a reflection of our emotional intelligence and our ability to adjust our behaviour to suit different circumstances. It also highlights that we have the power to choose how we respond and can adapt and perform in a manner that is suitable for the professional environment, the topic at hand and the needs of our audience.

The Art of Performing

When making changes to your communication style, discomfort might lead you to feel like you are 'acting'. There is some debate as to how much 'performing' is acceptable, necessary or desired, in professional situations such as a speech or presentation. Many professional voice users will already have some experience with performing; perhaps you found your way into your career through your ability to 'bring words to life' and enjoy doing so, but there are a significant number who find this is a daunting and often vocally tiring task. There are those who feel the throat 'tighten' as they read or present and hear a voice produced that they find difficult to recognise as their own; others feel inhibited and self-conscious when having to entertain or be seen to be 'performing'.

We would argue that entering a 'performance mode' is not the same as putting on an 'act'. When anyone embarks on something new, such as developing an alternative communication style, making changes to their vocal quality or developing new presentation skills, they may initially feel that it's an 'act'. It is natural to feel somewhat 'false' as you step outside your comfort zone and try something unfamiliar. This sense of 'acting' should not be seen as inherently insincere, deceptive or inauthentic. In the process of learning and growth, we often need to experiment with new and different approaches and behaviours. By temporarily adopting new ways of working, you can explore alternative methods that may enhance your effectiveness in the workplace, and decide whether they work for you, or not. This is a transitional phase, a means of acquiring new habits and refining your professional repertoire. While it may be necessary, for some, to don a metaphorical 'mask' during this developmental phase, professionals must remain mindful of the fine line between adaptive behaviour and losing their authenticity. 'Acting the part' should not mean compromising one's values, beliefs or personal integrity. It is vital to retain a sense of self and align any changes with one's authentic professional identity.

As mentioned earlier, the exercises in this book serve as a behind-the-scenes process to refine your communication skills. Some of these new habits will become ingrained, while others may not. It's perfectly acceptable to adapt and adjust based on the task at hand, granting yourself the best possible advantage and allowing you to create the desired impression. Ultimately, the goal should be to transition from 'acting the part' to a more genuine and integrated expression of the newly acquired skills which will come with familiarity, allowing the authentic self to shine through in all professional endeavours. This process should be driven by a desire for self-expression and growth, rather than feeling marginalised or pressured to conform. By embracing authenticity willingly and providing space for individuality, professionals can cultivate a work environment that celebrates diversity and encourages each person to contribute their unique perspectives and talents.

The Speaker's Mindset

Professional voice users must often contend with niggling doubts about their own ability. This is especially difficult perhaps when delivering to larger groups, or dealing with a disruptive class or a tricky customer, or doing something exposing and new, as it can undermine your status and confidence. Most of us have experienced thoughts such as 'I can't do this', 'I can't control this group', 'This team thinks I'm a pushover', 'This meeting is going so badly. It must be my fault', 'I should have prepared better' and so on, and sometimes this negative voice is very loud.

This negative self-talk can be just as damaging and demoralising as criticism from others. Once this inner voice takes hold, it is challenging to quiet its volume, which is why it must be confronted and challenged. Professional voice users often experience the familiar sensation of entering a room, whether it's a lecture hall, workshop, conference or courtroom, feeling defeated before even beginning. It's crucial to observe the impact of such an attitude on the body and how it subsequently affects our posture, breathing and, consequently, our vocal expression. Recognising these patterns and their physical manifestations is the first step towards addressing and overcoming them.

As discussed, 'good' communication is a complex interplay of various elements, including the voice, verbal expression, body language, vocal nuances and listening skills. Mastering these components in front of an audience can be intimidating, requiring self-awareness, deliberate practice and ongoing development. By cultivating an empowering mindset, embodying confident body language and harnessing the full potential of our voice, we can create a comprehensive and impactful communication experience. This mindset involves believing in our abilities, focusing on growth and possibilities and facing challenges with resilience. It fosters self-confidence, optimism and a proactive approach to achieving success. A focused and present mindset enhances clarity of thought, active listening and thoughtful responses. For professional voice users, it means believing in your vocal proficiency, embracing confidence, resilience and having a proactive attitude towards honing your skills, continuously seeking growth, remaining open to learning and approaching communication with enthusiasm and authenticity. This mindset empowers you to face daunting challenges, express yourself confidently, connect with your audience and leave a lasting impact through your communication.

But, we know, it is easier said than done.

We have intentionally refrained from using the term 'positive mindset' as it can sometimes be associated with 'toxic positivity', which may feel insincere, empty of real meaning and ultimately unhelpful. However, adopting an optimistic, hopeful and assured approach to a speaking assignment has proven to be highly beneficial and this approach is supported by scientific research around neuroplasticity, neurotransmitters and reduced stress levels. Positive thinking does not mean denying or ignoring negative emotions or challenges. It is about cultivating a balanced perspective and actively choosing to focus on positive aspects, solutions and possibilities. Authors such as Dweck (2017), Doige (2016) and Dispenza (2012), among others who focus on mindset, are recommended.

The 'Fear'

For many people, the thought of standing up and addressing a group would be their greatest fear. Globally, this fear – 'glossophobia'– is often considered the second greatest fear, second only to the fear of sharks! Speaking in public can elicit a range of physiological responses tied to our body's stress response system, commonly known as the 'fight-or-flight' response. When faced with the perceived threat of speaking in front of an audience, the sympathetic branch of the autonomic nervous system is activated, triggering the release of stress hormones like adrenaline and cortisol. These hormones prepare the body for action, increasing heart rate, blood pressure and respiration, which can, in fact, be very useful but often get in the way of performing well. The parasympathetic nervous system, which governs the body's rest and digestion functions, also plays a crucial role in public speaking. By engaging the parasympathetic system through deep breathing, relaxation techniques and calming strategies, individuals can counterbalance the 'fight-or-flight' response, promoting a sense of calm, focus and control. Balancing the activation of both the sympathetic and parasympathetic systems is key to managing the stress and anxiety associated with public speaking, allowing individuals to deliver their message with confidence and composure. It's very normal to have some fear around speaking publicly, and fear is a primal response to perceived danger. In an ideal world, speaking skills are learned by young people in school and university or professional training as they develop their confidence in interpersonal communication skills, and therefore the danger won't seem so apparent. If young people are given the opportunity to gain the experience and confidence needed for easy, structured and sustained public speaking, those fears need never materialise, and the adults of tomorrow will be much more confident and effective speakers.

Quick Strategies for Managing the 'Fight-or-Flight' Response

- Get to know the science. Recognise the physical symptoms, such as increased heart rate, sweating and shallow breathing. Understanding the science behind these reactions can help you reframe them as natural responses rather than something to be afraid of.

- Reframe. Instead of viewing your anxiety as a negative emotion, reframe it as excitement. Research has shown that reframing anxiety as excitement can help improve performance and reduce nervousness. (Brooks, 2013). Remind yourself that the adrenaline rush you feel before speaking can enhance your energy and engagement with the audience.

- Incorporate deep breathing, progressive muscle relaxation and mindfulness into your preparation routine. Practice these techniques regularly so that they become familiar and accessible during moments of stress.

- Imagine yourself confidently delivering your speech, engaging the audience and receiving positive feedback. Visualisation can help build confidence, reduce anxiety and create a positive mindset.

- Surround yourself with supportive individuals who can offer constructive feedback and encouragement. Practice your speech in front of a carefully chosen and trusted 'audience'. Their response can boost your confidence and provide valuable insights for improvement.

Building Confidence

The desire to feel confident when speaking in front of others, whether that is one person or one thousand, is a skill, and a mindset, that we gain by *doing*. Children gain confidence in reading, riding a bike, making friends, solving equations, playing instruments or anything they eventually become confident doing, through first believing they can by taking small steps, doing repetitive, playful and curious practice, getting advice from others, learning from their mistakes and celebrating their wins. Think of something you do confidently – whether that is baking, driving, knitting, football, parenting or doing your job ... how did you discover that confidence? Was it a magical ability given to you at birth? Or did it start with a desire to do it, lots of trial and error, and then slowly recognising your skill? Let's apply this formula to gaining confidence in public speaking.

Recommendations for Building Confidence

- Start with a 'development' mindset: focus on your motivation, what you hope to share with others and how you want your audience to feel. Recognise that you can make changes if you apply yourself to your goal.

- Break down public speaking into smaller goals, such as delivering a short presentation to a small group or participating in a speaking workshop. Gradually work your way up to larger audiences and more complex speaking engagements.

- Dedicate time to practice your voice and public speaking skills. Watch others, be curious about what works for you, what works for others, and do the 'work'. Be curious in your approach and self-reflection, rather than judgemental.

- As mentioned previously, take advantage of public speaking courses, workshops, drama or improvisation classes or Toastmasters clubs where you can receive constructive feedback and guidance from experienced speakers. Consider working with a voice or speech coach who can provide personalised advice and help you refine your speaking style.

- Understand that even experienced speakers make mistakes. Embrace any nervousness or hiccups as part of the learning process, and part of your authentic experience. Learn from each speaking experience, analyse what worked well and what could be improved, and

---

Continued

apply those lessons to future engagements. By reminding yourself of your aspirations, and learning to excuse the occasional badly handled situation, it becomes easier to rediscover the passion for what you do and find speaking publicly exciting and purposeful. Carrying demoralising thinking and low self-esteem from difficult situations into new challenges can only be limiting and ultimately damaging. It is worth remembering that good communication skills indicate that speakers not only respect their audience but also value themselves.

– Recognise and celebrate your growth as a public speaker. Take the time to acknowledge your accomplishments and feedback. Keep a diary of your presentations and speeches, what worked and what your goals are. You can also keep a private social media page where you can upload practice videos (perhaps that only you can see) to monitor your progress.

Some Useful Strategies to Ease the Effects of Fear and Anxiety Before an Event

– Creating a personal mantra can be a helpful strategy to counteract negative self-talk. Instead of relying on overly positive affirmations, such as 'It's all going to go brilliantly' or 'I'm the best', simple and truthful statements like 'This is where I want to be' or 'My hard work has got me here' can be more valuable. These authentic affirmations have the power to quieten the voice of doubt during moments of extreme stress and provide a grounded perspective.

– Take a mindful moment. Direct your attention to the sensations in your hands resting on your lap or desk. Shift your focus to your fingertips. Notice the sensation as your fingertips touch – can you feel the ridges? What is the temperature? What is the texture? Explore the sensation of touching your clothing or your chair. Pay attention to the textures, pressure and temperature. If your mind starts to wander, gently bring your focus back to the touch sensations. When you feel ready to conclude, take a deep breath, wiggle your fingers and slowly open your eyes. Transition back to your surroundings with a renewed sense of presence and calm.

Continued

- Practice self-compassion and kindness towards yourself. Recognise that it is normal to experience doubt and challenges and view them as opportunities for growth and learning. Set realistic expectations for yourself and avoid harsh self-criticism. Instead of dwelling on problems, focus on finding solutions and taking proactive steps forward.

- Engaging in meditation practices can support the retraining of our minds and help us to refrain from blindly accepting every negative thought or challenging emotion that might arise. By adopting this perspective, we can transform negative self-talk into a compassionate and generous narrative. This shift has the potential to enhance our self-esteem and empower us to invest our energy in activities that bring us joy, rather than allowing negative self-talk to hinder our progress.

- Journaling promotes self-awareness, reflection, rational analysis, emotional release, reframing and progress tracking. It provides a space to explore thoughts, challenge beliefs, express emotions and replace negativity with positivity. Consistency in journaling can lead to improved self-talk, self-knowledge and increased self-compassion.

- Regular practice is a powerful antidote to negative self-talk and a key to building confidence. It serves as concrete evidence of your abilities and provides you with the ammunition to challenge self-doubt. By actively engaging with this book, delving into the understanding and exploration of your voice, you establish a strong foundation for facing speaking engagements with the assurance that you have invested time and effort in preparation. Engaging in warm-up exercises, familiarising yourself with the space and being confident with your material, all contribute to directing your focus towards the task at hand rather than being hindered by internal doubts.

- Positive posture: as mentioned in the later section, 'Posture and Positioning', an open, lengthened and aligned posture can be energising and lead to a sense of 'readiness'.

- If you are about to present to an audience, it is a good idea to move to release some energy and do something physical rather than just worrying. If you have time before you speak take a walk, dance or take part in some relaxing movement such as tai chi or yoga.

- Engaging in regular physical exercise, such as jogging, swimming or dancing, can help release built-up tension and increase the production of endorphins, which are natural mood boosters.

Continued

- Music has the power to stimulate the release of dopamine, a neuro-transmitter associated with pleasure and positive emotions. It can also evoke memories of joyful experiences or create a sense of well-being. By selecting songs that resonate with you and have positive associations, you can harness the uplifting power of music to elevate your mood and create a positive mindset. Find your 'hype' song! Something energising and upbeat.

- Certain scents or wearing clothing associated with positive experiences can act as talismans, amplifying your emotional state and boosting your confidence when entering the speaking environment. Wear what makes you feel good.

- Refer to Chapter 3, 'Relaxation and Release of Tension' and Chapter 4, 'Breathing' for exercises on breathwork and tension release.

- Ensure you are well rested and well hydrated!

What if I Hate My Voice?

As mentioned in Chapter 9, 'Working with Variety', not liking your voice can be one of the limiting factors that prevents you being fully present when speaking. Accepting that your voice doesn't sound the way you hear it in your head to others is the first step. Your audience doesn't know what it sounds like in your head, so won't have the same dissociative experience as you do. Secondly, self-perception may not align with how others perceive your voice. Equally, you can never be 100 per cent in control of how your message comes across to others because of their own biases and perceptions, positive or negative. By working on the exercises in this book, you can develop a more objective assessment of your voice. You can identify areas of tension, recognise breath-related limitations and evaluate the level of resonance and variety in your voice. These elements can be improved with practice and dedication, allowing you to transform self-criticism into constructive action.

While this book is indeed focused on voice, it's worth considering that excessively worrying about how your voice sounds to others might not be productive. Remember the phrase 'What people think of me is none of my business'. It serves as a reminder to prioritise your own thoughts, actions and personal growth over being overly concerned with others' opinions. This doesn't mean you shouldn't care or strive to do your best, but rather it reflects a mindset of self-confidence, self-acceptance and a healthy boundary between your perception and that of others. Similarly, when it comes to your voice, it may be helpful to view your own opinion of it as 'none of your business'. Instead, focus on sharing your message effectively, maintaining vocal health and ensuring your voice serves as a channel for your message without being hindered by self-criticism. Strive to identify very specific areas for growth and take action to address them. However, maintain a balanced perspective by focusing on personal development, self-confidence and delivering your message effectively rather than being excessively preoccupied with others' opinions or your own self-criticism.

THE MESSAGE

The ability to convert ideas into words is fundamental to the communication process. There is no point in having the most wonderful appreciation and understanding of an idea without an ability to find words with which to transmit it fluently and imaginatively to others, and in a form relevant to the specific audience you are hoping to engage.

Effective speech is the process of getting an idea from one mind to another, both accurately and persuasively. There are so many of us who have attended lectures, conferences or board meetings and experienced the 'woolly talker'; individuals who know exactly what they mean but are, unfortunately, the only ones in the room who do. These speakers often converse in a vague, imprecise or ambiguous manner; use fuzzy or fussy language, often lacking specific details or clarity in their communication; and employ excessive jargon, convoluted phrases or overly abstract concepts that make it challenging for others to understand their intended meaning. This leads the listener to confusion, frustration, and an inability to action any request that has been made or focus on the information they are hoping to absorb. The 'woolly' speaker is likely been more concerned with showcasing their knowledge or just getting through the speech in one piece and has forgotten to consider the listener experience. Let's face it, we can all be a little woolly at times, whether we're 'off duty' and very relaxed or at the end of a long day, distracted by pressing requests, or less than enthusiastic about our topic, but the considered choice of our words, their arrangement and the way they are expressed, are the tools that will help us achieve our goals.

For every professional voice user reading this book the individual message they are sharing will be different. However, the structure, vocal and rhetorical techniques employed are likely to have similarities. We only have to look at a selection of TED Talks or political speeches to recognise that the basic formats of sharing a message follow similar, solid, principles. When

223

discussing 'the message', we will look at structure, subconscious messages and how to share your message most effectively.

The ancient Greeks held a deep appreciation for the power and artistry of communication, including how to convey a message effectively. Philosophers such as Plato and Aristotle placed great emphasis on the art of public speaking, persuasion and the role of rhetoric in influencing an audience, believing that effective communication involved carefully constructing arguments, appealing to emotions and presenting ideas in a clear and persuasive manner. They recognised that the way a message is delivered significantly impacts its reception and effectiveness. Plato, in his dialogues, explored the power of storytelling and the use of metaphors to convey complex ideas in a relatable and memorable way. Aristotle, in his work *Rhetoric*, outlined various persuasive techniques and principles that emphasised the importance of tailoring messages to specific audiences, organising thoughts coherently and appealing to the emotions and logic of listeners.

Across various cultures, there are traditions that align with the principles of Greek rhetoric, emphasising effective communication and persuasive storytelling. For example, in many African cultures, Griots serve as oral historians and storytellers who pass down cultural knowledge through captivating spoken word. They employ persuasive techniques, rhythmic language and storytelling to convey significant messages. Similarly, in ancient Indian culture, the Vedic tradition placed great importance on public speaking and persuasive communication. The recitation of sacred texts, such as the Vedas, involved precise intonation and rhythm, with scholars and teachers known as Rishis employing rhetorical devices in their discourses and debates. Indigenous cultures worldwide have a rich tradition of oratory, where skilled speakers communicate essential messages, cultural values and stories to their communities. They often incorporate metaphors, symbolism and gestures to enhance the impact of their message and engage the audience's attention. These diverse traditions share a common focus on the power of language, voice and delivery, to engage, inspire and influence others.

It is also important, in a participatory democracy, that all people – not just those from privileged backgrounds – develop the ability to speak confidently in public, to present effective and persuasive arguments through speech, and to examine critically but constructively the arguments presented by others.
Oracy Cambridge, The Centre for Effective Spoken Communication

Rhetoric has remained relevant and useful throughout history and continues to be valuable in modern society, whether in business, law, advertising, education, broadcasting, entertainment or politics. Rhetorical skills are crucial in negotiations and diplomacy, where the ability to persuade, communicate clearly and understand the perspectives of others is essential. Rhetoric plays a significant role in leadership and influence. Leaders who can articulate their vision, inspire their followers and effectively communicate their goals are more likely to be successful. In the era of social media and online platforms, rhetoric is vital for crafting compelling messages of influence and persuasion that can cut through the digital noise. Understanding how to use language effectively, appeal to emotions and engage online audiences is crucial for successful digital communication.

The following techniques help organise ideas, create a logical flow and enhance the persuasiveness of the message. Here are some common techniques used in rhetorical message structuring.

Structure Models

Introduction	Start with a compelling anecdote, thought-provoking question or interesting statistic to capture the audience's attention. Introduce yourself, describe your experience or unique perspective to establish your expertise on the topic which will encourage the audience to pay attention. Clearly articulate the main objective or central idea of your message.
Statement	State your main argument or position in a concise and compelling manner. This acts as a guiding statement for the rest of your message.
Body	Structure your main points logically, using a clear and systematic approach such as chronological order, cause and effect, problem and solution, or compare and contrast. Provide factual evidence, examples, expert opinions or statistics to strengthen your main points and enhance credibility. Acknowledge opposing viewpoints and refute them with well-reasoned counter-arguments.
Transitions	Use connecting ideas and transitional words and phrases to create smooth transitions between ideas and maintain a coherent flow throughout the message.
Emotional Appeals	Employ language which evokes emotions, e.g., vivid imagery, metaphors or personal stories, to engage and connect with the audience on an emotional level.
Appeal to Values and Beliefs	Tap into the values and beliefs of the audience, aligning your message with their concerns and aspirations.

Conclusion	Recap the key arguments and main ideas discussed in the body of the message.
	Provide a clear and compelling call to action, urging the audience to take a specific course of action or consider a particular viewpoint.
	End with a memorable quote, a powerful statement or a call to reflection that leaves a lasting impression.

The techniques for structuring messages in rhetoric are flexible and can be adapted to different contexts and communication mediums. The key is to create a logical, persuasive and engaging structure that effectively conveys your message to the intended audience. Trying different approaches will help you discover what works best for you and your audience. Below you will find some other examples of useful structures to help organise your material for presentations, speeches, interview responses or even in day to day conversation. Repetitive explanation in classrooms, pitching a new business, working in sales and delivering the same presentation over and over, coaching clients, working as any type of instructor, explaining processes or giving updates can be frustrating, vocally tiring and inefficient if not of high quality and easy to understand. The following structures work well.

–   **PPS**: Problem, Process, Solution.
    (P): Introduce the problem or issue you're addressing: what the problem is, why it matters, who it affects.
    (P): Explain the process or factors that contribute to the problem, delve into the 'how' and provide context, break down the problem into its components, explaining causes and effects.
    (S): Present potential solutions, strategies, or actions to resolve the problem. Clearly communicate how these solutions address the issues raised.
    PPS can be used to discuss a current scenario, or to describe how you approached a project you worked on in the past.

–   **PPF**: Past, Present, Future.
    (P): Begin by discussing the history of your topic, providing context or background information. Explain how the issue or subject has evolved over time and what significant events or developments have occurred.
    (P): Transition to the present and describe the current state or situation. Highlight key aspects or conditions that exist now, explain why they are relevant. Provide a snapshot of the 'here and now'.

(F): Conclude by looking ahead to the future. Discuss potential trends, challenges, opportunities, or what you believe should happen next. Offer insights, recommendations, or goals for the future based on the past and present analysis.

– **PEEL:** Point, Evidence, Explain significance, Link (back to point).

(P): Begin with a clear and concise statement of your main point or argument. This is your thesis or the central idea you're conveying. Make it specific and focused.

(E): Provide evidence or supporting information that backs up your point. This can include relevant data, examples, quotes, or facts.

(E): Explain why the evidence you presented is significant or how it supports your point. Analyse the evidence and show how it reinforces your argument. 'Connect the dots' for your audience.

(L): Conclude by linking back to your original point. Summarize the main argument and how the evidence and explanation support it. This reinforces the central message of your presentation.

– **Wh questions**: Why?/What?/How?/Who?/Where?/When?/What If?

Using **all** these questions ensures a comprehensive and structured explanation. They serve as helpful prompts, especially in impromptu speeches, to guarantee you address all aspects of your topic. Adapt the order, and the number, to suit your topic and communication style.

Why?: Explains the purpose and significance of your subject matter.

What?: Defines the topic or subject.

How?: Describes the process or method.

Who?: Identifies people or entities involved.

Where?: Specifies the location or context.

When?: Pinpoints the timing or timeframe.

What if?: This question can be useful for exploring hypothetical scenarios, potential outcomes, or alternative possibilities.

Other speech /presentation structures might include:

– **PASTA:** Problem – the problem at hand; Alternatives – alternative actions; Solution – chosen solution; Takeaway – the learning; Action – the action you are going to take.

- **PREP:** Point – the point of your argument; Reason – your reason for your point, or your 'why'; Example – an example to illustrate your point; Point – returning to your point.

- **SOAR:** Situation – describing your scenario, past or present; Obstacle – the problem or issue you are facing; Action – the action you took, or will take, to resolve it; Result – the outcome.

- **Visual brainstorming:** Mind maps/spider diagrams/tree diagrams are tools used to organise and represent information and capture and structure your thoughts, ideas or concepts. The central idea or main topic is placed at the centre of the mind map; related subtopics branch out from it. This will likely guide you towards what your topics and subtopics should be.

You can practice these techniques by selecting a current project to discuss or picking topics from the news to talk about, creating concise notes using your chosen structure, and then recording yourself while presenting. The more you use these techniques to plan, prepare and structure your presentations, pitches or interviews, the more adept you'll become at delivering well-crafted and polished talks even with minimal preparation or off the cuff/on-the-spot.

The focus is thus directed to delivering a clear message which your audience can easily absorb. It can remove some of the anxiety around knowing what to say, or in what order. Keep practicing and this 'muscle' will grow. There are some more exercises below which will help you with structured messaging and speaking without a script.

Suggestions and Strategies to Develop Structure Skills

Game: 'How to …'

You will be giving verbal instructions for a familiar task, for example: Cooking your favourite meal/Planning the perfect evening in/Sending an email/Doing a grocery shop/Wrapping a Present.

Give yourself a time limit and enforce it. You can make a few brief notes to refer to or choose one of the suggested structures. Record yourself delivering the instructions and review:

- Was there anything vital missing? Could someone easily replicate the task?
- Was there any unnecessary or distracting information?

Continued

- How might you say it or structure differently? What have you learnt?

Try again, either with the same topic or explaining some simple work tasks or processes. Play around with speaking for different lengths of time –1 minute, then 2 minutes, then 30 seconds and so on.

Finally, try this exercise with more complicated tasks, ideas or arguments, or a speech or presentation you are planning to deliver. 'Concertina' your time – move from a very brief explanation, to a much longer one.

- Notice the value in expanding and reducing the time. Pinpoint which aspects you need to improve upon.

Game 'I like ...'

Make a statement starting with 'I like ...' (or 'I dislike ...') and justify the statement with 'Because ...'

Limit yourself to one sentence. Repeat the information, but this time use two sentences, then three sentences, and so on ... Your argument can be expanded to allow for greater expression of ideas and freer use of language.

Game: 'Play Teacher'

Practice 'teaching' whatever you might be doing, whether that's making a cup of tea, walking the dog or putting together a deck of slides; 'narrate' your process out loud. It might be best to do this one at home, rather than in the office! This really helps with thought flow, observation of detail, clarity on how to share information through speech, and structure.

Game: Speechmaking

Practice structuring and delivering speeches, about all sorts of things, keep it lighthearted and fun! Some suggested topics: Celebrating your pet/Advertising your favourite chocolate bar/Giving a farewell speech for a co-worker/Presenting a lifelong achievement award/ Campaigning for election/Accepting an award/Explaining why you're the world's biggest fan of something/someone. Treating this as a game can make speechmaking more enjoyable and less intimidating.

Storytelling

The professional voice user has a powerful role as a storyteller in the world of work. Stories have been a fundamental part of human culture for thousands of years. Stories can shape our beliefs, trigger emotions and create connections between people. Our brains respond to narratives, and we are wired to seek out and remember stories. 'Storytelling' has become a buzz word in communication and in this context refers to the strategic use of narratives to convey information, engage audiences and make a lasting impact. It goes beyond simply sharing anecdotes or entertaining stories. Storytelling for communication is about well-crafted, purposeful, relevant narratives which are aligned with the objectives of the organisation or individual and their audience.

Our brains are wired to seek patterns and make sense of information. Stories provide a coherent structure that help us organise and remember information more effectively; information is more likely to be encoded into long-term memory and imagery stimulates the visual cortex and makes the story more engaging and memorable. When we engage with a well-crafted story, multiple areas of our brain are activated. The sensory and motor cortex light up as we imagine the events, the language processing areas activate as we process the words and the emotional centres of the brain respond to the feelings evoked by the story. Mirror neurons, which play a crucial role in empathy and understanding others' perspectives, are activated and our brains release neurotransmitters such as oxytocin (often called the love hormone or cuddle chemical!) which enhance feelings of trust and empathy.

Storytelling should be authentic and rooted in truth. It is not about fabricating stories or manipulating emotions for the sake of influence. Ethical storytelling requires transparency, honesty and a desire for a genuine connection with the audience.

Suggestions and Strategies

- Read books, watch TED Talks or attend workshops focused on the art of storytelling. Observe structure, techniques and delivery styles used by skilled storytellers in various fields.
- Look for opportunities to tell stories in different contexts, adapt your stories to different audiences, and observe the responsiveness of your listeners. Can you tell when the story is too long or doesn't have enough detail?

Continued

- Try using these tactics in social events as well as at work as that will help you build your confidence. Craft your stories to be concise and focused, emphasising the key elements but avoiding unnecessary details or lengthy explanations that could make the story drag on. Anecdotes are short personal stories that can be woven into conversations naturally. They provide a brief and engaging way to share experiences or make a point without prolonging the interaction. Even if you don't narrate a full story, you can still incorporate storytelling elements such as introducing a relatable character, describing a vivid scene or sharing a brief example to make your speech more engaging and memorable.

- Tailor your storytelling to the specific context, ensuring that the story adds value and relevance to the discussion without unnecessary digressions.

- Explore storytelling to communicate your personal or professional brand. Craft stories that highlight your values, experiences or achievements, and share them in your bio, your LinkedIn and social media pages, on your website or during job interviews.

- Embrace vulnerability and authenticity in your storytelling, as it helps build trust and emotional connection with the audience; this may mean sharing personal professional experiences (whilst taking care to protect your own boundaries). Authenticity builds trust and makes your stories more relatable and compelling.

- Utilise conflict and tension in your story. Conflict is a key driver of compelling narratives, whether internal or external; it drives the narrative and engages the audience's attention. Transformation or growth often comes from the catalyst of conflict.

- Instead of simply stating information, use descriptive language and vivid imagery to paint a picture in the minds of your audience. Engage their senses and create an immersive experience.

- Employ the skills you have gained working on the exercises in Chapter 7, 'Exploring Pitch', Chapter 8, 'Muscular Flexibility', Chapter 9, 'Working for Variety', and Chapter 10, 'Development and Control of Volume', to bring your story to life as much as possible, aligning your voice with your words and message and the atmosphere and mood you hope to create.

- Think story. Consciously respond to questions with a story structure rather than a list of information. Common structures include

Continued

linear (chronological), three-act (set up, confrontation, resolution), and hero's journey (embarking on an adventure, facing challenges, experiencing personal growth, and returning transformed), amongst others. Treat storytelling as a craft and be willing to revise and refine your stories depending on your goals and desired impact. Edit out unnecessary details, clarify your message and ensure that each element serves a purpose in the narrative.

Message Within the Message

Various subtle messages, conscious and unconscious, are conveyed by the tone of the voice and it is quite possible for the words to be 'saying' one thing and the voice to be 'saying' another. An example of this is where, in response to being asked how they are feeling, an individual may answer 'fine', yet it is apparent that they are not fine. Feelings of low self-esteem, tension, tiredness, sadness or boredom are all reflected in the voice. There are certain vocal qualities that are perceived as more friendly than others. A speaker with warm 'mellow' tones seems to be perceived as someone who can be trusted, is sincere and friendly, whereas a 'harsher', more forced, voice quality can appear aggressive and threatening. A relaxed vocal quality might be perceived as confidence and help you pass an interview; a voice that rises in pitch, seems to 'crack' and needs to be cleared constantly may signal to an audience that you aren't a confident or reliable expert.

Positive Messages

In both personal and professional settings, giving feedback is challenging, and sometimes risky. Having to make requests of others can be difficult and you may feel you are in murky communication waters. You may worry that you are 'nagging' or being negative, and it is tiring and often counterproductive. It can create tension and fatigue in our voices as we find ourselves repeatedly making requests or reprimanding others; it tends to escalate difficult situations and can foster a negative and unproductive atmosphere. The power of negative feedback lies in its judicious use. When employed sparingly, it can have a considerable impact. However, constant use diminishes its effectiveness. Employees often cringe at the words, 'Can we talk?', fearing a discussion about perceived shortcomings rather than receiving praise for their accomplishments. Genuine and well-deserved positive reinforcement should always be the foundation, as insincere, non-specific or hollow praise is quickly identified and undermines genuine efforts.

Employers, leaders and mentors understand the significance of both approval and disapproval for their employees, students or clients. However, in the fast-paced and often chaotic environments of busy workplaces or high-pressure projects, it can be challenging not to focus more on problems or opportunities for improvement, inadvertently neglecting to acknowledge minor successes. This is especially relevant when many individuals are working remotely, with reduced opportunities for casual social interactions. It is crucial to be mindful of this shift and ensure that communication with senior team members or colleagues doesn't solely revolve around identifying what is wrong. It is important to invest time and effort into adjusting the balance and providing meaningful recognition.

Framing the Feedback: Delivering the Message of Improvement

If you find yourself having to give negative feedback, it can challenge your counterparts' sense of self-worth and competence, be perceived as a threat to their self-esteem, lead to discomfort or resistance, trigger feelings of fear and failure and can evoke emotional reactions such as frustration, sadness or even anger. No wonder most of us dread giving negative feedback to others. It is common to fear negative reactions, defensiveness or potential retaliation from the recipient. It is natural to be hesitant to inflict those negative emotions on your co-workers. There may also be a fear of being seen as overly critical, unsupportive or mean-spirited, which can damage your reputation or likability. *How* you deliver feedback, and the recipient's self-confidence and desire for self-improvement, will influence how they respond.

Suggestions and Strategies for Giving Feedback

–   It is important that both the speaker and listener separate the feedback from self-worth. This can be encouraged with a focus on the behaviour or the issue at hand, not the person or their character. Use non-judgemental language, and focus on improvement, not blame.

–   Aim for a relaxed and composed tone of voice. Release any obvious tension and take a few breaths before beginning. Tension, constriction and breathlessness may lead to an aggressive, confrontational or emotionally charged tone. Strive for a balanced vocal quality. Avoid 'performing' a role of authority, or adopting an artificial or insincere tone; try to stick to the facts and move the conversation forward to a positive conclusion.

– Start with a smile to infuse your tone with warmth, consider a slower pace and lower volume. Show genuine care and concern for the person receiving the feedback. A warm tone helps to create a safe and supportive environment. Active listening techniques, with sparing affirmative sounds, connected eye contact and encouraging body language, will create an encouraging and compassionate atmosphere.

– Authenticity helps build trust and rapport with the person receiving the feedback. If it is useful for you to take some notes in to the conversation to help you, then that's a good idea. It can help with authenticity to have a structure and not get swept away by discomfort or adrenaline into a performative quality. If you recognise that you are 'putting on a voice', take a calming breath, check for tension, refocus your objective and continue.

– Don't accuse, but ask questions. As the person giving feedback, don't assume you know everything. Treat it as a conversation.

– Highlight the fact that the feedback is about specific behaviours or actions, not a judgement of personal value, and that receiving feedback is a chance to learn and develop. It will be easier to see this opportunity if you are able to share a plan of action, rather than just a list of negatives, and build on what is going well, rather than dwelling on what isn't.

– Seek to monitor the response of your listener and pivot the conversation if necessary.

– Offer opportunities for questions and clarification; engage in a dialogue, rather than delivering a monologue.

– After delivering the feedback, be open to the recipient's perspective and concerns. Engage in active listening and maintain a dialogue to foster understanding and collaboration.

– Combine negative feedback with positive reinforcement and recognition of strengths. This balanced approach helps to maintain a supportive and encouraging environment. This needs to be authentic as this much used feedback structure can feel a little insincere if not carefully considered.

– Find an appropriate time and private setting to deliver the feedback. This allows for a focused conversation without distractions or potential embarrassment.

Remember, the goal of feedback is to provide constructive guidance and support growth. Using a vocal quality that reflects respect, empathy and authenticity enhances the effectiveness of your feedback and promotes a positive and receptive atmosphere.

Here Are a Few Commonly Used Feedback Models

Situation **Behaviour** **Impact**™	E.g., 'During the team meeting [situation], when you interrupted others and spoke over them [behaviour], it made it difficult for everyone to express their ideas and disrupted the flow of the discussion [impact]'. (Center for Creative Leadership)
Describe **Express** **Specify** **Consequences**	This model helps to ensure that feedback is actionable and focused. E.g., 'When you consistently miss deadlines [describe], I feel frustrated and it affects productivity [express]. I would like you to develop better time management strategies and communicate challenges in advance [specify]. Otherwise, it can lead to delays and impact performance [consequences].' (Patton, Stone and Heen, 2011)
The Pendleton's **Feedback Model:**	This model is commonly used in the medical field but can be applied to other professions as well. It involves a two-way feedback process where both the giver and receiver provide input. The receiver starts by self-assessing their performance, followed by the giver sharing positive aspects and areas for improvement. Finally, the receiver summarises the feedback and develops an action plan for growth and development. (Burgess, van Diggele, Roberts et al., 2020)

Compassionate Communication

The nonviolent communication (NVC) model, developed by Marshall Rosenberg (2015) is a communication and conflict-resolution framework that emphasises empathy, understanding and mutual respect. While NVC is primarily used for resolving conflicts and fostering compassionate connections, it can also be applied to the feedback process or any difficult or appraisal conversation.

Observe

Start by describing the specific behaviour or situation you observed without judgement or evaluation. Focus on the facts rather than interpretations or assumptions.

Feel

Share your feelings about the observed behaviour, acknowledging that feelings are personal and subjective. Be honest and express your emotions using the phrase "I feel x" without blaming or criticising the other person. This step helps create a safe and empathetic environment. After expressing the feeling, you connect it to your underlying needs.

Need

Identify and communicate the underlying needs or values that were impacted by the observed behaviour. Connect your feelings to the core human needs that were either met or unmet. This step fosters understanding and empathy, allowing the other person to relate to your perspective.

Request

Clearly state your request or suggestion for a specific change in behaviour or action that would address the needs discussed. Make sure your request is realistic, specific and actionable. Encourage a collaborative problem-solving approach and invite the other person to offer their perspective and ideas.

This method promotes open and honest communication while reducing the need for defensiveness or conflict. It encourages true listening, empathy and understanding, promoting a cooperative and mutually beneficial feedback process. Practising NVC requires patience, self-awareness and a genuine intention to connect and find solutions together.

Knowing What to Say

Vocal problems may arise from the difficulty you may have in finding and using words effectively. Voice production is most effective when what is being said is important to the speaker and, subsequently, stimulating to the listener. Professional voice users are often conscious that a vocal difficulty began as a result of a lack of focus on oral skills in their own education and training and feel that they would like to offer a richer repertoire of verbal expression, to be more eloquent and articulate. Just as children need to be able to express themselves and explore ideas in order to develop, so do adults. If you have children of your own, one of the best things you can do for *both of you* is to read to them, teach them your traditional songs and rhymes, and expose them to language structure, sound and rhythm, whilst exploring your own abilities and storytelling strengths. If you don't have children, consider dedicating time to reading aloud or volunteering to read to others, such as in care situations or through organisations like Bookmark Reading (bookmarkreading.org). These activities offer a wonderful chance to expand your vocabulary, gain confidence in vocal expression and develop a passion for speaking well-structured and expressive language. By consciously speaking for the benefit of your audience, you become purposeful and diverse in your delivery, enhancing your overall communication skills.

Game: Show-and-Tell

Perhaps you did 'show and tell' at school, where you brought in a special item and spoke about it to your peers. The demands the exercise makes on children are those faced in everyday adult working life and as useful in adult life as skills in mathematics, science and written English. Show-and-tell builds skills including engaging an audience, physically taking command of the space, critical thinking, creating a narrative or a sequential structure, putting across an opinion by developing an argument and debating the pros and cons, using the voice artistically and applying the elements of emphasis, pause and other aspects of modulation.

Some show-and-tell topics for you to try:

Demonstrate how an object works or is constructed/Describe an object that has had a significant impact on society such as a postage stamp, a fork, a wheel, etc./Describe the personal significance and object has for you, such as a letter, a gift, a photograph or keepsake.

Strategies and Suggestions for Improving Impromptu Speech and Developing Vocabulary

- Join book groups, discussion groups or debating societies where you can engage in structured spoken conversations on various topics for the opportunity to express opinions, listen to others and develop persuasive communication skills.

- Seek opportunities to speak in public – giving presentations, speaking at events or participating in Toastmasters or similar organisations.

- Try an acting class, join an improv group or attend open mic performance nights or poetry slams, amateur dramatics, storytelling groups, oral history classes, Debate Mate, one-to-one lessons with a teacher from The Society of Teachers of Speech and Drama or work towards speech and drama certifications such as Trinity or LAMDA.

- Set aside development time; read, watch speeches and debates, listen to discussion, current affairs or narrative podcasts; spend time listening to audiobooks; or attend talks. Make notes, keep lists of words you like and try using them!

- Read poetry and great speeches aloud. Speaking the words of others can be the first step to being able to find words for oneself. English literature offers such an enormous variety of wonderfully honed and precisely constructed examples of the expression of every conceivable emotion. Verse or prose often has the power to unlock words and rhythms within individuals, giving voice to their thoughts and allowing them to express themselves. Poetry presents a unique opportunity to delve into one's own expressivity, to discover the perfect word for a feeling, to consider the arrangement of words, create atmosphere, and indulge in the exploration of vivid imagery and metaphor. It also encourages the personal exploration of deep emotions.

- Singing is a wonderful opportunity to establish the essence of easy, free, spontaneous voice use, and builds vocabulary, memory training and technical aspects of breath, pitch, communication and precision of sounds. Joining a choir brings a sense of companionship and offers the opportunity to be in a team and to perform safely without exposure.

- Invest in word games such as 'Articulate!', 'Taboo', 'Scattegories', 'Balderdash', 'Bananagrams', '20 Questions' or free online games such as 'Wordle' and crosswords.

THE MEDIUM

The 'Way' Rather than the 'What'

Your content will convey, more or less, the meaning to the listener, but the *way* the words are expressed will affect the impact that your message has on your audience. In terms of speech, articulation, voice quality and vocal variety underpin the way that words are expressed. In this chapter we will look additionally at pace and speed and pause, tone, emphasis and intonation.

Nonverbal cues, facial expressions and body language carry emotions, attitudes and add layers of meaning to our communication. Visual aids also have their place in supporting the message. Furthermore, the physical environment and setting in which communication occurs influence the overall medium of communication. This is explored further in the later section, 'The Context'.

Voice as the Medium

More on Clarity

In casual conversations with one or two individuals, the emphasis on precise consonant articulation may not be necessary. However, when speaking to a larger audience, it becomes crucial to prioritise clarity and ensure that the message is audible. Clarity of consonants can become important; for example, enunciating the final consonant in words such as 'find', 'debt' or 'dock' is important in order to avoid confusion with similar words such as 'fine', 'death' or 'dog'.

A game of 'broken telephone' can occur when your audience aren't sure which word you are using, and they supplement one of their choosing to 'decode' the message you are sharing. The danger is that there is too much energy expended by the listener in attempting to decode, or understand, the message and they get distracted by the mystery meaning or may 'switch off' entirely. With clarity of articulation, there is less need for repetition and as a result, less need to use the voice unnecessarily. The muscularity of speech is never fully present if the speaker is not mentally committed to the word; on the other hand, the enthusiastic communicator with a need to share ideas rarely has a problem being understood. Only when the synchronisation of thought and word occurs is language wholly energised; this energy brings a dynamic to language and produces the physical and vocal movement inherent in words.

Over-obvious manipulation of the dynamics of words is often seen as extravagant, over-assertive or arrogant. Some individuals feel that they would be exposing themselves by using an 'overstated' voice or that they could, or would, appear pedantic. In truth, it is possible to appear all these things if articulation is pushed or unrelated to the meaning behind it, but committed meaningful speech tends to engage the breath and muscles in the most positive way and produces energised language.

Accent and Dialect

Some professional voice users may have personal concerns that their particular accent is standing in the way of comprehension, if their 'audience' has a different accent to their own. You may have feelings about your own accent; we hope you love it or have neutral feelings about it. However, many people report that they are not comfortable with their regional or national accent and seek coaching from 'accent modification' coaches for a variety of reasons. These include which include being better understood by their colleagues and clients, wanting to feel more fluid in conversation, integrated or more confident about their pronunciation and intonation in a second language, or so that they can embody the level of their fluent English by adapting to the British English rhythm and pronunciation. This is personal choice, and there are many ways you can work on your accent, pronunciation, rhythm and intonation if that is what you choose to do.

First impressions formed due to an individual's accent are not ideal, but it is undeniable that such impressions do exist. Accents can unintentionally influence how people perceive and judge others. While this may not reflect the true character or abilities of a person, it is a societal phenomenon that we must recognise. It is important to embrace understanding, empathy and open-mindedness, appreciating that accent should not define a person's worth or capabilities. As we continue to progress towards a more interconnected and globally diverse world, we hold the hope that these biases and prejudices will diminish. As people from different backgrounds interact more frequently, we have the opportunity to cultivate a more inclusive and accepting perspective. By actively challenging and dismantling stereotypes associated with accents, we can look forward to a future where individuals are judged based on their unique qualities and abilities rather than merely their speech patterns.

Intrinsically, accents carry certain intonation patterns, which, according to the listener's individual perception, may appear to have more or less musical quality and therefore acceptability, depending on their individual preference. Musicality, however, has a hidden cost; individuals with a musical accent may be perceived as lacking authority. The inflection pattern inherent in a musical accent, which adds a more melodic quality, can at times be falsely interpreted as questioning and uncertain.

Discussion about accents and the assumptions that are made about accents, should be challenged, otherwise change will never occur. Nevertheless, we are aware that accent is, for some, an emotive issue. A professional with a non-local accent may be positively perceived or conversely, the difference may become a basis for derision. The media does nothing to break down stereotypical assumptions about regional accents, but, rather, reinforces them. Adults seldom change their accents dramatically. As individuals grow older, their brain's plasticity decreases, making it harder to acquire new phonetic patterns and modify existing ones. Adults have already established strong language and speech patterns, which are deeply ingrained through years of practice. Accent modification requires conscious effort, retraining of muscle memory and significant practice to override well-established habits. However, most of us are 'vocal chameleons'; slightly adapting our speech according to changing situations – the phenomenon of the 'telephone voice' is well recognised.

Adults, however, rarely make a conscious decision to change their accents unless for very specific political or socio-cultural reasons. Some adults adapt their accent unconsciously, blending with their peer group and depending on how they identify with the places they work and live. Accent often plays a role in personal identity, cultural affiliation and social belonging and it's important not to forget how personal accents are in this respect. The richness of regional and national accents should enhance a workplace, and professional voice users should not feel outside pressure to seek to eradicate their accent. Professional voice users should instead attempt to ensure clarity and vocal spontaneity, whatever their accent. Distinctions should be made between clarity and accent so that all professional voice users can enjoy the opportunity to develop eloquence and a joy in communicating verbally. Clarity can be embraced by employing the techniques from the chapters on muscular flexibility, resonance, volume and vocal variety, using pause and eye contact, a moderate pace and a confident mindset. If you are concerned about your accent, consider: am I intelligible? Does my intonation match my meaning in the language I am speaking? If not, is it affecting intelligibility? Am I aware of where the stress should be for the sake intelligibility? Nevertheless, if, for whatever reason, you do wish to speak in a different accent from your own we recommend working with a skilled dialect or accent modification coach.

More Meaning in Your Message

Our voice is an incredible instrument that extends beyond the mere transmission of words. It holds the potential to add layers of meaning and depth to our communication. From the nuances of tone and pitch to the strategic use of volume and pace, our voice becomes a versatile tool for conveying emotions, emphasising key points and establishing genuine connections.

Modulating the Message

Modulation of the voice is an important feature of communication. It encompasses the many elements we have already considered and other elements we will explore in this chapter such as pace, pause and emphasis. A common concern for professional voice users is feeling their voice is contained within a very narrow range and it does not move naturally in response to thought or word. Modulation is not simply a technical changing and varying of the voice with no regard for the thought that produced it. Movement of the voice through a series of cadences without reason produces a sound just as unconnected to mind and action as a dull monotonous voice. Ideally, the voice should respond to changes in thought, these thoughts being reflected by a variety of subtle vocal changes. If, however, tension or stress levels are high, it is likely that this natural delivery will be inhibited. When the individual is relaxed and at ease, the voice moves effortlessly and naturally through its entire range, the movement reinforcing the intention of the language rather than distracting from it. Refer to Chapters 6, 7 and 9 respectively on resonance, exploring pitch and working for variety to develop easy modulation.

Suggestions and Strategies

- Select a well-known advertising slogan or familiar phrase (see below) and repeat it multiple times, each time emphasising a different word. Experiment with modulation by changing the pitch, volume and duration of specific words (specifically the vowel length) to convey different meanings or emotions.
- Now try reading it again, this time vocally highlighting the words that you most wish to convey to your listener, with the voice responding to this 'need' to share information.

Absence makes the heart grow fonder. An apple a day keeps the doctor away.
The early bird catches the worm. Better late than never.
Actions speak louder than words. Easy come easy go.
Laughter is the best medicine. The pen is mightier than the sword.

- Storytelling with emotion: choose a short story or passage from a piece of fiction and practice infusing it with emotion. Focus on using vocal modulation to convey different moods, such as excitement, sadness or suspense. Experiment with changes in pitch, pace

Continued

and emphasis to effectively communicate the intended emotional impact. Try this with content from work, even if it feels strange at first. Deliberately aim to convey a distinct mood or tone. Start by choosing a single emotion for the entire passage and then, in a second attempt, transition through multiple emotions, either pre-selected or spontaneous.

Emphasis

Emphasis is always present when a speaker is clear about the message that they are conveying, just as energy is present when the speaker has a 'need' to be heard. You only have to listen to a group of enthusiasts debating a subject close to their hearts to understand this, or think of your own speech style in moments of urgency. Emphasis is the art of giving prominence or importance to specific elements of our communication. By strategically emphasising certain words, phrases or ideas, we can guide our listeners' focus and enhance their understanding. It helps us communicate our intentions, emotions and convictions with greater impact. Speech without emphasis would be dull, monotone and the meaning would be hard to identify.

What We Emphasise

–   'Content words' that carry the main meaning or message of a sentence – often nouns, verbs, adjectives and adverbs.
–   New and important information.
–   Contrast or comparison words – 'today it's *sunny*, tomorrow it's *cloudy*'.
–   Emotional or expressive words – 'I'm *extremely proud* of you!'

Again, we are reducing the effort the 'audience' needs to put in by revealing the essence of our information to them.

How We Emphasise

– Intonation, which refers to the rise and fall of pitch in speech, plays a role in emphasising certain parts of a sentence. A change in pitch (usually higher) can act as a mark of emphasis on a word: 'I want *that* one'. Rising intonation can indicate a question or uncertainty, while falling intonation can signal a statement or emphasis.

– Greater volume or loudness compared to the surrounding words. By increasing the volume, we create a contrast that makes the emphasised elements stand out and capture the listener's attention.

– Pausing before or after an emphasised word or phrase can create emphasis and give the listener time to process the highlighted information. A brief pause can draw attention and add weight to the emphasised element.

– Elongating a word draws attention to it. It signals to your audience that this part of the sentence is crucial or requires special consideration. It's like shining a spotlight on that word.

There is also emphasis within individual words. A primary stressed syllable is the syllable within a word that receives the greatest emphasis. In English, the primary stress is often marked by a louder and longer vowel sound, a higher pitch or a combination of both. It helps to distinguish between different words or word forms, convey meaning and maintain the natural rhythm of spoken language.

Our body language, facial expressions and gestures can reinforce verbal emphasis and convey additional layers of meaning. Gestures, facial expressions and body movements can reinforce the emphasised words or phrases, adding clarity and impact to the message.

The best way to work on your emphasis is to read aloud, listen to public and political speeches (where you may encounter some overemphasis which can be equally exhausting for the 'audience'!) and play a game of 'What?!'.

Game: What?!

You'll need a trusted friend for this one, preferably someone you can be playful with!

Deliver a speech or piece of verse or prose. Your partner will say 'What?' whenever a 'key' word is not emphasised, not emphasised *enough*, inaudible or they need you to work harder to share the idea.

Continued

You'll begin to notice how often a 'key' word comes up, how much eye contact you start to make to effectively share the word, idea or feeling and how much energy you need to offer your 'audience' to prevent them from repeating 'What?!'.

This is not about being loud, or shouting; try exploring many different tactics to make your message clear, using pitch, duration, pause and varying volume.

If you feel any tension creeping in due to the pressure of being made to repeat yourself, try and laugh it off, or pause the game for a bit! You can 'What?' yourself by practising out loud and going back over key words if you feel they don't hold enough weight.

Vocal Colour

As we discovered in Chapter 9, 'Working for Variety', vocal colour is heard when a voice is well connected with the breath, has range and is capable of pitch change. Most individuals display their true vocal colour when they laugh. A free, generous and unforced sound is able to develop warmth and resonance, and to convey subtle changes of thought and emotion. Vocal colour is comprised of many elements, including your anatomy, breath support, muscular flexibility, emotion and intonation.

Intonation

Intonation, one element in the constellation of our individual vocal DNA, describes the way in which a voice alters during speech. It is the melodic pattern created by the variation of pitch levels and contours during verbal communication. Intonation plays a crucial role in conveying meaning, expressing emotions and adding nuance to spoken language. It helps in distinguishing between different types of sentences (declarative, interrogative, exclamatory, etc.) and conveying the intended emphasis and intention behind the words. The intonation pattern used, for example, when asking a question, is very different from the one used to express an opinion. In a situation in which a speaker feels under-confident, a questioning vocal tune may be used because it seems to produce an impression of politeness and conciliation. This, sometimes known as 'upspeak', also known as uptalk or high rising terminal, is a speech pattern characterised by a rising intonation at the end of declarative statements or sentences, giving the impression of a question. It is called 'upspeak' because the pitch of the voice tends to go up instead of falling at the end of a sentence. This 'tune' can often be heard in the voices of people who work with young children, animals or vulnerable adults because it does not sound threatening or aggressive. When used inappropriately, however, it can give the impression of being uncertain and tentative, which may be far from your intention.

Each language and dialect have an inherent 'tune' that expresses emotion and attitude. Even after a relatively short exposure to a language that is not their own, most individuals become aware of the 'tune' of the language. This then allows them, when listening to an exchange between speakers, to make an educated guess as to whether the speakers are having an argument, exchanging pleasantries or asking questions just by the way in which the individual voices are moving through the pitch range.

Upspeak

Upspeak is often associated with younger generations and has gained attention in popular culture, along with vocal 'fry' and 'fillers'. Upspeak is more often associated with women, but it is not exclusive to any gender. Upspeak faces criticism for conveying uncertainty or a lack of confidence, and its interpretation can vary depending on the context and cultural norms. However, upspeak can also indicate turn-taking in conversation, a desire to be polite, to be inclusive or gain affirmation from the listener, to indicate an openness to a response from the audience or to invite an alternative opinion. Used consciously and sparingly, it can be a useful tool in working with a team, brainstorming ideas: a vocal tactic to show you are open-minded and inviting certainty from others. Samara Bay writes in *Permission to Speak* of upspeak, vocal fry and fillers: 'they are choices, and practical ones at that. They may be just the right tool for the job. But they may not, and we must wield them with care' (2023). It is important to be aware of whether you are using upspeak in places that aren't helpful to you, and if it is a repetitive habitual feature of your speech. If your intention is to make a clear, final and indisputable statement, or if your goal is to appear more authoritative, it may be more useful for you to avoid this seemingly questioning tone and spend some time practising using downward inflection to indicate conviction and confidence. Try statements such as 'The End', 'I have no doubt', 'I believe in you' with a downward inflection which corresponds with the statement, and note the sound of certainty.

Definitive Statements

Another extreme is the continual use of the 'definite statement tune', used effectively by those in high status or authoritative positions and generally used by newscasters, because it is perceived as being 'the truth' and not to be questioned. Although this is a confident and assertive tune, if used inappropriately or continually, it can make your listener feel that there is no space or opportunity to ask questions or share ideas, or that they are being hit over the head again and again with the same energy or view; it can feel repetitive and ultimately dull. Audiences respond well to vocal variety which reflects the feeling behind the message rather than rhythmic and tonal repetition that soon becomes uninspiring.

Try this exercise, record yourself, and note the different results that are produced.

N.B. It can be useful to move your hand up as your voice rises or lower it as it falls.

Try saying 'This is critical'.

a. With a rising intonation as if your voice is climbing the stairs on the word 'critical'.
b. With a falling intonation, creating the sound of a definitive statement, using a 'high to low' tune on the word 'critical'.

Try this with phrases you use regularly. For example:

I'm not sure.	Let's find a time in the diary.
Thank you.	I need a raise.
This must be complete by tomorrow.	My name is…

Listen to your recording and consider which tune suits each phrase best.

The ideal intonation for your speech varies depending on the context, language and cultural norms. However, in general, an ideal intonation pattern is characterised by a natural and varied pitch range that reflects the meaning, emotion and emphasis of the speaker's message. It involves appropriate rises and falls in pitch, pauses and stress on important words or phrases.

Revisit Chapter 7 on Pitch and Chapter 9 on Vocal Variety for more of these exercises. Start implementing variety and awareness at work, making a note of the different responses or results you achieve and how it feels. It can be uncomfortable to begin with to use a different intonation, to make statements rather than questions, or invite responses when you are used to making demands. Knowing this may help you remain curious about your communication and vocal options.

Speed, Pace and Rate

Does Your Speed Reflect Your Need?

Some of the most common communication concerns brought to coaches is 'I speak too fast', 'I know that I speed up when I'm under pressure', and, less regularly, 'I'm too slow' or 'People switch off when I'm speaking because my thoughts take too long to form'.

The bigger concern is at what speed does your audience need you to speak? Think about being the passenger in an open-top car on an hour-long journey. If you travelled at 200 miles per hour along the motorway, never stopping, this journey might feel exhausting and you might step out of the car dizzy and windswept; equally, if the driver did 5 miles per hour all the way the journey would be tedious, you'd cover far less ground in an hour and you might be inclined to get out and walk! Travelling at one speed only is predictable, tedious, tiring and ultimately doesn't take care of your 'passenger' and their needs. When it comes to speed, natural variety is one of the major tools we have to look after our 'speech passenger', our 'audience'.

It's important to remember that we all have different natural speeds of speech and there is no one-size-fits-all ideal tempo. Various ancient systems, such as Ayurvedic medicine, the Chinese five-elements philosophy and culture and the four Hippocratic temperaments, delve into different personality types and energies. These systems recognise that individuals possess unique characteristics that can manifest in their communication style, including the speed at which they speak. Ultimately, finding your own comfortable speaking pace is key. The crucial element is being aware of how your speech speed affects your message delivery and how others understand you, in order to make conscious adjustments and ensure your message is clear and well received. Experimenting with different speeds and finding a balance that allows for effective communication while staying true to your natural style can enhance your overall communication skills.

Just as stress can affect your pitch, pace is often altered by pressure or nerves. Understanding your 'normal', gives you a benchmark to aim for, even when under stress. Knowing whether you tend to get faster or slower when adrenalin is coursing through your system can be helpful, allowing you to monitor and adjust during a speaking event. An undesirably fast pace has unwanted knock-on effects; a fast pace raises pitch, or makes it mono-tone, meaning it gets lost as your speech becomes one long sentence with few pauses and the major message you are sharing becomes one of fear, boredom or embarrassment.

I Speak Too Fast!

What does 'too fast' really mean? Do you speak so fast that your words run together and are not discernible from one another? If so, that may well cause some difficulties for your listener and you may want to learn how to adapt your speed. 'Rate' is the speed at which an individual word or group of words is spoken. To process information effectively, it is important to speak at a reasonably 'digestible' rate: neither too fast nor slow. 'Pace', on the other hand, can be thought of as the overall energy and rhythm of the delivery of an entire speech so that individual words can be spoken clearly and concisely, but the general pace can be driven forward energetically. This means that speech may have clarity, energy and precision as well as a sense of the 'drive' of language flowing in rhythmic cadences.

It is believed that listeners can process between 500 and 800 words per minute, although individual processing speeds may vary. However, the challenge with fast speech lies not only in the speed of the words but also in other factors that can make it difficult for listeners to comprehend and follow the message – clarity, reduced emphasis or information overload.

We might speak extremely fast because our mind is elsewhere and we have forgotten about our audience, or we want to get off the 'stage' as quickly as possible, or for positive reasons such as speaking with a sense of excitement or urgency. However, speaking rapidly can have implications for effective communication. Consider individuals you know who speak at a fast pace, with rapid delivery. This style is often observed in meetings where a fast talker dominates the conversation, leaving little room for interruptions and allowing limited time for others to fully grasp the content. In such cases, speech may sound staccato and excessively regular, lacking vocal variation and pauses.

If you consider yourself a 'too fast' speaker you may recognise some of these causes:

- Unconsciously speeding up your speech because of heightened adrenaline or the desire to finish speaking quickly. See Chapters 3 and 4 on tension release and breathing. Focus on your audience and *their* needs.

- Rapid pace of speech may reflect your enthusiasm and desire to convey information quickly. Can you think of other ways to utilise your enthusiasm other than speed? Perhaps varying your pitch, slowing down over an exciting part, playing with volume or using physical energy.

- Some individuals naturally have a fast-speaking style as part of their speech pattern, influenced by cultural or regional factors, or personal habits, developed over time. For them, speaking rapidly may feel more comfortable and natural. Pause can still be used between phrases and pitch can remain varied.

- You may find you are speaking at a fast pace and not pausing to avoid being interrupted. Some interruptions occur, however, because people are trying to piece together the information you are sharing. Ensure that you are you using emphasis and pause, allowing your idea to fully form and conclude so that your audience doesn't need to interrupt to complete the 'jigsaw'. Surprisingly, speaking rapidly can actually encourage interruptions, as it may give the impression that your speech lacks careful consideration. Taking your time to speak thoughtfully reflects a well-thought-out idea, and your conversation partners are more likely to allow you to finish without interruption.

- Speakers with fast cognitive processing speed may speak quickly because their thoughts and ideas are processed rapidly. Their speech rate aligns with the speed at which their mind generates and organises information, resulting in faster delivery; for those speakers, not having to repeat themselves may be the incentive to introduce a more moderate pace.

- Rushing through our speech can stem from a desire to hold onto a thought, but speaking rapidly increases the risk of losing track of that thought. Instead, prioritise delivering your ideas effectively to your audience by incorporating pauses that allow them to process the information and using word emphasis to highlight key points. Before a meeting, take a few minutes to contemplate what you want to say and consider jotting down brief notes (avoiding full sentences) to help you stay on track if needed.

I'm Too Slow!

At the opposite end of the spectrum, if you are uncertain about facts or simply unsure as to what position to take on an issue or, for some, extremely nervous, an individual may slow speech down excessively, become hesitant and frequently introduce fillers such as 'er' and 'um', appearing to weigh up each word. A slower pace may become a form of unconscious protection, avoiding commitment to delivery. The words can become so disparate it can become hard to find meaning between the gaps, the speaker may be perceived as demonstrating uncertainty or 'liking the sound of their own voice', and again the listener may then just 'switch off' and disregard what is being said.

If speech is overly slow:

- The words can begin to disconnect and meaning is lost.
- You lose control of focusing your audience's attention on specific key words as every word sounds important.
- Your audience may start to 'fill in the blanks' and make assumptions about what you are going to say and consequently you may be interrupted more. It is important to maintain their interest and attention by avoiding predictability in your speech.
- Overly slow or consistently slow speech may be interpreted as a lack of enthusiasm or knowledge, frustrate your audience or mean you get cut off.
- Some audiences may perceive this regular, consistently slow speed as conceited, long-winded and overbearing.

Speaking at an excessively fast or slow pace can indicate a lack of focus on the audience's experience. To create a more impactful and audience-centred speaking experience, it is important to find a balanced pace that allows for clear and coherent delivery while considering the audience's ability to follow along. A moderate, balanced pace in speech signifies the speaker's commitment to their audience and confidence in their ideas or opinions. It reflects their ability to think ahead and maintain control over their words and allows for careful consideration, ensuring the speaker can articulate their thoughts effectively. While a moderate pace is important, it is equally crucial to let the content dictate the pace of delivery to sustain the listener's interest. It is vital to avoid a monotonous – whether fast or slow – rhythm that becomes predictable and detached from the intended message; variety of pace is important. Adapting the pace to match the significance and tone of the content enhances engagement and ensures that the delivery remains purposeful and meaningful.

Suggestions and Strategies

If you are concerned about 'speed', it is worth asking yourself the following questions:

- Does my voice sound energised?
- Do I sound engaged in my message?
- Are the words themselves overly fast/slow?
- Am I using pause? Too much or too little?
- Is there animation in my face or body whilst I am pausing? Or do I appear as if my 'battery' has run out?
- Can I link words together more or do they need some separation for coherence?
- Am I using key word emphasis and variety?
- Am I clear? Could I articulate more to aid clarity or am I being too careful?
- Am I attempting to demand the attention of my audience through a faster/slower pace, and are there other ways I could do this?
- Am I clear on what I want to say next?
- Am I filibustering? (Using delaying tactics or obstructing conversation with either a too rapid or a too laboured pace.)

You might be alerted to 'monospeed' or lack of variation in your speed by:

Listener's reactions: are you often asked to repeat yourself, do your audience look confused or appear overwhelmed? Do your audience appear disengaged, distracted or struggling to maintain eye contact while you're speaking? This might indicate that your pace is not working for them. People may find it challenging to stay engaged when the information is delivered at a singular speed without pauses or variations.

Incomplete thoughts: if you find it challenging to complete your thoughts or speak coherently it may be because you're rushing through your thoughts and words or trying to get out of the spotlight quickly. Breath is going to help here – the brain loves oxygen for thinking. Breathing between thoughts will give you the 'fuel' to get to the end of a thought or sentence and let your audience know that you are structuring your speech for their benefit.

The way English is structured means our key word often is found at the end of a sentence, so if you are cutting off before you get to that key word your audience may feel very confused.

Breathlessness or physical discomfort: if you frequently run out of breath or experience discomfort while speaking, it could be a sign that you need to slow down and allow for more breath.

Becoming aware of your speaking speed and learning to use different speeds requires conscious observation and practice. Here are some suggestions to help you develop this skill:

- Choose to be conscious of your speaking speed and find opportune moments and low-stakes scenarios in which when you can 'try out' alternative paces.
- Incorporate variety and modulation into your speech.
- Ask trusted peers for feedback on your speaking speed. You can also record yourself occasionally to check in with your speed, making a note of points that are missed or laboured and whether you notice external factors that make you increase or slow your speed.
- Observe audience responses and adjust your speed accordingly to ensure effective communication.
- Use material that supports your practice – for example, a highly energised piece of text about a race might lend itself to a fast pace, and a text describing a lazy Sunday afternoon might lend itself to a slower, more leisurely place. Television and radio commercials are useful to listen to, to hear this principle in action.

Elevator Pitch Challenge: deliver an 'elevator pitch' – a concise and compelling speech to 'sell' your idea or opinion in a limited time of 30 seconds or one minute. The challenge encourages you to communicate your ideas succinctly and persuasively within a short timeframe, but be purposeful about not rushing.

Speed Variation: select a piece of text, such as a paragraph from a book or a newspaper article. Read it aloud multiple times, each time varying your speed. Start with a slow and deliberate pace, then repeat the passage at a moderate speed and, finally, read it quickly. Pay attention to how the meaning and impact of the text can change with different speeds of delivery.

Remember, mastering different speaking speeds takes time and practice. Regularly evaluating and adjusting your pace will allow you to adapt to different contexts, connect with your audience and effectively convey your message.

> We often forget that pace is a choice, and you can use it creatively for the impression you choose to make.

Pause

It takes confidence to hold your ground, to remain silent without losing concentration; this often leads to limited use of pauses in our speech. Yet, crucial communication takes place in the time allowed by a pause. One piece of information can be digested before another is presented. Workplace dynamics or 'company culture' may be fast-paced and demand efficient communication, which in turn may lead speakers to edit out pauses. In a fast-paced meeting culture longer or more frequent pauses might be seen as inefficient. Furthermore, in highly pressurised environments some individuals prefer to avoid the spotlight and the attention which comes with speaking; as a result, they may speak rapidly with fewer pauses to escape focus quickly. In cultures where only assertive, rapid speakers are perceived as authoritative, individuals who speak slowly or use pauses may feel that their voice is undervalued, and therefore aim to eradicate pauses. However, the efficiency of your speech and the presence of pauses are not mutually exclusive.

Pauses are a natural part of speech, rather than a technical element that we should learn to perform. They serve various purposes and contribute to effective communication. Just as silence can speak volumes, well-placed pauses in speech can convey meaning, emphasise key points, allow for reflection and create a sense of rhythm and flow. The beauty of the pause is that our words get a second life, so to speak; they can resonate in the listener's mind, settle and allow them to reflect, build suspense, create impact or signal transitions in conversation. Not all pauses are created equal, and nor should they be, and they don't necessarily need to be long, but you may wish to pause for slightly longer if you are asking your audience to process something complicated or imagine something new.

- Pausing should save you time, as you won't have to repeat yourself, or follow up with an email.

- Using a pause, rather than fighting to speak over a noisy group of people, can be a valuable crowd control mechanism.

- Pausing allows you pose rhetorical questions to your audience – questions that don't require an answer but create a connection between the speaker and the listener.

- Pauses provide a valuable space for reflection and thought, both for the speaker and the listener. It allows individuals to fully absorb what has been said, contemplate its meaning and formulate a response or question.

- Pauses help with humour: when we pause before the punchline of a joke, a pause lets us know that 'here comes the funny bit!' The pause focuses attention on the key element of the joke and will help the punchline. Pausing will invite your audience to laugh. A speaker who is confident that they're funny will deliver the punchline and pause for the laughter because they know it's coming. If you are unsure of your joke, delivering the punchline and racing to the next joke, your audience will be denied the opportunity to laugh; they'll feel shut out. Brave the silence. If you do get the laugh you are hoping for, don't 'step on it'; let your audience enjoy themselves and hold off on resuming your speech until they can hear you.

- Pausing at appropriate intervals demonstrates confidence, control, and that you have a roadmap for your speech and you know where to rest. It may instil confidence in your listeners, if they feel confident that you are comfortable and prepared.

- Pausing strategically can help improve overall speech fluency. It provides moments to breathe, collect thoughts and avoid rushed or fragmented speech.

When you receive feedback suggesting that you should pause more in your speech, it can be helpful to understand how to implement this effectively. A pause should not be a complete stop or a frozen moment but rather, as described by Cicely Berry (2007), 'a poise' or an organic, vibrant moment, just before the next phrase.

> When you pause while maintaining eye contact with your audience, it creates a moment of anticipation and emphasis. It allows the audience to absorb and process the information you've just shared, and it signals that something important or impactful is about to follow.

Suggestions and Strategies

To incorporate pauses into your speech, consider the following tips:

- Take natural pauses at commas, periods or other punctuation marks to allow for a moment of reflection and to guide the flow of your speech. With regular practice of reading aloud and pausing at punctuation, you will gradually develop the ability to incorporate pauses naturally into everyday speech.

- Pause to ground yourself, to slow down and breathe. The breath will allow you to use a variety of volume, pitch and tone. You may not need to breathe every time you pause.

- Pause briefly between different points or concepts to give your listeners time to process and absorb the information before moving on.

- Pause for the 'unsaid', the metaphorical raised eyebrow, or wink, to the audience. It deepens the sense of your communication being a conversation rather than just a one-way street.

- Prioritise pauses before and after important or impactful statements. This can help draw attention to the significance of those points and allow them to resonate with your audience.

- Treat pauses as deliberate moments of connection. Use them to establish eye contact, engage with your audience, or to build anticipation before delivering a punchline or important message.

- Experiment with different lengths and placements of pauses during your practice sessions. Pay attention to the natural rhythm and flow of your speech and adjust the timing of pauses accordingly.

- Watch the news and observe the use of pause by broadcasters and politicians. Observe when they pause, take note of what work works for you and what you find plodding or pedantic.

- Observe skilled speakers, such as TED Talk presenters, public speakers or actors known for their delivery. How do they use pause to highlight key ideas, allow for audience reaction or create a sense of anticipation?

Using the guidelines above try applying pause to this excerpt:

A hundred years ago her great-great-grandfather, Seymour Parry, who ran away with Conway's daughter, had walked down Bond Street. Down Bond Street the Parrys had walked for a hundred years and might have met the Dalloways (Leighs on the mother's side) going up. Her father got his clothes from Hill's. There was a roll of cloth in the window, and here just one jar on a black table, incredibly expensive: like the thick pink salmon on the ice block at the fishmonger's. The jewels were exquisite— pink and orange stars, paste, Spanish, she thought, and chains of old gold; starry buckles, little brooches which had been worn on sea green satin by ladies with high head-dresses. But no good looking! One must economise. She must go on past the picture dealer's where one of the odd French pictures hung, as if people had thrown confetti—pink and blue—for a joke.

Mrs Dalloway in Bond Street, Virginia Woolf (1922)

Sound Bite

Remember, the goal is not to *force* pauses into your speech but to allow them to emerge naturally, enhancing your communication and creating a sense of poise and presence. With practice and mindfulness, you can master the art of pausing and make it a valuable tool in your expressive repertoire.

Vocal Spontaneity

A more difficult aspect for any of us to master is the skill of making information sound new. You may have taught the same course for many years, delivered your sales pitch a hundred times, your weekly update may feel repetitive, or you've described a process more times than you care to remember. The truly effective communicator can impart information as though it was as fresh and new to them as it is to the listener. When enthusiasm is natural, not pushed or forced, and the speaker uses breath freely without any postural or tension problems, most of the aspects that determine an 'interesting' voice are present. Sometimes, however, a habit of sounding monotonous has developed over a few years and, indeed, may have been a vocal habit for you as a child or an adolescent. Habits such as vocal monotony can develop during a period of insecurity or vulnerability and frequently, when the phase passes, the habit may remain. For some, the idea of standing up and reading or speaking in front of their peers is terrifying; the jaw tightens and all vocal variety is suppressed. For others, a vocal quality is assumed as part of a survival strategy, such as the adolescent 'chill', 'street cred' approach, which may involve a very limited use of range. Vocal 'fry' or 'creak' may fall under this umbrella of adopted 'casual' vocal qualities. Vocal fry is the lowest vocal register, typically produced at below 70 Hz., resulting from a long closed phase in the vibratory cycle of the vocal folds. As a consequence, slower vibrations are produced and this results in the lower, creaky sound. This quality often emerges at the end of sentences when a speaker's airflow weakens. While not physically harmful to your voice it can become a habitual speech pattern that influences how listeners perceive you. Some radio personalities incorporate vocal fry into their speech in an effort to come across as more natural, relaxed, and accessible to their audience. Some individuals use vocal fry in an attempt to assert casual, relaxed authority by adopting an artificially deeper pitch, a trend more commonly observed among, but not exclusive to, younger women. Some listeners may perceive it as authoritative and casually assertive, while others may find it grating and associate it with disinterest, boredom, or a lack of ambition due due to reduced pitch and volume variation caused by insufficient breath. In professional and public speaking contexts, the use of vocal fry can be a divisive issue. Some people may consider it unprofessional or while others see it as a way to connect with a more informal and youthful audience. Ultimately, the impact of vocal fry on spontaneity, authority and credibility depends on the audience's preferences and the specific communication situation.

As we've discussed already, there are many other ways of achieving a natural, engaging quality or displaying authority rather than using vocal fry – for example using pace, pause, intonation, volume modulation and vocal variety.

Refer to the exercises in the previous chapters (particularly 'Release of Tension', 'Resonance', 'Pitch' and 'Working for Variety') to help find more vocal spontaneity and resist monotony, the sound of fatigue or disinterest.

By actively practising and embracing opportunities to speak in various settings, such as assemblies, work events or conferences, you can cultivate modulation, music and spontaneity in your speech. While business and industrial courses may offer effective speech formulas, it's important to tailor those techniques to your own unique style and message. Using cookie-cutter approaches or recognisable sales patter and tactics may not feel natural or authentic to you. Instead, focus on gaining practical experience and making gradual adjustments to your voice and delivery. Clarify your specific motivation or intention behind your speaking engagements as this will guide your delivery and connect you more deeply with your audience. Additionally, prioritise your overall well-being and vocal health to ensure you have the energy and vitality to engage your listeners effectively.

As you continue to practise and refine your skills, you'll gradually build the confidence to step out of your comfort zone and embrace methods that mirror natural, easy and engaging speech. Remember the mantra 'feel the fear and do it anyway' (Jeffers, 1998) and trust in the foundations you've developed through observation, experimentation and learning from others.

Not always relying on a script can help to enhance vocal spontaneity and naturalness in communication; you have the freedom to express yourself more authentically and adapt your delivery in response to the audience and the moment. This allows your voice to reflect your genuine thoughts and emotions, leading to a more engaging and dynamic communication experience. Speaking impromptu or with brief notes encourages you to rely on your knowledge, expertise and understanding of the topic, rather than relying solely on memorised lines. This can give your voice a sense of spontaneity and flexibility, as you respond in real-time to the flow of the conversation or presentation. It allows for more organic and interactive exchanges with your audience, fostering a deeper connection and engagement. It is important to note that speaking without a script requires adequate preparation and familiarity with the subject matter. It's not about improvising or speaking without any structure or direction. Instead, it involves having a clear understanding of your key points, main ideas and supporting examples, which allows you to speak more freely while maintaining coherence and clarity.

Vocal Tone

Vocal tone refers to the quality or character of someone's voice, which conveys emotions, attitudes and additional layers of meaning beyond the literal words being spoken.

Vocal tone is an amalgamation of the elements we have already explored in this book, including pitch, volume, timbre and intonation. It influences the overall mood and emotional impact of the communication, allowing the speaker to convey sincerity, confidence, warmth, authority, excitement, empathy and many other qualities.

The choice of vocal tone can greatly affect how a message is received and interpreted by others. For example, a warm and empathetic tone can make someone feel understood and supported, while a confident and authoritative tone can command attention and convey expertise.

Using the wrong tone can devalue the work you have done on vocal variety, modulation and healthy voicing, leading to misinterpretation, emotional disconnect or reduced credibility. It is crucial to match our tone with our intended message and the attitudes we wish to convey; if the intention is clear, generally tone follows.

The following exercise encourages us to embrace the exploration of different vocal tones.

Playing with Tone

Confident: assertive, self-assured, poised.

Friendly: approachable, amiable, welcoming.

Informative: knowledgeable, factual, informative.

Thoughtful: reflective, considerate, introspective.

Compassionate: Warm, caring, empathetic.

Authoritative: firm, commanding, in control.

Enthusiastic: energetic, upbeat, sincere, excited.

Assertive: direct, determined, self-assured.

Motivational: inspiring, encouraging, uplifting.

Professional: polished, business-like, formal.

Serious: Grave, earnest and solemn.

Playful: fun-loving, light-hearted, mischievous.

Calm: serene, composed, tranquil.

Persuasive: influential, convincing, compelling.

Sincere: genuine, heartfelt, authentic.

Curious: inquisitive, interested, probing.

Supportive: Nurturing, comforting, reassuring.

Diplomatic: tactful, sensitive, balanced.

- Select a tone from the provided list or choose an appropriate tone of your own for a forthcoming speaking engagement.

- Choose a short text to use as your practice material. It can be a quote, a dialogue or a brief paragraph.

- Take a moment to connect with the chosen tone of voice and understand the emotion or attitude it represents. Consider which situations would require this tone.

- Experiment with your voice's pitch, volume, pace and overall delivery to convey the desired emotion or attitude. Record yourself.

- Listen to the recording and assess how well you captured the intended tone. Take note of any areas for improvement or adjustment.

- Repeat with different tones from the list. Challenge yourself to explore a variety of emotions and attitudes to expand your vocal range and versatility.

- After practising several individual tones, try blending them together within the same text. Explore transitions between different tones to create a nuanced and engaging vocal performance.

- Practise with different texts and contexts to enhance your adaptability. Consider what tones you'd choose for certain types of audiences.

- Identify the tones that come more naturally to you, that are most useful to you at work and those that require more practice.

This is great practice, to flex your vocal colour, modulation and variety 'muscles'. When presenting or speaking at work, consider the appropriate tone for what you hope to achieve, what tone will your audience respond best to, what will help you achieve your goals? Always remember if the intention is there your voice will follow suit. To borrow the title of Janet Feindel's book, 'the thought propels the sound' (2009).

The Message: Body Language

Body language has a voice of its own. Just as the voice carries tone, pitch and emotion, our bodies express a multitude of messages through subtle movements, gestures and postures, conveying intricate nuances that support, or alter our words. This silent dialogue adds depth and authenticity to our communication, revealing our true intentions, feelings and attitudes. It becomes a powerful companion to spoken words, where words and gestures work in concert, amplifying the impact of our message and forging deeper connections with others.

> Ideally, body language and gesture come naturally and spontaneously, reflecting our authentic emotions, thoughts and intentions. Instinctive body language is more effective in establishing rapport, building trust, and creating a positive connection with others. It allows us to communicate nonverbally in a way that is authentic and aligned with our true selves. Developing awareness of how we are expressing ourselves, returning our focus to our message, and trusting our instincts can enable us to communicate with others in a more meaningful and impactful way.

Gesture

Gesture provides a natural reinforcement to what is being said. In general, gesture has cultural implications and roots; different cultures and languages will use gesture in different ways and with varying regularity. Paralinguistic features of communication encompass various aspects of communication beyond spoken words, including gesture, body language and facial expressions. These elements play a crucial role as they have the power to alter the intended message. This is often described as 'nonverbal communication', and within this category 'body language' is frequently used to refer to all the means other than speech by which individuals communicate messages, beyond, in support of, or in contrast to, the words. As with vocal variety, gesture should be the result of thought processes and should stem from the desire to communicate those thoughts and ideas to the listener. Imposed or learnt gesture is quickly identified as artificial. Excessive and unrelated gesture distracts from, rather than adds to, the message being conveyed.

N.B. Gesture is most effective when the speaker is sufficiently relaxed to integrate mind, body and speech in a cohesive whole.

Self-Assessment and Building Awareness

1. Film yourself speaking to camera while narrating a story that you are familiar with, such as a memorable holiday experience, the plot of a film or a work event you participated in. As you watch the recording, pay attention to the moments when you naturally use gestures to enhance your meaning. Observe how regularly you use gestures and if there is a pattern to their usage. Do you find yourself gesturing more when you want to emphasise a point? Or perhaps when you are trying to establish a connection with your audience? Or when explaining complex ideas? Take note of these patterns and consider how they contribute to your communication.

2. Film yourself trying to sell an object, such as a pencil or cup, to the camera, being sure to employ plenty of enthusiasm and physical energy in your delivery. Review the video and observe how you used gesture compared to the previous recording. Reflect on the impact of using more gestures. Did it help in delivering the message effectively, or did it become a distraction? Notice any changes in your voice as you employed more gestures. Were you louder or more emphatic? Did it result in vocal variety, and if so, did it sound natural or forced?

3. Film yourself describing a task you don't enjoy, such as a housework chore or a tedious process at work. Review it and notice if you use any gestures, if your voice has variety, if there are any noticeable facial expressions, what level your energy is at and if you use emphasis in the same way.

Reflect on your answers to these questions. Take note of how incorporating additional gestures influenced your energy level and tone. Did it increase your overall energy and make your delivery more engaging?

Continued

Did it alter the tone of your voice in any way? Be mindful of any habitual gestures that may not enhance your speech. Are there certain gestures that you unconsciously rely on, which do not add value to your message? Identifying these gestures can help you refine your body language and make it more purposeful and effective. This self-observation can provide valuable insights into how your nonverbal and verbal communication aligns with your feelings and perceptions of different tasks or experiences. Keep in mind that adopting new speech styles can initially feel unnatural.

Gesture and Finding Your Words

Gesture serves a purpose beyond the message conveyed to your audience – it has the power to ignite and stimulate your brain. The neuroscience behind hand gesture and memory suggests that there is a strong connection between the two (Kelly, Manning and Rodak, 2008). Some actors use movement to memorise lines, and some individuals find gestures energise their thinking. The act of gesturing involves both motor movements and cognitive processes, engaging different neural pathways simultaneously. These activations create a link between the physical movements of the body and the cognitive processing of information. It is suggested that individuals who use hand gestures during learning or teaching tasks tend to have improved memory recall compared to those who do not gesture. By engaging multiple brain regions gestures can aid in remembering and effectively conveying your content, so the next time you feel that you are losing your train of thought, or that you might be drawing a blank, about to cut yourself short or use unwanted filler sounds, try gesturing or moving, to get the brain engaged.

Gesture should not be confused with 'mime'. Instead, it can serve as a valuable tool to help you express your thoughts and ideas effectively. Certain gestures, such as a juggling motion or a weighing-up gesture, can assist you in finding the right words or ideas. By employing gestures such as these, you signal to your audience that you are engaged in thoughtful consideration or reflection. You don't have to inform them that you are 'thinking', the gesture does it for you. This message can put your audience at ease and assures your listener that there is more to come, minimising their discomfort or concern that the conversation has come to a halt or that they need to worry about you! Thus, gestures play a crucial role in supporting your speech and maintaining uninterrupted and engaging conversation.

263

If you find that your gestures are lacking or that your delivery is not effectively connecting with your audience, it can be helpful to explore and experiment with different gestures. Finding gestures that personally resonate with you and align with your content can enhance your message and aid in memory recall. Remember, the goal is to achieve a natural and seamless connection between your content, your identity as a speaker and your physical expression. So don't hesitate to try out different gestures and discover what works best for you. Consider:

Beat gestures are subtle rhythmic or repetitive movements of the hands or body that align with the natural flow of speech. They can help establish a cadence or rhythm in your delivery, making it easier to maintain listener attention, highlight key points and enhance the overall expressiveness of communication.

Spatial gestures involve using physical space to represent relationships or positions between objects or ideas. Mapping information onto a spatial layout or using gestures such as pointing or directing attention can help individuals indicate specific objects, locations or people; enhancing shared understanding and reducing ambiguity.

Iconic gestures visually depict or represent the shape, size or movement of objects or ideas. They can help reinforce the mental imagery associated with the information, a kind of 'belt and braces' approach to the message your audience is receiving. In the workplace they can aid in conveying complex ideas, demonstrating processes or illustrating data. Iconic gestures help make information more tangible and memorable.

Metaphoric gestures: by using symbolic hand movements or body actions, individuals can add depth and meaning to their verbal messages. For example, a speaker extending their arms as if embracing the opportunities that lie ahead visually represents the speaker's vision.

Gestures That Might Tell a Different Story

Habitual, unintentional or unconscious gestures that are unrelated to your content can distract your audience and undermine the impact of your spoken message. These gestures are typically not intentional but arise from habits, nervousness or cultural influences that impact body language. They can include repetitive movements like fidgeting, or playing with clothing or objects, as well as excessive hand gestures or facial expressions that are irrelevant to the material being discussed. These 'leaked' gestures can draw attention away from the message, making it challenging for the audience to stay focused on the speaker's words, or even feel that the speaker is being authentic.

> Imagine a host saying 'Welcome everyone, we're so happy to have you here, we're confident you are going to have a great night' whilst fidgeting with their sleeve, or tapping their foot – would you believe them? Do you trust that they are happy you are there? Are you convinced they are confident about hosting, or might something else be going on for them? Furthermore, the gesture might inform the voice, and the delivery might be affected, consequently sounding less committed or energised.

Let the Medium Match the Message

We believe the most important aspect of gesture or body language in general is that it is in line with the meaning of your message. Used in harmony with your message, purposeful, energetic, clear and congruent gestures can support and emphasise verbal messages and body language can facilitate rapport and influence interpersonal interactions.

The **direction** of your gestures can add meaning and emphasis to your speech. For instance, gestures that move outward or upward can signal expansion, growth or positive outcomes. On the other hand, gestures that move inward or downward can convey containment, limitation or negative aspects. The voice should mirror these gestures accordingly.

The **speed** of your gestures can influence the energy and impact of your communication. Faster gestures can convey enthusiasm, excitement or urgency, while slower gestures can indicate thoughtfulness, reflection or emphasis on specific details. Varying the speed of your gestures throughout your speech can help maintain engagement and capture attention, and your vocal quality should follow.

The **intensity** of your gestures reflects strength or magnitude. Some gestures can be subtle and gentle, while others can be more expansive and dynamic. The intensity of your gestures should match the emotional tone and emphasis of your speech and your voice.

Suggestions and Strategies: Building Awareness of Habitual Gestures

1. Record yourself in an online meeting; leave it running for some time so you forget you are filming and can observe yourself in your natural 'gestural state'!
2. Film yourself for 1 to 2 minutes introducing yourself as if at an event (seated).
3. Film yourself standing up delivering a speech – your own, or a well known speech.

   – Notice if you have repetitive gestures *which do not add* to your message – such as picking your nails, rocking back and forth, clapping your hands. What happens to your voice in these moments?

   – Become aware of these habits. Do they serve you? Are they comforting? Would you rather not include them? Are they an outlet for nervous energy?

   – Make a choice whether to use them. You may feel they give you a personal flair, add to your vocal quality, and are not negatively impacting your message, if so, great!

   – If you would rather reduce these habits and explore alternatives, continue filming and observing yourself over the next weeks and months. Determine if you prefer to replace these habits with something else or aim for more stillness in your gestures. By cultivating deep focus on your purpose, your audience and your connection with them, you can redirect your energy away from excessive hand, feet or facial movements. If unwanted, anxious energy continues to manifest despite your shift in focus, consider exploring other outlets for releasing that energy, such as:

   Warming up and releasing some adrenaline before you speak.

   Muscular tension release.

   Calming breath.

   Energetic delivery.

   Energised focus on your listener.

   Emphasising vocal variety and modulation.

- Be aware that using repetitive gestures may create a repetitive vocal quality.
- Contradictory gestures can send mixed signals and lead to misinterpretation. The audience may focus more on the gestures rather than the verbal content or your vocal delivery, resulting in a disconnect between what is being said and what is being conveyed through body language.
- Be culturally sensitive. Gestures can vary significantly across different cultures, and what may be appropriate in one cultural context can be offensive or misunderstood in another. Inappropriate gestures that go against cultural norms or customs can lead to cultural misunderstandings, sensitivity issues or even unintentional offence.
- Let your gesture be the supporting actors, and your message the star of the show. Strive for balance; let your gestures complement and enhance your overall message without becoming the centre of attention.

Posture and Positioning

Positioning and Status

How an individual is positioned in relation to another person or persons is very important; each position 'says' something. Positioning can affect the interaction that takes place in significant and predictable ways. An intriguing discovery is that individuals who are in tune mentally, or who respect each other, tend to mirror the other's posture, whereas those who are not compatible show definite signs of defensive body posture, arms crossed, leaning away and lack of eye contact. It is a useful tool of observation which helps in meeting facilitation, to assess team well-being and to know when to adapt your style or approach your audience.

What Your Positioning 'Says'

While it may not always be feasible to choose where you sit or stand, your position when speaking can have a predictable impact on the ensuing interaction. For example:

- Sitting or standing side by side with someone suggests a sense of cama-raderie, partnership or alignment in a shared goal or interest; it is the recognised co-operative position, but is more rarely seen in formal situations.

- Sitting directly opposite someone can create an atmosphere of competi-tion, confrontation or interrogation, which can make interviews or one-on-one meetings feel intimidating. In the era of online meetings, we often find ourselves in this opposing position, sometimes with multiple participants, leading to a sense of being 'in a firing line'. To alleviate any potential tension, consider finding a way to maintain eye-level contact while adopting a more relaxed positioning, such as sitting at a slight angle. This subtle adjustment can help create a more comfortable and inviting environment for your conversation partner. When considering interview situations, visiting the doctor or speaking with someone in authority, the 'opposite position' appears to be the preferred position, although more doctors are introducing a diagonal position vis-à-vis the patient, and this is something you can also achieve with in-person meetings.

- Standing behind someone may indicate a position of support or of defer-ence, allowing the person in front to take the lead.

- Positioning oneself at the centre of a group can signify authority or lead-ership, while positioning at the periphery may convey a sense of detach-ment or being an outsider. By strategically considering one's position in relation to others, you can influence the dynamics and outcomes of the interaction before you begin to speak, fostering connections, asserting authority or establishing rapport.

Positioning and Distance

Distance from another person or group of people would not at first sight appear to be an important aspect of communication, but it has been rec-ognised as having a considerable effect and for those who were the subject of the relatively recent social distancing measures during the COVID-19 pandemic, distancing has a long afterlife, where many of us remain cau-tious of being too close to others. Previous studies highlighted appropriate distances for specific communication situations: up to 0.5 metres for inti-mate social situation; 0.5 to 1.5 metres for personal situations and talking to friends or colleagues; 1.5 to 3 metres for social or consultative situations; beyond 3 metres for public or group speaking situations. Communication styles are influenced by distance. When communicating with a large group, we must not only consider audibility, but also acknowledge that within that group those nearby and those at a greater distance may perceive our communication differently. The person closest to the speaker might experience a more personal communication style and those at the back of the space will experience a more social, consultative or public communication style, and their responsibility as a listener within that dynamic may also lessen. This can be resolved by the speaker including the back of the room, by spending more time making eye contact with those at the back. Make sure you are audible, your posture is inclusive and you are not 'shutting anyone out', and, if you can, deliberately move around your speaking space to achieve a mix of personal and social and consultative positioning with all listeners. With a large audience you may choose to use attention-grabbing techniques, such as compelling visuals, dynamic body language and interactive activities, to maintain interest and participation. Speaking to a smaller group, who are closer to you, you have the advantage of more personal interaction, allowing for more nuanced communication, a conversational tone and direct engagement with individuals.

Managing Eye Contact

With the rise of remote working, video conferencing and social media, our reliance on digital communication platforms has increased significantly. This shift has impacted the way we engage in eye contact since it is mediated through screens. We have adapted to making eye contact through webcams, seeking to maintain a sense of connection even in virtual interactions. As our societies become more diverse and interconnected, there is a growing recognition and appreciation of cultural differences in eye-contact norms. We have become more aware that eye-contact practices vary across cultures and have developed a greater sensitivity to understanding and respecting these differences. There has been a heightened emphasis on inclusivity and understanding neurodiversity in recent years. This has led to increased awareness of different eye-contact preferences and challenges faced by individuals with diverse neurological profiles. We have become more accepting and accommodating of individual differences, fostering an environment where everyone's communication preferences and comfort levels are respected.

In very general, neurotypical terms, aiming for genuine presence in a conversation and being respectful of people's differences will guide your eye contact to be responsive and authentic.

As a speaker:

–   Eye contact can be active, and not always on your audience, as you engage in visual, auditory and kinaesthetic thinking, tapping into memories and imagination.

–   Laser-like fixed eye contact can be uncomfortable for your listener, as they may feel 'pinned down' and unable to escape your gaze.

–   It can be effective to make eye contact when making a key point, and a pause can be a convenient place to do this at the end of phrases, thoughts or sentences, or when you're expecting a response.

–   The duration of eye contact can vary.

–   Be aware that if you don't make much eye contact your audience may interpret this as you being disconnected from your message, and from them, whether this is true or not.

As a listener:

–   The passive listener in general takes on the bulk of the responsibility of maintaining eye contact.

–   Be aware that if you make very limited eye contact, the speaker may interpret this as you having little interest in them or their content.

It is important to approach the topic of eye behaviour with caution; it is not an exact science, and these suggestions should be used as a general guideline rather than an absolute truth.

Group Eye Contact

'W' formation eye contact refers to a pattern of making eye contact with multiple individuals or points in a room by gently moving your gaze in the shape of a 'W' over the audience including the front left, back left, centre, back right, and front right sections. Instead of fixating on one person or area, you intentionally shift your focus to engage with different individuals or sections of the audience. This metaphorical gesture of forming a loose 'W' back and forth with your eyes reminds you to create a sense of inclusiveness and connection, allowing you to establish rapport and engage with a broad range of people during your communication. The aim is to create a balance between making brief eye contact with larger sections of the audience and with individuals, ensuring that each person feels seen and acknowledged.

It is important to be aware that performed without authenticity, the 'W' formation can possibly appear mechanical or contrived. It may not allow for genuine, meaningful eye contact with individual audience members, as the speaker's attention is constantly shifting. Additionally, in some cultural contexts, prolonged or direct eye contact may be perceived differently or make people uncomfortable. Ultimately, the effectiveness of the 'W' formation and any other eye-contact technique depends on various factors, such as the speaker's style, the size of the audience and the cultural norms. It might be a good place to start from if you are new to addressing large audiences and until you find your own style. Random scanning can give a more natural and spontaneous feel to your eye contact, making it less predictable, trying to connect with different individuals by looking into their eyes for a few moments and varying the duration of your gaze. Although you can't practise with your actual audience, when you rehearse, scan the room and practise connecting with 'individuals' so you become familiar with the feeling; otherwise shifting your gaze in front of a live audience can feel quite 'risky' and stiff. You can also practise this silently in any space where there is a large crowd of people, at a train station or in a restaurant, just by scanning the group and letting your eyes rest occasionally on individuals. Always consider the specific context and adapt your eye-contact approach accordingly to establish a genuine connection with the audience.

Suggestions and Strategies

–   If you can move around and approach your audience, be mindful of physical contact and respect personal boundaries. Avoid making physical contact without prior consent, as people have different preferences and cultural norms regarding personal space.

–   To effectively address interruptions, distractions or challenging participants, it is crucial to respond promptly and assertively. Establishing clear expectations and ground rules is key to maintaining a productive and respectful environment. In addition to verbal communication, utilising physicality can enhance your ability to captivate the audience, maintain their attention and avoid distractions. One aspect of physicality is projecting assurance and authority. Stand tall, maintain good posture and use confident body language to convey your expertise and command of the situation. Use assertive body language with discretion, such as firm hand gestures and appropriate spatial positioning. Your physical presence can instil confidence in the audience and discourage disruptive behaviour.

- Pay attention to nonverbal cues, such as crossed arms or leaning away, as they may indicate a sense of discomfort or disengagement. Adapt your approach and delivery style in response to these cues, aiming to create a more engaging and comfortable experience for your audience. By being sensitive to nonverbal signals; you can tailor your communication to better connect with your audience and create a positive environment.

How Can I Have More Presence?

Physical presence is a combination of body language, posture, movement and self-assurance. The exercises in the book on posture, relaxation, breathing, vocal impact through variety, resonance and pitch, will all lead you towards more presence. Moving with intention into a room and knowing your purpose for being there will also give you a greater sense of presence.

- Stand tall, but not rigid – imagine you have a helium balloon attached to your head, creating length in your spine.
- Walk with deliberate and conscious movements, rather than rushing or shuffling. Take confident strides and maintain a steady pace.
- Look around the room and make brief eye contact with those present. This makes you feel more present, aware of your surroundings and engaged with the people in the room.
- Project a sense of warmth and approachability through your facial expressions and body language, coming from within.
- Stand or position yourself in a way that occupies an appropriate amount of space. Avoid slouching or hunching over, as it can diminish your presence.
- Be aware of the room's dynamics and adjust your behaviour accordingly. Adapt your volume, tone and energy level to suit the environment and the occasion.

Developing 'presence' takes practice and self-awareness; embody it at home and on your commute to work, or walking down the street. By consciously incorporating these techniques into your posture and everyday manner, you can cultivate a confident and impactful presence when entering a room.

The author Viv Groskop talks about the concept of 'happy high status' in her book of the same name (2023) and this concept is a great lens through which to view presence. Individuals who exhibit happy high status are often perceived as approachable, self-assured and positive. They radiate an aura of confidence and happiness, which can have a positive impact on their interactions with others. It's important to note this idea of high status is not about being arrogant or dismissive of others. It is about having a positive mindset, feeling good about oneself and radiating that positivity and confidence in a way that uplifts and inspires those around you.

Cultivating 'happy high status' involves finding fulfilment in one's personal and professional life and responding to change or mistakes in an easy-going, unflappable way. It is about being authentically happy and embodying a sense of inner strength and positivity that elevates your interactions and the overall atmosphere around you. Now if that isn't a recipe for presence, we don't know what is.

> The green reed which bends in the wind
> is stronger than the mighty oak which breaks in a storm.
> —Confucius

An Exercise for Presence

Visualise yourself feeling peaceful and content, exuding positive energy. Take a few deep breaths, let go of any tension. Stand tall, relax your shoulders, keep your chin level, with soft eyes gazing at the horizon. Let your head 'float'. Maintain an open and relaxed stance, keeping a sense of openness. Let a subtle, genuine smile form on your lips. Allow it to reach your eyes, creating a warm and inviting expression, extending the warmth outward.

THE CHANNEL

In the context of the communication model, the primary channel used is the vocal-auditory channel. Overall, the vocal-auditory channel encompasses the use of spoken words, vocal elements and body language to effectively transmit and receive messages in verbal exchanges. The channel has been thoroughly explored in the earlier chapters of this book and in the previous sections covering vocal pace, tone and body language.

THE NOISE

In the communication model, 'The Noise' refers to any factor or element that interferes with the smooth and accurate transmission of a message from the sender to the receiver. It can disrupt or distort the intended communication process, leading to a potential loss or misinterpretation of the message.

In earlier chapters we discussed some of the external environmental factors that create disturbances in communication, such as loud background noise, poor acoustics or interruptions. Physical noises such as these can make it difficult for the receiver to hear or understand the message clearly. The communicators' mindsets may also introduce another type of 'noise'. For instance, internal distractions or mental barriers, including factors such as preoccupation, personal biases or emotional states which impede the speaker's ability to share their message effectively or the receiver's ability to fully grasp the message. Relaxation, preparation and focusing on your purpose can quiet this noise. Unfamiliar, or fussy vocabulary, jargon or ambiguous terms, complex and unhelpful structures, or information 'buried' by a lack of clarity, can lead to confusion or misinterpretation of the message by the receiver. Adding to this, unhelpful volume levels, lack of clarity, or a misplaced vocal tone can produce a lot of 'noise'. Differences in beliefs, values, customs and norms can also create interference in communication, as can biases regarding diversity and disability. In modern communication, technology can contribute to 'noise'. Poor Wi-Fi, dropped calls, distorted audio or glitches in video conferencing can all hinder effective communication. And last, but not least, any voice disorder or vocal 'issue' can create 'noise' for both the speaker and the listener.

It is important for communicators to be aware of these potential sources of noise. Having a healthy 'working voice', being aware of the message you are sharing, preparing well, maintaining calm, tailoring your speech to your audience and their needs, using clear and concise language, choosing appropriate communication channels, adapting to cultural and access differences and ensuring a conducive physical environment all help to overcome the noise and enhance the overall effectiveness of the communication process.

Hearing the Full Picture

The wearing of masks during the pandemic was a communication challenge for us all, and particularly for those who are deaf or hard of hearing. As the 'receiver', we couldn't get the visual data (from looking at people's mouths when they speak) to help decode the sound or message we are receiving. Lip-reading both helps and confirms understanding; most of us use it to aid comprehension (to differing degrees). If a speaker cannot be seen, the listener needs to listen more attentively. As speakers, we had to articulate more clearly behind the mask, to make up for the lack of visual input. For many, this extra effort to articulate from behind an obstacle such as a mask was instinctive. The need to communicate can drive clearer articulation.

Consider what your listener needs to hear from your presentation or speech and let that drive your articulatory clarity, volume and physical embodiment of your message.

Context, Clothing and Comfort

We have discussed the unfortunate, but undeniable, reality of first impressions. In certain contexts, the choice of attire can influence how the message is received and perceived by others. Issues related to clothing choices can carry emotional weight for both the speaker and the listener. Wearing something overly casual, 'unsuitable' or culturally insensitive can create a form of 'noise' that diverts attention from your intended message and hinders effective communication. Rather than focusing on the content, your audience may become preoccupied or distracted by your clothing choice, which may not align with your intended aim.

Consideration of diversity, including different cultural perspectives, abilities and sensitivities, can guide your choice of clothing and reduce any potential distractions associated with inappropriate attire. This does not mean you should blend into the background, but rather aim to ensure that your appearance supports and enhances your communication through thoughtful forward planning. By being conscious of the diverse needs and perspectives of your audience, you can create an inclusive and engaging environment that allows your message to shine through.

Equally, you will have a lot of psychological 'noise' if you are wearing something that doesn't feel authentic, or something you don't like or isn't comfortable. Your unique attire can in fact be very useful in communication – you can incorporate distinctive pieces into your outfit that draw attention and serve as conversation starters, such as a statement accessory, talisman, colourful garment or a unique pattern. Wearing clothing that reflects your personality, interests or culture can attract people who share a similar taste and initiate conversations or response based on these visual cues. When we wear clothing that we feel comfortable and confident in, it can boost our self-esteem and make us feel relaxed and prepared to speak confidently.

When using your voice at work, it is important to be comfortable. Posture affects breath and voice production, and it makes sense to have a solid, balanced, foundation for speech. If possible, it's best to opt for footwear that provides balance, good support and allows you to move freely. Similarly, clothing that restricts your movement or constricts your breathing can make you feel uncomfortable and limit your ability to speak naturally. Choose clothing that stays in place and doesn't require frequent readjustment. Constantly tugging at your clothes or fussing with your appearance can be distracting for both you and the audience. Be aware, if you are using a mic, if any of your clothing or jewellery is noisy – does it interfere with the microphone or create any distractions as you speak or move? If you are going to be on camera, there are a few items of clothing to avoid. Intricate patterns, busy prints or stripes can cause a visual distortion known as the moiré effect on camera. Materials that are highly reflective, such as metallic or sequined clothing, can create distracting glares or reflections, and give your face a 'glitterball' effect, or shine light into the audience.

Paralinguistic 'Noise'

Fillers, such as 'um', 'uh', 'like' or 'you know', are sometimes a natural part of speech, but excessive use of fillers can hinder effective communication. They can create 'noise' for both the speaker and the listener. Speakers may feel that fillers reveal their insecurities, interrupt their flow or make them sound monotonous. For listeners, fillers can be distracting, hinder understanding or give the impression of disinterest. However, it's important to note that fillers have a place in speech.

From a linguistic perspective, fillers serve as language-processing mechanisms. They help bridge gaps between thoughts, organise ideas and serve as cognitive markers during speech production. While fillers may be disliked because they reveal moments of uncertainty or anxiety, they also demonstrate authenticity and relatability. Fillers can help maintain the flow of conversation and signal engagement and processing of information.

Occasional use of fillers for brief moments of thought-gathering or transitioning between points can be useful. They act as temporary placeholders while formulating the next sentence or idea. The key is to be aware of habitual and repetitive 'fillers' that may hinder communication rather than enhance it. Instead, strive for conscious, spontaneous and intentional speech.

Suggestions and Strategies

If you wish to become more aware of how often you use fillers and learn to reduce them, replace them with alternative sounds, words, pauses or gestures, or simply want to become conscious and present in your speech, try this challenge.

- Choose a topic to speak about – start with something familiar but that you don't necessarily talk about on a regular basis. For example, a topic from the news, what your dream home looks like, where you would like to travel and why.
- Record yourself talking for 1 to 2 minutes, consciously trying not to use fillers.
- Listen back and make a note of the regularity of fillers, what fillers you are using and notice whether you can pinpoint why you use them. Habit? Not knowing what to say? Finding the perfect phrase?
- Increase the length of the challenge over time and make the topics harder, or work-related.

What happens when you are very comfortable with a topic? What happens when the information is not so familiar?

Notice how you employ fillers differently in distinct contexts. Play the game above with friends, and give them permission to trigger a loud noise each time you use a filler. You could download a free 'airhorn' app on your phone, or use any other annoying noise. It's a swift and amusing way to recognise and deter fillers! It's important to have fun, as you don't want to become overly self-conscious when you talk, but by paying attention to your speech patterns, you can catch yourself using fillers in real-time, and eventually even before you utter them. Like any behavioural change, eliminating fillers requires practice and repetition. Awareness gives you choice, and if you are going 'filler-free', you may discover you are using gesture, facial expression and pause more regularly, choosing your words more deliberately, in place of relying on fillers. Listen to BBC Radio 4's show *Just a Minute* for another, more challenging, version of this game.

THE FEEDBACK

The feedback loop in the communication model is an essential component for effective communication. It allows for the exchange of information, understanding and adjustment based on the response received. Feedback can take various forms, including verbal and nonverbal cues, questions, comments or even silence.

In the communication process, feedback serves multiple purposes. Firstly, it confirms that the message has been received and understood by the recipient. It helps to ensure that the intended meaning has been accurately interpreted and that any misunderstandings or confusion can be clarified. Feedback also provides an opportunity for the sender to gauge the effectiveness of their message and make any necessary adjustments or improvements.

Positive feedback can reinforce effective communication strategies, while constructive feedback can highlight areas for improvement and further development.

Moreover, feedback encourages active engagement and participation from both parties involved in the communication. It fosters a sense of openness, encourages dialogue and promotes a collaborative environment where ideas and perspectives can be shared. By actively seeking and providing feedback, individuals can enhance their communication skills, build stronger connections and ensure that their message is accurately conveyed and understood.

We looked at feedback structures that you might use in 'The Message'. There is also the feedback you might be giving to your communication partner as a listener, the feedback your audience gives you and the feedback you may be giving unawares.

Active Listening – Communicating Through Listening

Be Aware of the Feedback You Are Providing to Others

Active listening plays a crucial role in the feedback process, one that the communicators can control. Active listening is a communication technique that involves fully focusing on, understanding and responding to the speaker, when you are the listener, or by both sender and receiver in a two-way conversation. Active listening will enrich your response when it is time for you to speak.

Misconceptions about active listening need to be addressed. It is important to recognise that active listening is an intentional process that requires genuine engagement, empathy and a thorough understanding of the speaker's message.

Active listening is often misunderstood as simply nodding, smiling or showing agreement without truly engaging with the speaker's message. However, active listening goes beyond passive agreement and involves actively processing and comprehending the information being conveyed.

Many people mistakenly believe that active listening simply means waiting for their turn to speak and formulating a response in their mind. However, it requires fully focusing on the speaker's words, without interrupting or interjecting prematurely. Undivided attention is given to the speaker; the listener should avoid multitasking and immerse themselves in the communication process. Active listening is not solely about memorising specific details or facts but involves understanding the overall message, intent and emotions conveyed by the speaker, as well as the underlying, possibly unspoken, meaning and context of the communication. While nonverbal cues like maintaining eye contact, nodding and using appropriate facial expressions are important components of active listening, they alone do not define active listening. True active listening involves mentally processing and internalising the speaker's message, rather than relying solely on nonverbal signals.

Here are some key elements and strategies for active listening:

–   Eliminate distractions and focus solely on what the speaker is saying. Maintain eye contact, lean forward slightly and show genuine interest in their words.

–   Put yourself in the speaker's shoes and listen with empathy and compassion, acknowledging the speaker's emotions; validate them. This helps to establish a connection and create a safe space for open communication.

–   Allow the speaker to express their thoughts fully without interrupting or interjecting. Interrupting can disrupt their flow and make them feel unheard or dismissed.

–   Nodding, smiling or using brief affirmations like 'I see' or 'hmm' indicates that you are actively engaged and encourages the speaker to continue sharing. Use appropriate body language and facial expressions to convey attentiveness.

–   Periodically summarise or paraphrase what the speaker has said to confirm your understanding. This technique helps to clarify any misunderstandings and ensures that you are on the same page.

- If something is unclear or you need further information, ask relevant and open-ended questions to seek clarification. This demonstrates your interest in understanding the speaker's message completely.

- Suspend judgement and refrain from making assumptions about the speaker or their message. Withhold any personal biases or preconceived notions.

- Pay attention not only to the speaker's words but also to the emotional undertones of their message. Try to understand the subtext and emotional context, as this can provide valuable insights into their communication.

- Provide thoughtful and relevant responses to the speaker's message. This may involve offering support, sharing your own perspective or asking follow-up questions to deepen the conversation.

- Sometimes, silence can be an essential part of active listening. Allow moments of silence for the speaker to gather their thoughts or express themselves fully. Avoid rushing or filling in the gaps with unnecessary comments.

- Let the speaker know that you are there to support them. Express your willingness to listen, offer help if appropriate and provide reassurance that their feelings and experiences are valid and important.

It's Written All Over Your Face!

Empathetic listening extends your focus beyond the immediate conversation to your surrounding environment; it is about being fully in the present moment, paying close attention to the speaker's emotions, body language and micro expressions. When practising empathetic listening, micro expressions displayed by the person you are speaking to can be valuable indicators of underlying emotions that may not be explicitly expressed in words. For example, a fleeting expression of sadness while discussing a seemingly positive topic might indicate unexpressed unease or discomfort. However, it's essential to remember that facial expressions should be considered in conjunction with other nonverbal and verbal cues, as well as the overall context of the communication. Micro expressions can provide valuable information, but they are just one piece of the puzzle. Being sensitive and respectful to the speaker's privacy is crucial, as not all expressions are intentionally revealed or meant to be interpreted, and you shouldn't publicly draw attention to them.

As a speaker, paying attention to your audience's subtle, and possibly unconscious, nonverbal cues is important. A slight furrowing of the eyebrows or a brief narrowing of the eyes may alert you to confusion, while a slight upward turn of the corners of the mouth, brief nod and slightly raised eyebrow may show agreement and connection. By observing these cues, you can adjust your communication. If you notice confusion, you can rephrase or elaborate on the point. Reinforce key ideas when you see agreement. Signs of boredom or disinterest should prompt you to modify your delivery style or pace. Being aware of nonverbal cues helps you create a more impactful and engaging experience for your audience.

We're not proposing you 'mask' your facial expressions, but sometimes, under stress, your body's instinct may be to display emotional cues more prominently, and this may be something you'd rather be in control of. If you worry that your face is 'leaking' information:

- Relaxation and release of tension are key to being able to approach communication in a neutral way; breathing can help you remain calm, and may help with any intense internal feeling that is being unconsciously exposed.

- If you find that your face is revealing something that you feel you mustn't say, it's important to explore the underlying reasons behind it. It could be a sign that you are feeling silenced or restricted in expressing yourself, which can manifest through your facial expressions. For example, as a teenager, maybe you rolled your eyes without realising it, belying frustration, anger, anxiety or distaste. When we don't have the opportunity to address an issue openly, these emotions can often surface on our faces. If this is the case, it can be helpful to identify the root of this sense of being silenced or restricted. Is it due to a specific work environment, cultural norms or personal dynamics? Once you understand the causes, you can begin to explore strategies to address them such as more support, being more assertive or striving to build a workplace environment in which you feel you can express yourself.

- Again, filming yourself in meetings is a great way of becoming conscious of what others see. Alternatively setting a goal of 'self-awareness' even just one day a week might be enough for you to become mindful of the messages conveyed by your facial expressions.

- Zone in on the speaker and actively listen; this will direct your focus from yourself to the speaker.

If you are concerned that your face isn't giving enough feedback, or you may have been told you are 'unreadable', work on active listening; shine your light onto the audience to listen empathetically rather than simply waiting to respond, and remember just because you are not speaking, you are still communicating. Tension is the most common cause of a 'frozen' or inexpressive face. If you have worked on the exercises in the book, you will already have explored and gained more mobility. Working on poetry is also a great way to let your 'message reach your face'. Engaging in reading material with vivid imagery and emotional content, such as poetry, can be remarkably effective in honing your ability to reflect the message through your facial expressions; you can develop a heightened sensitivity to the emotions conveyed and learn to subtly embody them. This practice can be particularly valuable when transitioning to delivering a presentation or speech. Facial mobility, in conjunction with vocal pitch and variety, plays a vital role in creating dynamic and expressive communication; as you express different emotions on your face, your vocal inflections and tones naturally follow suit.

While facial expressions are a significant part of nonverbal communication and can convey emotions and intentions, it is essential to understand that not everyone communicates or interprets facial expressions in the same way. Individuals with neurodiverse characteristics or conditions such as autism spectrum disorder may have different ways of expressing or perceiving emotions, which may not align with neurotypical expectations. It is crucial to approach communication with an open mind, respect for diversity and an understanding that different people may have varying styles of expressing themselves nonverbally. Sensitivity and empathy towards individual differences can foster more inclusive and effective communication, allowing for a broader range of expressions and interpretations beyond the neurotypical norm.

Silence the Critic on Your Shoulder!

Imagine you are standing on stage, delivering a great speech, in the zone, making great eye contact with the audience ... and you catch someone in the third row shaking their head and sighing ... suddenly you lose your thread, the heat starts to rise up your neck and your voice begins to shake ... the little voice on your shoulder says, 'Oh no, they're hating this. It's because you're boring and you don't know what you're talking about. You should give up'.

Whilst we can gain a lot from observing the feedback we are receiving from our audience during a presentation or speech, it can be so disheartening when you catch a less than enthusiastic facial expression or see someone with their arms firmly crossed. A little voice on your shoulder might tell you that you are doing a bad job and you might feel your confidence slipping away. This is a common but uncomfortable feeling which can throw you off track. 'Shooing', 'tickling' or 'shushing' the invisible critic sitting on your shoulder is a great way to overcome this challenge. Form a strong visual image of you brushing, or shooing, them off your shoulder and silencing them! Imagine using a water pistol or a cannon ball – whatever works. Yes, the critical thought is still in your mind, but you acknowledge it is not useful to you in this moment; you two can talk later! You might find it helpful to give your 'critic' a foolish costume, imagine them as a naughty child or give them a funny voice, so you can recognise they are silly and unhelpful.

Preparation is a great way to quiet the critic; before you speak, work on relaxation and breathing. Counter negative self-talk with positive affirmations grounded in truth that reinforce your confidence and abilities. Visualise yourself delivering a successful speech, with composure and an engaged audience, to boost your self-assurance. When negative thoughts arise, reframe them into more positive perspectives and remind yourself of your preparation and competence. Another helpful technique is to shift your focus from self-judgement to the needs and interests of your audience. By directing your attention outward, you can regain your momentum and engage with your listeners effectively. Finally, practice self-compassion and treat yourself kindly, understanding that mistakes are part of the learning process. If the inner critic persists, keep calmly acknowledging it and then 'shooing' it off your shoulder as a symbolic way to dismiss its influence and continue with confidence. With consistent practice, these strategies can help you silence the inner critic and deliver your speech with poise and conviction. While we know feedback from your audience is important, recognising that a single audience member's expression may have nothing to do with your speech at all – they may have a pressing worry, the beginnings of a migraine or a personal issue to deal with after your speech – can be extremely advantageous.

THE CONTEXT

The context refers to the circumstances, environment or situation in which the communication takes place. It encompasses various factors that influence how the message is created, transmitted, received and interpreted. It includes the physical setting, cultural and social norms, time, place and the relationship between the sender and the receiver. The context plays a significant role in shaping meaning and understanding of the message. It helps determine the appropriate language, tone and style of communication. For example, the way you communicate with your friends may well be different from how you communicate with your colleagues in a professional setting.

Understanding the context is crucial for effective communication because it helps ensure that the message is tailored to the specific situation and the needs of the receiver.

In the introduction to this book we explored the diverse range of professional voice users and their various contexts. Voice actors, radio hosts, podcasters and television presenters operate in different environments, both live and pre-recorded, whether in-person or remotely. They face the challenge of heavy vocal loading to captivate their audience, convey emotions effectively and deliver information with clarity, expression and emotion. Professionals engaged in public speaking, such as executives, politicians and motivational speakers, communicate with individuals one-on-one, address groups of colleagues and deliver compelling presentations across a variety of settings. In these situations, projecting confidence, clarity and authority through their vocal delivery is crucial.

Educators, trainers and instructors rely heavily on their voices to impart information in demanding environments such as classrooms or training sessions. They must inspire learners, maintain clarity, manage vocal variety and ensure their voices are healthy, audible and engaging.

In every professional role, there are variables in the context, and throughout any given day, multiple contexts may arise that require effective performance. Recognising and adapting to these varied contexts is essential for professional voice users to excel in their respective fields.

Self-Assessment and Building Awareness

This is a useful context checklist for you to use to define and respond to the context you will be working in. Regular use of a list like this will help with preparation, reduce unwanted surprises and improve confidence on the day.

- What is the purpose of the event?
- What is the event format (conference, workshop, panel discussion, etc.)?
- How much time will be allocated for your presentation?
- Who is your audience (demographics, background, knowledge level)?
- What are their expectations or what are your desired outcomes for your presentation?
- Are there any specific challenges or concerns you should be aware of?
- What is the size and layout of the venue? Will you be able to visit beforehand?
- Is there any audio-visual equipment available? Are there any technical requirements? Will you be able to practise before the event?

Continued

- Is there anything unique about the venue that may affect your delivery (acoustics, lighting, etc.)?
- What key messages or takeaways do you aim to communicate?
- Are there any specific subjects or examples you should include or avoid?
- How confident are you with the subject matter? Do you need to conduct additional research or gather more information?
- Are there any specific points or areas you want to emphasise or focus on? How will these considerations shape your speech, and does your structure align with their significance?
- Have you communicated with the event organisers regarding their expectations?
- Are there any specific guidelines or requirements you need to adhere to?
- Is there a specific tone or style they prefer for the event?
- How much time do you need to set aside to prepare?
- Would you like to practise your delivery? If so, how many times?
- Do you have a plan to manage any potential nervousness or anxiety?
- How much time are you able to commit to warming up or preparing just before the event?
- Will you be able to find a private space to prepare?
- Are there any specific techniques or strategies you plan to use for effective delivery?
- Will there be an opportunity for audience feedback or evaluation? Will there be a Q&A session?
- How will you measure the success of your presentation?
- What steps will you take to reflect on your performance and improve for future events?

Key Context and Communication Guidelines

It is impossible to cover every eventuality for professional voice users, as there are as many possible contexts as there are professional voice users, but the suggested scenarios below should give you a good example of how to assess and prepare for your own speaking context.

Presentations and Speeches

When speaking at a conference or large event, there are several key contextual considerations to keep in mind:

Audience	Tailor your content, language and examples to resonate with them and meet their values, specific needs and expectations.
Topic Selection	If speaking at an event, ensure your presentation adds value and provides insights or solutions related to the conference focus. Are there questions that are seeking to be answered? What might other delegates be speaking about?
Clear Objective	Clearly define the purpose and objective of your presentation. What do you want your audience to learn, understand or take away from your talk? Structure your content and delivery to align with your objective.
Preparation	Develop a clear and logical structure for your presentation, incorporating key points and supporting evidence. Practise your delivery to ensure a smooth and confident performance. Ensure you have water.
Time	Respect the allocated time for your presentation. Practise and time your delivery to ensure that you can cover all the essential points within the given time frame and to avoid rushing or exceeding the allotted time. Look at the clock when you begin so that you are aware of what time you start.
Engaging Opening	Capture the audience's attention from the start with a compelling opening. Use a powerful anecdote, a thought-provoking question or a surprising fact to pique their interest and set the tone for your presentation.
Organised Structure	Organise your content in a logical and coherent manner. Use a clear introduction, well-defined key points and a conclusion. Create smooth transitions between sections to guide your audience through the presentation.
Visual Aids	Utilise visual aids to enhance your presentation. Keep them visually appealing, concise and supportive of your key points. Ensure any your visual aids are clear, well designed and support the key points of your presentation without overwhelming the audience. Avoid overcrowding slides with excessive text. Avoid turning your back to read them; glance at them to trigger your memory.
Engaging Delivery	Speak with enthusiasm, energy and confidence. Consider posture. Use appropriate vocal variation, intonation and pacing to keep the audience engaged. Make eye contact with individuals throughout the room to create a connection.
Body Language	Pay attention to your body language. Stand tall, maintain an open posture and use natural gestures to convey your message. Move purposefully around the stage or speaking area to command attention and create visual interest.

Audience Interaction	If appropriate, encourage audience participation and interaction. Incorporate activities, questions or discussions to keep the audience engaged and involved. This can include Q&A sessions, audience polls, group activities or case studies. Encourage participation and create opportunities for discussion.
Adaptability	Be prepared to adapt to unexpected situations or changes in the presentation environment. Stay flexible and responsive to the audience's needs and feedback. Address questions or concerns promptly and adjust your approach if necessary.
Closing Impact	End your presentation with a strong and memorable closing. Summarise the key points, provide a clear takeaway message and leave the audience with a call to action, a thought-provoking question or a compelling story that reinforces your main ideas.
Q&A and Feedback	Be prepared to answer questions after your presentation. Anticipate potential questions and have thoughtful responses ready. Embrace feedback from the audience and use it as an opportunity for growth and improvement.
Networking Opportunities	Connect with attendees, fellow speakers and industry professionals. Be approachable, open to conversations and ready to share insights beyond your presentation.
Post-Talk Feedback	Follow up with interested attendees, exchange contact information. Communicate with organisers or attendees to gain insights for improvement and future engagements.
Professionalism	Dress appropriately, be punctual and show respect to other speakers and attendees. Be prepared to adapt to unforeseen circumstances and handle any technical or logistical challenges gracefully.

Even if formal speeches are not a regular part of your professional role, it is crucial to prioritise preparation. Simply hoping to come up with something on the spot will not suffice. The fear of speaking diminishes once you begin preparing. With adequate preparation, your voice will remain controlled and confident. It is natural to experience some tension or stage fright, which can be beneficial as it provides an adrenaline rush and sharpens your wits.

Teaching, Training and Workshops

Manage Your Environment	Are you able to maintain level eye contact with your group, is the room acoustically suitable for you to speak easily and to manage noise control? Consider any adjustments to seating or set up you need to make. Be sure not to disappear behind a desk, move around the space and encourage participants to do so if appropriate. Be mindful of any physical limitations or disabilities that individuals may have and aim for accommodations for accessibility and inclusivity.

Clear Communication	Use clear and concise language, avoid jargon or unnecessarily complex terms that might be confusing. Provide explanations, examples and visual aids to enhance understanding.
Active Listening	Pay attention to any concerns, ideas and contributions. Show empathy and understanding, creating an inclusive and supportive environment.
Nonverbal Cues	Convey enthusiasm, interest and attentiveness, creating a positive learning atmosphere.
Engaging Delivery	Vary your tone, pace and volume to maintain interest and attention. Incorporate storytelling, real-life examples, multimedia resources and interactive activities to make the content engaging and relatable.
Clarity of Expectations	Clearly communicate your expectations regarding conduct, participation and performance. Set clear goals and objectives for each session.
Adaptability	Different students have different learning styles and preferences. Consider incorporating a variety of teaching methods, such as visual, auditory and kinaesthetic techniques, to cater to diverse learning needs.
Positive Reinforcement	Provide constructive feedback, encouragement and praise to students. Acknowledge their efforts, progress and achievements. Foster a positive and supportive environment that motivates students to actively participate and learn.
Empathy and Respect	Demonstrate empathy and respect towards students. Show genuine care for their well-being, interests and challenges. Create a safe and inclusive space where students feel comfortable expressing their thoughts, asking questions and seeking help.
Two-Way Communication	Encourage open dialogue and two-way communication. Create opportunities for students to ask questions, share ideas and engage in discussions.
Vocal Health	Ensure you are well hydrated all day and take opportunities for vocal rest. Use visual props to attract the groups attention to limit excessive volume.

Facilitating or Hosting a Meeting

Agenda and Structure	Prepare a well-organised agenda with specific topics, allotted time for each item and a logical flow. Share the agenda in advance with participants.
Participant Engagement	Encourage active participation from all attendees, invite different perspectives and ensure everyone has an opportunity to contribute to the discussion.
Time Management	Keep the meeting on track and manage time effectively. Ensure you can see a clock.

Communication	Clearly and concisely communicate the purpose, expectations and desired outcomes of the meeting. Encourage open and respectful communication among participants.
Techniques	Guide the discussion and maintain a productive atmosphere, use brainstorming, consensus-building and decision-making processes. Be vigilant for any conflicts that may arise and manage them effectively.
Active Listening	Actively listen to participants' input, ideas and concerns. Demonstrate attentive listening through nonverbal cues, paraphrasing and asking clarifying questions.
Visual Aids and Materials	Use visual aids, such as slides or handouts to enhance understanding and provide visual support.
Meeting Etiquette	Set clear expectations for meeting etiquette, such as speaking in turn, avoiding interruptions and respecting diverse viewpoints. Address any disruptive behaviour.
Decision-Making Process	Establish a clear process for reaching consensus or making final determinations. Ensure that decisions are well documented and communicated to participants.
Follow-Up and Action Items	Summarise key discussion points, decisions made and action items at the end of the meeting. Assign responsibilities, set deadlines and follow up on progress.
Continuous Improvement	Seek feedback from participants on the meeting process and facilitation. Use this feedback to improve future meetings and adjust as needed.

Networking Events

Clear Objectives	Define your objectives for the networking event. Are you looking to make new connections, promote your business or gather information?
Elevator Pitch	Prepare a concise and compelling elevator pitch to introduce yourself and your work. Clearly articulate who you are, what you do and the value you offer.
Active Listening	Show genuine interest in others by asking open-ended questions, actively listening to their responses and demonstrating attentiveness.
Authenticity and Professionalism	Be authentic and genuine in your interactions while maintaining a professional demeanour. Be respectful, courteous and mindful of your body language and tone of voice.
Networking Etiquette	Introduce yourself with a confident handshake, maintain good eye contact, be aware of personal space, avoid interrupting others, ask open-ended questions and engage in professional conversations. Be mindful of dominating any conversations.
Value	Focus on creating value in your conversations. Offer insights and share relevant information. Look for ways to build mutually beneficial relationships.

Follow-Up	Consider sending personal follow-up emails or LinkedIn invitations to continue the conversation and maintain the connection.
Preparation	Research attendees and speakers to facilitate meaningful conversations. Knowledge and context can help you engage in more targeted and relevant discussions.
Impression	Dress appropriately and comfortably for the event, consider your language and communication style and present yourself as a professional in your field.
Positive Attitude	Maintain a positive and approachable attitude throughout the event. Show warmth and enthusiasm and be open to new connections and opportunities.
Follow Event Guidelines	Respect event organisers' instructions, adhere to timeframes for activities and be mindful of any designated networking areas or formats.

Virtual Communication

The exponential increase in digital communication during the past decades has altered the balance between verbal and written communication that we engage in, reducing the verbal content and increasing the written or digital element. Digital advancements have revolutionised communication and technology has transformed the way we interact. Even medical consultations have shifted to online platforms, reducing the need for face-to-face visits. Many individuals prefer texting over phone calls and experience varying levels of unease or annoyance when receiving calls.

The increasing reliance on digital communication methods can contribute to, or reinforce, anxiety around in-person communication. Digital platforms offer benefits such as the ability to review and edit communication, reduced pressure for immediate responses and limited social cues to process, making them more comfortable for some individuals. The COVID-19 pandemic further impacted mental health and increased social anxiety for many people. Disrupted routines, physical distancing measures and a shift to remote work and online interactions reduced face-to-face connections and introduced new challenges into negotiating social situations. These changes, coupled with the need for virtual interactions, being 'on camera' and interpreting social cues through screens, added to the desire for stress-free, calm and effective spoken communication.

Technology has both positive and negative impacts on speaking skills. Virtual communication platforms enable interactions across distances, enhancing communication skills and exposure to different accents, languages and cultures. However, relying heavily on digital communication can reduce face-to-face interactions and diminish the practice of in-person conversation, affecting speaking skills. Children's increased screen time and passive engagement can limit their expressive abilities and erode their range of expression. This can lead to communication difficulties when they enter school. The pandemic's social distancing measures have also impacted adults' communication, causing, for some, feelings of social awkwardness, decreased fluency and reduced confidence in speaking due to the lack of regular interactions. For others, the shift to remote working and virtual platforms meant they were required to participate more actively in verbal expression, and many became comfortable with digital communication in a way they hadn't been previously. People adapted to video calls and online meetings, actively participating in discussions and presentations. Some individuals sought out alternative methods like online communities or virtual educational programmes to maintain verbal communication and improve their speaking skills.

To mitigate any negative impact of increased remote working on their speaking skills, individuals should actively seek face-to-face conversations, engage in public speaking opportunities and spend time developing their 'working voice'. Balancing digital communication with real-world interactions is essential for maintaining and improving speaking skills comprehensively.

Lights, Camera, Action

The visibility of the speaker plays a crucial role in effective communication and understanding. Consider the impact when a lecturer faces away from the audience or a presenter solely focuses on their PowerPoint slides with their back to the room. How much do we miss of their message? How quickly do we lose interest?

In the context of online meetings and presentations, having your camera on can greatly enhance the delivery and retention of information. It shows your active presence and engagement. As a listener, turning your camera on can be seen as an act of generosity, ensuring the speaker feels supported and not as if they're speaking into an empty room or void. However, it is important to acknowledge digital fatigue as a real issue for many individuals. If you're feeling fatigued, it is crucial to prioritise self-care and take breaks from being on camera, if possible and permitted in your company culture. Fatigue can affect your vocal delivery and undermine your confidence. Each organisation may have different guidelines for online meetings, and it is essential to adhere to them accordingly.

When experiencing digital fatigue, here are some strategies to consider:

- **Turn off self-view:** constantly seeing your own image on the screen can increase self-consciousness and impact your confidence. By disabling the self-view option you can focus more on the content and interaction without being overly conscious of yourself. The way we view ourselves in digital spaces can influence how much we interact, how we present ourselves and our overall communication effectiveness.

- **Check in on areas of tension:** pay attention to any physical discomfort or tension in your body. Take short breaks to stretch, relax your muscles and release any built-up tension. Being physically comfortable can contribute to better focus and engagement.

- **Stay hydrated and ensure comfort:** drink water and maintain proper hydration levels throughout online meetings. Also, make sure you are seated in a comfortable ergonomic chair with good posture to prevent unnecessary discomfort or distractions.

- **Look away from the screen:** give your eyes a break by periodically looking away from the screen. Set your gaze on something in the distance, allowing your eyes to refocus and rest from the constant digital display. This can help reduce eye strain and provide a refreshing change of perspective, keep your energy up and help you to actively participate.

- **Consider using a standing desk or changing locations:** if feasible, try using a standing desk during online meetings or endeavour to switch locations within your workspace. Changing your physical position can promote blood circulation, increase energy levels and prevent excessive sedentary behaviour.

Remember, it is important to find a balance between optimising virtual interactions and taking care of your physical and mental well-being. Implementing these strategies can help create a more natural and meaningful meeting experience while prioritising your overall health.

The Picture

When considering digital communication, there are several contextual factors to consider:

- **Technology and platform:** familiarise yourself with the functionalities of your platform, such as chat features, 'hand' gestures, screen-sharing and document collaboration. Understanding the technology you are using will help you navigate the digital environment and the opportunities for communication available to you effectively.

- **Audience and purpose:** consider who your audience is and the purpose of your communication. Are you communicating with colleagues, clients or a larger audience? Is it formal, informal, a presentation or a collaborative project? Tailor your communication style, tone and content to ensure your message resonates with the intended audience.

- **Communication and expectations:** consider the cultural and professional context in which you are communicating. Different industries, organisations or regions may have specific guidelines or expectations for digital communication, including camera-use and level of participation.

- **Environment and distractions:** create an appropriate digital environment for communication. Choose a quiet and well-lit space with minimal distractions. Consider whether using a virtual background feels authentic to you. Minimise interruptions and distractions, such as notifications, background noise or visual clutter, to maintain focus and engagement.

The Big, or Small, Picture

Carefully curating your image on screen can help you to shape perceptions, control distractions and project a polished and engaging virtual presence. The look of the 'window into your world' can ensure attention remains focused on your face and your content. Blurring your background during an online meeting can be a personal or practical choice. While it can create a sense of detachment or disconnection by removing environmental context, some find it helpful in minimising distractions and maintaining privacy. For others, the digital frame they occupy on the screen offers a glimpse into their world and can be used as a canvas for self-expression. By carefully selecting personal items, décor or background visuals, individuals can add touches of their interests, hobbies or unique style to their video frame. This allows them to infuse their personality into the digital space, fostering a sense of connection and authenticity with others. By showcasing glimpses of who they are beyond their professional roles, individuals can foster a more vibrant and human connection with their virtual audience.

- Ensure that you have adequate lighting in front of you, preferably natural light from a window or a well-positioned artificial light source. Avoid having a bright light source behind you, as it can create a silhouette effect and make your features unclear.

- Position your camera at eye level or slightly above. This helps to avoid unflattering angles and minimises the appearance of double chins or distorted facial features! Consider using a laptop stand or a separate webcam if needed.

- Avoid wearing overly distracting patterns or colours that may not translate well on camera. Pay attention to grooming and personal presentation to convey your desired image.

- Maintain good posture to appear engaged and confident. Make eye contact with the camera rather than constantly looking at your own video feed. Use hand gestures and facial expressions appropriately to enhance your communication.

- Test your audio and video settings before the meeting to ensure clear and crisp audio quality. Use headphones or a dedicated microphone if needed. Check your internet connection to avoid disruptions or lag during the call.

Making eye contact with the camera during virtual meetings can feel strange, as it requires looking directly into the lens rather than at the faces on the screen. In a live setting, listeners naturally provide visual feedback to the speaker, such as nodding, smiling or other facial expressions, which can encourage the speaker and demonstrate active listening. When we stare at the camera without any visual feedback, it can create a disconnect between the speaker and listener, potentially reducing the speaker's motivation and affecting the overall dynamics of the conversation. Without visual feedback and natural interaction, our vocal variety and expressiveness may be diminished. On the other hand, for the audience, when you make eye contact with the camera it creates a sense of connection as they perceive you are looking directly at them.

Suggestions and Strategies

- Move the video window as close as possible to the camera so that the faces on the screen are closer to your line of sight and you appear to be looking in the direction of your listener. This can create a more natural eye contact experience.

- Looking directly into the camera may be sustainable for a presentation, but not useful for a conversation. For those coaching or teaching, or as a health practitioner online, it may be more important to have visual feedback from your audience/client.

- If you choose to make eye contact with the camera visualise the faces of the participants as if they were behind the lens; imagine that you are looking directly at them as you speak. You should also shift your gaze occasionally to check participants' reactions or engage with them. Return your focus to the camera periodically to maintain that connection. The more you practise, the more comfortable you will become with making eye contact with the camera. Over time, it will feel more natural and become a regular part of your virtual communication.

Non-Verbal Communication on Camera

Visual communication is a crucial aspect of effective virtual communication. It is essential to remember the power of gestures and body language. Even though your audience may not be physically present, using gestures can help convey meaning, add emphasis and maintain engagement. Gestures such as hand movements, facial expressions and body posture, can enhance the clarity and impact of your message. They provide visual cues that complement your verbal communication and make your presentation more dynamic and engaging. When you use gestures while speaking, it activates your body, and this too translates to your voice. This increased physical engagement can lead to improved resonance, clarity and overall vocal variety. Gestures can help you express emotions, emphasise key points and create a sense of rhythm and flow in your speech. They provide a dynamic connection between your words, body and voice, making your communication more compelling and expressive.

Virtual Voice

When it comes to presenting in an online meeting, the fundamental principles of effective communication remain consistent with in-person settings. However, there are additional considerations that come into play.

- Remember that your voice is amplified in the online setting, so you don't need to shout or raise your volume excessively. However, it is important to maintain an energetic and dynamic delivery. Even though you have the assistance of a microphone, your enthusiasm and energy will still play a significant role in capturing and holding the audience's attention.

Maintain a lively and engaging tone throughout your presentation to keep listeners interested and connected to your message.

- Online participants may already be experiencing screen fatigue or have been attending back-to-back meetings throughout the day. By utilising vocal variety, you can inject energy and keep their attention. Avoid falling into a monotonous tone, pace or volume, which can lead to disengagement and a loss of interest. Instead, strive to infuse your voice with enthusiasm, expressiveness and variation in pitch, tone and volume. Use emphasis and pause effectively and modulate your voice to convey different emotions and intentions.

- Mute your microphone when not speaking and familiarise yourself with how to turn it on and off! It lends a false quality to speech because we can't just chip in as we would in an in-person conversation, but background noise can be very distracting, and starting to speak whilst on mute can make you feel embarrassed and affect your delivery when you can be heard.

- Microphones follow the rule of 'rubbish in, rubbish out'. A microphone is not necessarily the solution for lack of clarity as it may merely make you mumble more loudly! Microphones can also enhance aspects of our speech which we wouldn't hear if we weren't amplified. 'Mouth sounds', often referred to as 'clicks', 'pops', or 'smacks', are unwanted noises that can occur, and be exaggerated, through a microphone, whether you are at a conference, on a podcast or recording a voiceover. The more you use a microphone, the more aware of them you become! These sounds are often due to a dry mouth and what may feel like 'sticky' or 'thick' saliva. In general, hydration is the solution. If dryness persists despite good hydration it is worth consulting your GP. Bear in mind sedatives, muscle relaxants, antihistamines, anticholinergic agents, diuretics, antidepressants, blood pressure and pain medications can all contribute to a dry mouth.

- Record and review: set up a practice presentation and record yourself delivering it. Then, watch the recording and assess your performance. Take note of areas in which you feel you can improve, such as body language, vocal tone, clarity of speech; be specific with your feedback so you can make incremental changes.

- Time yourself: if you have to present within a time limit, practise delivering your presentation within a specific time frame to avoid

Continued

rushing or going over the allotted time. Ensure you are relaxed, breathing well and warmed up.

- Conduct mock Q&A sessions: enlist the help of a colleague or friend to simulate a Q&A session after your presentation. Practise responding to various types of questions, maintaining clarity and confidence in your answers.

- Observe: observe others during online interactions and create your own 'advice' for best practice online communication.

- Collaborate: host a training session for your colleagues to facilitate open discussions and exchange insights on effective online communication. Encourage feedback and tips for improving virtual communication. Foster a supportive and engaging communication culture within your team.

Introducing and Thanking Speakers

You may be comfortable delivering your own material, but at a conference or similar event, be given the responsibility to introduce or thank another speaker. Prior research on the speaker's background, achievements and connection to the organisation or industry should be included in the introduction. When expressing gratitude, take notes during the speech and highlight the most memorable points in the concluding remarks. Even informal occasions like introducing a guest speaker can generate tension for the person officiating. To alleviate this, self-help strategies can be implemented. The speech should be practised multiple times, preferably in front of a real 'audience' such as a partner or colleague. It is essential to practise aloud rather than silently or in one's head. If practising with an audience is not possible, recording the speech using a mobile phone can help with feedback, although it lacks the experience of communicating with live listeners. During rehearsals, focus on maintaining proper alignment and weight distribution, standing firmly yet relaxed and occupying the space with confidence. It is generally recommended not to carry a large number of papers to the podium; instead, bullet points on index cards or a tablet with notes can be more manageable. It's advisable to avoid memorising the speech word-for-word but have notes as a guide for prompts in case of any anxious slips. When delivering the speech, make direct eye contact with the audience, engaging with various individuals without fixating on one person. Allow for pauses to let important points sink in and maintain your natural vocal energy and intonation. Remember that minor mistakes are not catastrophic; as the audience is typically supportive and wants you to succeed. If making speeches is a regular part of your role or if you wish to improve your skills, as we have already mentioned, you could consider joining organisations like Toastmasters, debating clubs or speaking clubs to further develop your abilities.

This chapter has explored some of the various aspects of effective communication. We began by looking at the Communicators, the part the individual plays in communication and acknowledging that nervousness is natural, and shared some strategies to manage it, of which there are more in Chapter 3, 'Relaxation and Release of Tension', emphasising the importance of preparation and practice. Next, we looked at the message itself, and discussed the significance of speech structure, emphasising the value of clear organisation for the audience. 'The Medium' considered techniques to help your voice carry the message, and we then looked at body language as a powerful aspect of communication, influencing how messages are perceived. We explored the significance of posture, gesture, eye contact and facial expression in conveying confidence and engagement. Intensive work on 'The Channel' – the voice and body – can be done using the information and material in Chapters 2 to 10. 'The Noise' – psychological, physical and technical – was investigated, and 'The Feedback' was identified as a crucial tool for improvement. We emphasised the importance of active listening, empathetic understanding and validation when providing feedback, and how to monitor self-criticism and process feedback you receive when speaking.

We considered the diverse contexts of communication, particularly digital communication and highlighted the importance of adapting to digital platforms, including managing technical aspects, maintaining visual presence and balancing real-world interactions with digital communication.

Conclusion

The context in which the information, exercises, strategies and solutions outlined in this book will be applied will be different for each reader, depending on the specific vocal and communication demands that you encounter. The essential work undertaken by those who choose to enter the world of the 'working voice' is reliant on a flexible and free vocal mechanism and on the ability to convert thoughts and ideas into sounds, words and language. The fact that we take our voices so much for granted, and generally think about them only when they do not work effectively, is an indication of the general resilience of the voice and the synchronicity of thought and speech. When a problem does occur, it is often the result of an altered balance between the production of voice and the effort levels required to sustain easy and effortless voicing.

This book will have been successful if, through its cocktail of information, it helps to steer professional voice users towards a greater understanding of their own voice and acts as a lifelong resource. Our aim is to provide the necessary support, information and guidance to allow you to remain for as long as you want in your role – that of a professional voice user.

Appendices

Appendix A: Your Voice Profile   302

Appendix B: Voice Diary   312

Appendix C: Voice Care Recommendations   312

Appendix D: Voice Warm-up   314

APPENDIX A: YOUR VOICE PROFILE

The Voice Profile was designed to provide a tool which will allow you to examine potential areas of vulnerability or challenges that may contribute to your overall vocal quality. It offers you a point-in-time visual profile and may also be used to provide robust visual reinforcement of change over time as you use it to chart change.

You can download or photocopy the Voice Profile and use it to record your vocal quality at a specific time, examining how certain factors within the overarching categories of physical health, mental health and environmental health may be contributing to producing, sustaining and varying your voice in order to communicate effectively. This will allow you to evaluate the possible impact of each factor in terms of its collective contribution to, or maintenance of, a voice problem and its effect or influence on communication in general.

The Voice Profile is not a therapeutic tool, but it can be used to provide a concrete method of identifying specific areas of concern. Completing the Voice Profile on subsequent occasions will allow you to note changes in voice quality and vocal performance over time and offer you a tool with which to consider the impact of certain components of your communicative style and vocal effectiveness and thus refocus your attention over time.

As this book has shown, voice is an amalgam of a number of different factors used to produce, sustain and vary voice in order to communicate effectively. If we accept the dependency and interdependency of these factors, then to single out one specific factor or another as the cause of a problem would, self-evidently, be to miss the point. It is important to be aware of all contributory factors within our vocal environment to properly evaluate the possible impact of each factor in terms of its collective contribution to, or maintenance of, a voice problem.

While our perspective in this book is on the 'working' voice rather than the 'problem' voice, we are examining measures you can take to prepare your voice for the extensive work it does in withstanding the demands of your occupational role. We are looking to suggest measures you can take to prevent problems and offer solutions. For that reason, we have isolated and highlighted factors that may affect or influence communication in general and voice in particular. Some of the questions may be similar to those that are contained in the self-awareness questions in each chapter, but the Voice Profile does not negate those questionnaires, rather it provides a composite picture of your voice.

The Voice Profile examines the potential impact of a number of specific factors on the voice. These factors are addressed before each set of questions in ten different sections:

- Section 1 **General Health**
- Section 2 **Vocal History**
- Section 3 **Vocal Health**
- Section 4 **Vocal Care**
- Section 5 **Vocal Demand**
- Section 6 **Vocal Status**
- Section 7 **Voice Genogram**
- Section 8 **Anxiety and Stress**
- Section 9 **Social Functioning**
- Section 10 **Environment**

The following points summarise the main attributes of the VP, which:

- Provides a stand-alone, 'at a glance' screening tool which you can complete in your own time.
- May be used as a template for achieving change in a specific area of vulnerability such as voice use in an occupational setting.
- Provides a method of focusing on what you feel is of concern.
- Provides a way of confirming change in several areas within your physical and vocal environment.
- May be used to self-assess vocal change.

As you go through the questions, simply tick the yes or no square in each section. Once you have completed each section then count all the 'yes' responses and, using the Voice Profile sheet, hatch the squares related to the section. As you complete the sheet you will see in which sections you've recorded the most responses and so your personal profile emerges.

Section 1: General Health

Questions in this section relate to your medical history and your current health status. The aim of the questions is to collate information on health issues that may affect or compromise voice production.

Many health factors have the potential to adversely affect the vocal tract and voice production in general for example:

- Various medications may have an adverse effect on the vocal tract.
- Discomfort or pain from various disorders or poor habitual posture may have a negative influence on posture and spinal alignment. Similarly,

303

flattening of the lumbar spine results in flattening of the diaphragm and reduced airflow, with the ensuing negative impact on voice production.

- The use of inhaled corticosteroids may be a causative factor in bowing of the vocal folds due to steroid-induced dyskinesia. Dyskinesia is the name given to involuntary, erratic, writhing movements of the face, legs and trunk which may also cause extended muscle spasms of the intrinsic laryngeal musculature. An additional factor may be a lack of proper attention to vocal hygiene, for example, not gargling after using your inhaler, which can cause oral thrush.

- Hoarseness after cardiac surgery, although it is often transient, is a common occurrence. Following cardiac surgery, patients may limit the movement of the ribcage in an attempt to reduce post-operative pain. This can become habitual, with obvious effects on their breathing method and, therefore, on their voice production.

	Section 1: General Health	Yes	No
1.	Do you take any medications regularly (e.g., blood pills, HRT, anti-depressants)?		
2.	Do you have any allergies?		
3.	Do you have any joint or muscle problems?		
4.	Have you any mobility problems?		
5.	Do you have any chest problems affecting your breathing?		
6.	Do you have asthma?		
7.	Do you regularly use inhalers?		
8.	Are you ever short of breath?		
9.	Do you have recurring viral illness (e.g., postviral fatigue syndrome, Long Covid)		
10.	Have you ever had open-heart surgery?		

Section 2: Vocal History

Questions in this section relate to your vocal history. The aim of the questions is to collate information on factors which could be implicated in the onset of a voice disorder, whether in the recent or long-term history. The questions focus on the severity of voice loss, its impact on your activities and any previous advice or treatment you may have been given.

Numerous physical factors may contribute to disorders in the vocal tract and a voice disorder, such as:

- Infections of the nose, sinus passages, pharynx or any part of the upper respiratory tract can lead to acute or chronic inflammation, dryness and irritation in the vocal tract and generalised fatigue.
- Any reduction in hearing acuity, or perception, may result in an adjustment to the way in which you produce voice.
- Surgical procedures or traumatic injury to the larynx may have a good surgical outcome; it doesn't preclude inadequate or ill-advised voice use in the post-operative period.

	Section 2: Vocal History	Yes	No
1.	Have you ever noticed any change in the way your voice sounds?		
2.	Were you ever hoarse as a child?		
3.	Have you ever completely lost your voice?		
4.	Do you often have throat infections?		
5.	Have you ever had any surgery to your throat?		
6.	Have you ever had a traumatic injury to your throat?		
7.	Have you any recurring ear, nose or throat problems?		
8.	Has a problem with your voice ever limited your activities?		
9.	Have you ever sought advice from anyone regarding your voice?		
10.	Have you ever had speech and language therapy due to a problem with your voice?		

Section 3: Vocal Health

Questions in this section relate to your current vocal health. The aim of the questions is to collate information on the condition of the vocal tract with reference to irritation, increased secretions, throat-clearing, discomfort, a feeling of a 'lump in the throat', recurring gastroesophageal reflux, laryngeal pain, discomfort, dryness, coughing, swallowing difficulties or whether it takes you a lot of effort to talk. While these may not make it difficult for you to be understood, as vocal quality may be largely unaffected, they can negatively impact on your quality of life, and they are very often early indicators of a vocal tract disorder.

	Section 3: Vocal Health	Yes	No
1.	Do you have a hoarse voice?		
2.	Does your throat or mouth feel dry?		
3.	Do you often want to clear your throat?		
4.	Do you regularly have a lot of catarrh?		

5.	Do you regularly have gastroesophageal reflux (e.g., heartburn or indigestion)?		
6.	Do you ever feel as if you have a lump in your throat?		
7.	Do you ever feel tension or constriction in your throat?		
8.	Does your voice ever feel tired?		
9.	Do you feel any pain or discomfort when you use your voice?		
10.	Does it take a lot of effort to talk?		

Section 4: Voice Care

Questions in this section relate to your vocal care. The aim of the questions is to collate information on voice care issues that may affect or compromise voice production such as misuse of the voice through shouting, smoking, alcohol or caffeine intake, lack of hydration, dietary habits and lack of awareness of voice care.

Vocal care is closely related to vocal health, with certain aspects from each being interrelated. For many, voice care is frequently considered very little, or not considered at all. Voice is not anything that is really thought about until it goes wrong, so preserving the voice is not an issue people think about; they open their mouth and voice comes out! When the voice becomes challenged, however, certain habits need to be considered and we hope that as you've read through this book certain previously neglected aspects of voice care have emerged for you to think about.

	Section 4: Voice Care	Yes	No
1.	Do you smoke?		
2.	Do you drink a lot of tea, coffee or other drinks containing caffeine?		
3.	Do you drink less than two litres of water a day?		
4.	Do you frequently eat dairy produce and/or carbohydrates?		
5.	Do you frequently eat hot and spicy food?		
6.	Do you often shout?		
7.	Do you often use your voice when you have a sore throat?		
8.	Are you ever hoarse after a night out?		
9.	Do you worry about your voice?		
10.	Do you feel you neglect to care for your voice?		

Section 5: Vocal Demand

Questions in this section relate to the vocal demands you may experience. The aim of the questions is to collate information related to incremental voice care over time and to allow you to assess the extent and nature of your vocal load.

The relationship between heavy vocal demand and the potential for vocal misuse has been recognised by professional voice users for many years. The following critical risk factors, associated with excessive vocal load are:

– The length of exposure – time.
– The frequency of vibration – pitch.
– The vocal loudness – acceleration of the tissues of the vocal folds.

For some of you, despite the heavy vocal demands made on your voice you'll be able to sustain phonation without compromising quality. Fifty years ago, Morton Cooper (1973) said, 'Voice disorders are not due to overuse of the voice; they are due to misuse and abuse of the voice. A voice well used is essentially never overused'. A very encouraging message, for those willing to put in the time to look after their voice!

	Section 5: Vocal Demand	Yes	No
1.	Do you use your voice a lot at home or at work?		
2.	Do you have to speak for long periods without rest?		
3.	Do you feel that you use your voice too much?		
4.	Do you put too many demands on your voice?		
5.	Do you have to talk over background noise (e.g., children, television, music, equipment)?		
6.	Would you have to leave your current occupation if you lost your voice?		
7.	Have you ever had to change your job because of a problem with your voice?		
8.	Do you regularly meet with anyone who is hard of hearing?		
9.	Do you feel that your voice deteriorates the more you use it?		
10.	Does your voice recover with voice rest?		

Section 6: Vocal Status

Questions in this section relate to your vocal status issues which might affect or compromise voice production. The aim of this section is to collate information on your perception of your vocal quality, adequacy, stamina and flexibility in all types of voice use.

This section is all about your perception of how your voice has changed.

	Section 6: Vocal Status	Yes	No
1.	Do you feel that your voice has altered over the past year?		
2.	Do you feel that your voice has altered in loudness?		
3.	Do you feel that your voice has altered in pitch?		
4.	Does your voice quality vary during the day?		
5.	Do you feel that your voice is less flexible than it used to be?		
6.	Does your voice ever break?		
7.	When you speak or sing, are you ever uncertain about how your voice will sound?		
8.	Do you frequently find it difficult to make yourself heard?		
9.	Are you unhappy with how your voice sounds?		
10.	Do people ever comment adversely on your voice?		

Section 7: Voice Genogram

Questions in this section relate to your voice genogram. The aim of the questions is to collate information about aspects that might affect or compromise voice use, such as family and cultural values and social training.

Family and cultural values and social training determine your view of yourself and how you relate to those around you. Your voice serves to reflect not only your emotional state and personality but also your physical state and your previous life history and experience.

For most, voice is a valued and central part of your identity, whether this is your natural voice or perhaps the voice that you have found for yourself. The voice reflects your emotional and personality characteristics.

This section also looks at your current lifestyle and personality but also examines what previous experiences have shaped your world view and your view of yourself. Even small changes in the manner or production of speech will influence vocal quality. As an example, extensive or invasive orthodontic treatment may limit mouth opening and result in altered oral resonance. Changes in the manner and place of articulation, either because of a phonological disorder or arising from the use of different phonemes when speaking in a different language, may impose changes in the resonance of your voice, so this needs to be considered.

	Section 7: Voice Genogram	Yes	No
1.	Do you feel that your voice does not match your personality?		
2.	Have you ever wished that you had a different personality?		
3.	Do you dislike your own voice?		
4.	Did you ever alter your own accent to blend in with others?		
5.	Do you ever speak a different language (i.e., not English) within the home?		
6.	Did you ever have any speech problems?		
7.	Did you ever have orthodontic treatment as a young adult?		
8.	As you grew up were you often asked to 'keep your voice down'?		
9.	As you grew up did you often feel your opinion was not valued?		
10.	Do you have difficulty recognising people by their voice alone?		

Section 8: Anxiety and Stress

Questions in this section relate to aspects of stress and anxiety within your personal social and work environment. The aim of the questions is to collate information on your experience of anxiety and stress issues, such as a personal level of stress, anxiety and muscular tension which might affect or compromise voice production.

The relationship between emotion and physical state has been well documented not only throughout this book but also in the wider context of investigations into how psychological factors influence physiological functioning and is particularly prevalent in a world which has turned its attention to mental health and well-being. Factors such as personality characteristics, emotional reactions to acute or chronic life stressors and emotional disturbances such as chronic anxiety affect the movement of the vocal folds through increased levels of intrinsic and extrinsic laryngeal muscle tension.

	Section 8: Anxiety and Stress	Yes	No
1.	Do you worry a lot?		
2.	Are you a tense person?		
3.	Have you ever had any major stress in the past?		
4.	Do you ever feel unable to cope?		
5.	Do you feel stressed by some aspects of your life?		
6.	Do you feel that in general there are too many demands placed on you?		
7.	Do you often get angry?		
8.	Do you easily get into arguments?		
9.	Do you have difficulty 'winding down' and relaxing?		
10.	Do you ever have feelings of fear, dread or panic without cause?		

Section 9: Social Functioning

Questions in this section relate to your social functioning and social adaptation. The aim is to collate information on your ability to function socially in terms of relationships, personal environment and degree and place of social contact.

The ability to function within society is an important human right, well documented in terms of the freedoms extended in all democratic countries and particularly enshrined in all aspects of the Equality Act in the UK. Social functioning is dependent on an ability to communicate with others through the use of a common language, but communication does, of course, encompass other forms of nonverbal language such as signing, body language, dress and facial expression. The experience of voice-loss includes a sense of isolation and distress with accompanying periods of depression. In view of the noted distress experienced as an aspect of a voice disorder, or voice dysphoria, it is important to consider how far-reaching this effect is and how much your ability to function socially has been compromised by your voice concerns.

	Section 9: Social Functioning	Yes	No
1.	Does your voice prevent you from having more outside interests (e.g., clubs, classes)?		
2.	Does your voice prevent you socialising (e.g., pubs, clubs, restaurants)?		
3.	Does your voice deteriorate after socialising?		
4.	Do you feel your voice has inhibited you from making social contacts?		
5.	Would an improvement in your voice quality change your life significantly?		
6.	Do you have difficulty imagining your voice being better?		
7.	Do you feel that you could have more regular contact with friends and family?		
8.	Do you feel excluded from your circle of friends and family?		
9.	Do you feel that you are not in charge of your life?		
10.	Do you feel that you should have more involvement in community life?		

Section 10: Environment

Questions in this section relate to your environment. The aim is to collate information on environmental issues that might affect or compromise voice production, such as the work and home environment, air quality, noise and pollution and the acoustic properties of those areas in which you spend periods of time throughout the day.

We've already discussed environmental and acoustic issues in this book, but one of the issues to remember is that the noise level in some domestic or care situations might be even higher than in many office workplaces.

	Section 10: Environment	Yes	No
1.	Are you in a dry atmosphere for any length of time during the day?		
2.	Do you often work in conditions with poor air quality?		
3.	Do you find the temperature level uncomfortable, either at home or at work?		
4.	Are there times during your week when you are in a difficult acoustic environment?		
5.	Would your voice benefit from adaptations in your workplace?		
6.	Do you talk to people at some distance from you?		
7.	Do you sit in one position for long periods of time?		
8.	Does your work cause physical discomfort (e.g., Back pain, stiff neck/shoulders)?		
9.	Do you have many changes of environment during the day (e.g., indoors/outdoors)?		
10.	Do you feel that you have insufficient breaks during your day?		

Once you have answered the questions in each section, count all the 'yes' responses, fill in that number of squares related to the section using the Voice Profile sheet below. If you have three 'yes' answers for a General Health, for example, fill in the first three squares, if you have said 'no' to all the questions on a particular topic you will have a line of blank squares. This will help you recognise the contributing factors to your voice concern.

Your Voice Profile   **Today's Date**

General Health										
Vocal History										
Vocal Health										
Vocal Care										
Vocal demand										
Vocal Status										
Voice Geneogram										
Anxiety and Stress										
Social Functioning										
Environment										

How to Use Your Voice Profile

This is a reflection of how certain factors are affecting your voice at this moment.

Revisit the Voice Profile to note changes you've manage to effect in voice quality and vocal performance and monitor the impact of certain components of your communicative style and vocal effectiveness.

Elements of your Voice Profile may be useful as a guide to prioritise your needs. For example, if you score high in Anxiety and Stress, it may be worth spending more time focusing on Chapter 3, 'Relaxation and Release of Tension'.

APPENDIX B: VOICE DIARY

Complete every section of this chart every day using the following scale:

1 = voice rest, 2 = easy voicing, 3 = possible vocal stress, 4 = vocal loading / intense activity.

	Morning	*Afternoon*	*Evening*	*Overall Voice Quality*
Monday				
Tuesday				
Wednesday				
Thursday				
Friday				
Saturday				
Sunday				

APPENDIX C: VOICE CARE RECOMMENDATIONS

In order to protect your voice, avoid:

- Talking above loud background noise at social or sports events, or above office or machinery noise.
- Smoking or vaping.
- Chemical irritants and dusty conditions.
- Recreational drugs.
- Spicy foods and dairy products that may affect your voice.

- Excessive use of the phone or mobile.
- Drinks that cause dehydration, such as tea, coffee and carbonated soda drinks.
- Dry atmospheres.
- Eating a large meal just before going to bed at night as it may cause reflux.
- Extensive voice use when emotionally challenged; the voice is closely linked with emotion and therefore vulnerable during times of tension, anxiety, depression or anger.
- Whispering and continuing to talk if your voice is hoarse, or you are losing your voice.

Try to:

- Keep alcoholic drinks to a minimum.
- Be aware that hormonal changes such as the menopause, pregnancy or menstruation may affect voice quality.
- Keep up your daily intake of water.
- Be aware of the colour of your urine. Pale-coloured urine indicates an adequate level of hydration. However, some medication and food, such as beetroot, can alter the colour of urine.
- Warm up the voice gently before prolonged speaking.
- Use a humidifier or water spray to moisten the air in centrally heated offices or homes.
- Keep physically fit and mobile in an effort to maintain effective respiration, reduce areas of tension and encourage vocal flexibility.
- Get an adequate amount of sleep each night.
- Take preventative measures to reduce the effect of allergies, irritants and changes to the mucosal lining of the nose and lungs, such as asthma.
- Steam when required, particularly when ill and before prolonged periods of speaking.
- Sip water or swallow if you feel you need to clear your throat as vigorous throat clearing can damage your vocal folds.
- Monitor changes in your voice quality carefully and be aware of any increased tendency to cough or feel dehydrated particularly after changes to your medication.
- Rest your voice when possible.

APPENDIX D: VOICE WARM-UP

Build Your Own Warm-Up

Try to do some of each of the exercises already included to warm up or warm down your voice. You can build your own bespoke warm-up from your favourite exercises in the book.

Ideally a warm-up involves some exercises for:

- Tension release – the whole body, the neck, shoulders, face, jaw and vocal tract.
- Posture – balance and alignment.
- Breathing technique and control.
- Vocal tract release of tension.
- Balanced resonance.
- Voice production, pitch range and voice projection.

The following short warm-up exercise gives you an example of how the warm-up incorporates all of the above.

Warm-Up One

Start by working on exercises to loosen up your body:

- Gently push your shoulder blades together and feel the 'opening' of the front of your chest as you do so. Do this three times.
- Lift your shoulders slightly and then release them. Do this three or four times.
- Using two fingers of your right or left hand gently push your chin into your neck and feel the stretch of your muscles down the back of your neck. Do this three times.
- Imagine that your head is balanced on the top of your spine on a greasy ball bearing.
- Move the head very smoothly in a nodding 'yes' motion.

Move on to exercises to loosen your jaw:

- Take your hands up to your cheekbones and gently stroke the jaw downwards allowing the muscles to release and lengthen.
- Imagine that the jaw is heavy and let its weight carry the jaw downwards. Monitor whether or not your teeth are clenched, if they are, release the tension and feel the separation of the top and bottom teeth.

Breathing out:

- Sigh out to a count of five on an /ff/. When the lungs 'empty' simply allow them to refill.
- Sigh out, on a count of six, on an /ss/. Repeat the refill process.
- Sigh out, on a count of seven, on a /th/. Repeat the refill process.
- Sigh out, on a count of eight, on a /sh/. Repeat the refill process.

Moving the voice:

- Hum any familiar tune. Purse the lips as you hum and maintain space between the upper and lower teeth in order to encourage the voice to be placed forward on the lips and in the mask of the face.
- Siren from your lowest note to your highest note using the sound /n/ or /ng/.

Lips and tongue:

- Purse the lips and then circle them first one way and then the other. Start at the right-hand corner of your mouth circle to the left-hand corner and then up towards your nose. Reverse the action.
- Repeat the same action with the tongue and make sure you stretch it and attempt to complete the full circle without missing out any section.

You can follow these steps by moving into sound and words with tongue-twisters or by using some of the text you are about to speak. As you go through the different stages of the warm-up, do make sure you continue to monitor any tension that may creep in at any point.

315

Express Warm-up (when pressed for time!)

- Let go of a long sigh through an open mouth.
- Check your shoulders.
- Relax your jaw.
- Place your fingers around your waist and release these sounds in short sharp bursts of air:
  /sh/ /sh/ /sh/
  /v/ /v/ /v/
  /fff/ /fff/ /fff/
  /zzz/ /zzz/ /zzz/
  /sss/ /sss/ /sss/
- Whilst humming, tap or gently 'bash' your chest.
- Use the phrase 'ha ha', as if you have solved a mystery, raising the eyebrows.
- Using an /n/ or /ng/, siren the sound.

Resources
Organisations and Resources of Interest

Professional Organisations

–   Society of Teachers of Speech and Drama. www.stsd.org.uk
–   LAMDA. www.lamda.ac.uk
–   The Royal College of Speech and Language Therapists. www.rcslt.org
–   Trinity College London. www.trinitycollege.com

Podcasts

We recommend listening to podcasts; in general, they are an excellent way to observe others communicating, using their voice, interviewing and using storytelling structure and there are many voice, speech and communication podcasts available. If you'd like some suggestions, then try the following.

Speech, Communication and Self-Development Podcasts

–   Paul Meier, *In a Manner of Speaking*; Elizabeth Day, *How to Fail*; Viv Groskop, *How to Own the Room*; Steven Bartlett, *The Diary of a CEO*.

Storytelling Podcasts

–   *This American Life*, *The Moth*, BBC Sounds podcasts, amongst many others.

Poetry Resources

We recommend looking for poetry anthologies that will give you a wide choice of poetry from which to self-select. If, however you'd like some suggestions then try the following:

- The Poetry Foundation. www.poetryfoundation.org
- The Poetry Society. www.poetrysociety.org.uk
- National Poetry Library. www.nationalpoetrylibrary.org.uk/online-poetry/poems
- Suggested poetry anthologies:
  - *Staying Alive: Real Poems for Unreal Times* (Bloodaxe Books)
  - *Poems for Every Day of the Year* (Macmillan)
  - *Poem for the Day: One and Two* (Chatto & Windus)

Organisations Interested in Promoting Oracy Skills

- Oracy Cambridge, at Hughes Hall, the University of Cambridge, has been working to recognise the value of good spoken communication for all children in a diverse range of contexts – the arts, education, law, health, social care counselling, management and other work situations – and considering how to develop a greater awareness of the importance of developing talk skills and of ways that this can be pursued in practice. www.oracycambridge.org
- The English-Speaking Union (ESU) is an international educational charity that aims to promote understanding and communication between people of different cultures and backgrounds through the English language. They offer programmes and resources to enhance public speaking and debating skills among young people, with a focus on inclusivity and diversity. www.esu.org
- Voice 21 is a UK-based charity that advocates for the teaching and development of oracy skills in schools. They work with educators to integrate speaking and listening skills into the curriculum and provide training and resources to support inclusive oracy education. www.voice21.org
- The Speaker's Trust is a charity that focuses on developing communication and presentation skills in young people. They offer workshops, mentoring and public speaking competitions to help individuals from

diverse backgrounds build confidence and effective communication skills. www.speakerstrust.org

- The Kalisher Trust helps young people develop the power of advocacy and supports those who aspire to become criminal barristers. www.thekalishertrust.org
- The Communication Trust. www.thecommunicationtrust.org
- English Speaking Board. www.esbuk.org

Organisations to Access Help with Bodywork and Postural Issues

- The Feldenkrais Guild UK. www.feldenkrais.co.uk
- Society of Teachers of the Alexander Technique. www.alexandertechnique .co.uk
- Yoga and tai chi instructors can be found locally and online.

Organisations to Help with Voices in Transition

- Trans Unite is an online resource and directory of local and online support groups for trans and non-binary people in the UK. www.transunite .co.uk
- The International Association of TransVoice Surgeons was established to improve the knowledge of voice care of the transgender community and develop high-quality techniques for voice gender affirmation surgery. www.transvoicesurgeons.com
- Individuals attending the NHS Gender Identity Clinic have access to Voice and Communication Therapy. More information on their website. www.gic.nhs.uk/services/speech-and-language-therapy/

References and Further Reading

Abitbol, J. (2006). *Odyssey of the Voice*. San Diego, CA: Plural Publishing.

American Institute of Stress. Available at: www.stress.org/workplace-stress/ [Accessed January 2023].

Anderson, C. (2016). *TED Talks: The Official TED Guide to Public Speaking*. New York: Houghton, Mifflin Harcourt.

Atkinson, A. (2008). *Speech-making and Presentation Made Easy*. London: Vermillion.

Bay, S. (2023). *Permission to Speak*. London: Penguin Audio.

BBC Speeches, Media Centre. Available at: www.bbc.co.uk/mediacentre/speeches/ [Accessed August 2019].

BBC. (2016). *France Law*. Available at: www.bbc.com [Accessed January 2023].

Bernieri, F., & Petty, K. N. (2011). The influence of handshakes on first impression accuracy. *Social Influence* 6: 78–87.

Berry, C. (2007) *Your Voice and How to Use It*. London: Virgin Books.

Berry, C. (2000). *The Actor and the Text*. London: Virgin Books.

Boston, J., & Cook, R. (2009). *Breath in Action*. London and Philadelphia: Jessica Kingsley Publishers.

Brooks, A. W. (2013). Get excited: Reappraising pre-performance anxiety as excitement. *Journal of Experimental Psychology*. www.doi.org/10.1037/a0035325.

Brown, B. (2018). *Living Into Our Values PDF*. www.brenebrown.com [Accessed March 2023]. *Dare to Lead*. Penguin Random House.

Burgess, A., van Diggele, C., Roberts, C., & Mellis, C. (2020). Feedback in the clinical setting. *BMC Medical Education* 20(suppl2): 460.

Carey, D., & Clark Carey, R. (2010). *The Verbal Arts Workbook*. London: A &C Black Publishers Ltd.

Centre for Women and Democracy. *Political Speeches by Women*. Available at: www.cfwd.org.uk/quotations-2/political-speeches-by-women [Accessed August 2021].

Centres for Disease Control and Prevention. (2020). Outbreak of lung injury associated with e-cigarette use or vaping. www.cdc.gov/tobacco/basic_information/e-cigarettes/severe-lung-disease.html.

Cloud, H. (2017). *Boundaries: When to Say Yes, How to Say No To Take Control of Your Life*. Grand Rapids MI: Zondervan.

Cooper, M. (1973). Modern Techniques of Vocal Rehabilitation, 2nd edn, Springfield: Charles C Thomas.

Cooper, Y. (2020). *She Speaks – Women's Speeches That Changed the World, from Pankhurst to Greta*. London: Atlantic Books.

Cuddy, A. (2012). TED talk. *Power Poses* [Accessed November 2022].

Dispenza, J. (2012). *Breaking the Habit of Being Yourself* (6th edn). Rakuten Kobo. Kobo Writing Life.

Doige, N. (2016). *The Brain's Way of Healing*. London: PenguinBooks Publishing Group.

Dweck, C. S. (2017). *Mindset - Changing the Way You Think to Fulfil Your Potential*. London: Constable & Robinson.

Erikson, T. (2019). *Surrounded by Idiots*. London: St. Martin's Essentials.

Fabrigar, L. R., & Krosnick, J. A. (1995). Attitude importance and the false consensus effect. *Personality and Social Psychology Bulletin* 21(5): 468–79.

Feindel, J. M. (2009) *The Thought Propels the Sound*. San Diego CA: Plural Publishing Inc.

Gallo, C. (2014). *Talk like Ted*. London: MacMillan.

Gilovich, T., Medvec, V. H., & Savitsky, K. (2000). The Spotlight effect in social judgment: An egocentric bias in estimates of the salience of one's own actions and appearance. *Journal of Personality and Social Psychology* 78(2) 211–222.

Government Equalities Office. (2013). *Equality Act 2010: Guidance*. Available at: www.gov.uk/guidance/equality-act-2010-guidance [Accessed June 2023].

Goyder, C. (2020). *Find Your Voice*. London: Vermillion.

Groskop, V. (2023). *Happy High Status*. London: Penguin Books (2018) *How to Own the Room*. Bantam Press.

Health and Safety Executive 2021/2 Labour Force Survey. Available at: www.hse.gov.uk/statistics/causdis/stress /stress.pdf [Accessed March 2023].

Jeffers, S. (1998). *Feel the Fear and Do It Anyway*. London: Ebury Publishing.

Judge, T. A. Erez, A., Bono, J. E., & Thoresen, C. J. (2002). Are measures of self-esteem, neuroticism, locus of control and generalised self-efficacy indicators of a common core construct? *Journal of Personality and Social Psychology* 83(3): 693–710.

Karpf, A. (2006). *The Human Voice*. London: Bloomsbury Publishing Plc.

Kelly, S. D., Manning, S. M., & Rodak, S. (2008). Gesture gives a hand to language and learning: perspectives from cognitive neuroscience, developmental psychology and education. *Language and Linguistics Compass* 2(4): 569–588.

Lindsey, G. (2019). *English After RP: Standard British Pronunciation Today*. London: Palgrave Macmillan.

Linklater, K. (2006). *Freeing the Natural Voice*. London: Nick Hern Books.

Martin, S. P. (2021). *Working with Voice Disorders* (3rd edn). Abingdon Oxon and New York: Routledge.

Martin, S., & Darnley, L. (2013). *The Voice Box*. London: Speechmark.

Mathieson, L. (2001). *Greene and Mathieson's The Voice and Its Disorders* (6th edn). Chichester: John Wiley & Sons.

Moses, P. J. (1954). *The Voice of Neurosis*. New York: Grune and Stratton.

Mugglestone, L. (2007). *Talking Proper* (2nd edn). Oxford and New York: Oxford University Press.

Nelson Mandela Foundation. Speeches. Available at: www.nelsonmandela.org/content/page/speeches [Accessed July 2022].

Oracy Network. Available at: www.esu.org/our-network/oracy-network [Accessed February 2023].

Patton, B., Stone, D., & Heen, S. (2011). *Difficult Conversations – How to Discuss What Matters Most*. London: Penguin Books.

Peters, S. (2011). *The Chimp Paradox*. London: Vermilion.

Pierrot, A. (2009). Breath in action. In J. Boston, & R. Cook (Eds.), *Effects of Posture on Diaphragmatic Breath*. London and Philadelphia: Jessica Kingsley.

The Poetry Society. Available at: www.poetrysociety.org.uk [Accessed December 2023].

Rosenberg, M. B. (2015). *Nonviolent Communication: A Language of Life*. Encinitas, CA: Puddle Dancer Press.

Rotter, J. (1966). Generalised expectancies for internal versus external control of reinforcement. *Psychological Monographs* 80(1): 1–28.

Storr, W. (2019). *The Science of Storytelling*. London: Collins.

Tawwab, N. G. (2021). *Set Boundaries and Find Peace*. London: Piatkus Books.

Toastmasters International. Available at: www.toastmasters.org [Accessed February 2023].

The Royal College of Speech and Language Therapists. Available at: https: www.rcslt.org [Accessed May 2023].

Verdolini, K. (1997). The vocal vision. In M. Hampton & B. Acker (Eds.), *Principles of Skill Acquisition Applied to Voice Training*. New York: Applause Books.

Woolf, V. (1937). *Mrs Dalloway in Park Lane*. London: Hogarth Press.

Index

4–7–8 breath 82

accent modification 240–241
accents 240–241; resonance 103
acid reflux 23–24
acoustic influences on projection
    193–194
acting 215–216
active listening 278–284, 288
actors/voiceover artists/broadcasters,
    resonance 112
Adam's apple 12
ageing: pitch 117–120; vocal quality 12;
    volume 185
alcohol 22–23
alignment; exercises for neck and head
    42–43; posture 33
allergies 26
altering pitch 123–124
androgens 118
anxiety 140; strategies for easing
    220–222; stress management 55;
    Voice Profile 309
anxiety checklist 50
art of performing 215–216
articulation 10, 239; warming up 158
articulators 138; emotional tension
    139–140; exercises for 148–149
assessing your vocal variety 168–169
asthma 120
atmospheric dryness, limiting 21
audience decoding, hindering 208–209
authenticity 213–215, 234
awareness exercises, smooth voicing 92

backs 17
balanced resonance 98
beat gestures 264

body language 261; eye contact 269–
    271; gesture 261–267; positioning
    268–269; posture 267–268; presence
    272–273
bowling 125
box breathing 81
breath control, exercises for 76–78
breath diary 79–80
breath release, exercises for 78–79
breath support 9
breathing 68–71; breathwork
    techniques 81–82; exercises for
    74–79; practical advice 73–74; rapid
    strategies for 82–83; self-assessment
    71–73; self-awareness 71–73
breathwork techniques 81–82
breathy onset 91
broadcasters, resonance 112
bulimia 24
business of communication 204

calling 201
caring for your voice 14–15
Cat-Cow pose 145
changes to voice 11–12, 23–24
channels, vocal-auditory channel 273
chest resonance 99; exercises for
    107–108
clarity 136, 184–185, 239, 241
clothing, comfort 275–276
coaches, resonance 111
cognitive reassurance 56
cognitive relief 56
cold remedies 25–26
comfort, clothing 275–276
communication 203; active listening
    278–284; body language see body
    language; business of 204; channels

273; compassionate communication 235–236; context 283–285; feedback 278; hindering audience decoding 208 209; impromptu speech 237–238; introducing/thanking speakers 297; knowing what to say 236–237; medium *see* medium; message *see* message; noise 274–277; nonviolent communication (NVC) model 235; pauses 254–257; self-assessment 206–207; speaker's mindset 216–222; speed of speech 248–253; spotlight effect 203–204; virtual communication *see* virtual communication; vocal spontaneity 257–259; vocal variety 163–165; vocal-auditory channel 273
communication model 205–206, 208, 273, 278
communication personal inventory 207
communicators 205, 207–208
compassionate communication 235–236
confidence: building 219–220; posture 37
connected speech 151
conserving your voice 14–15
consonant clusters 152–153
consonants: clarity 239; consonant clusters 152–153; final consonants 151–152
constriction 84–86; exercises for 88–90; practical advice 91–92; self-assessment 87–88; stress 86; vocal loading 86; volume 85–86
context 283–285; clothing and comfort 275–276; communication 206; guidelines for in-person communication 285–287; for teaching, training, workshops 287–288; when attending networking events 289–290; when hosting a meeting 288–289
contradictory gestures 267
control of volume 193–194
COVID-19 25; masks 274; work-life balance 54
creak 257
cultural perspectives, clothing 275
customer-support agents/telephone operators, resonance 111–112

danger zones, awareness of 201
decoding 208–209, 239

deconstruction 84–86, 96; strategies for 95–96
definitive statements 247–248
dehydration 85
dialects 240–241
diet 23–24
digestive problems 23
digital communication *see* virtual communication
digital fatigue 291–292
direction of gestures 264
disability discrimination 137
discrimination: disability discrimination 137; against women 114
distance, positioning and 268–269
drug use, cannabis 172
dynamic posture 31
dyskinesia 304

early warning signs and symptoms of voice changes 12–14
effective speech 223
effortful voicing 12
Elevator Pitch Challenge 253
elite vocal performers 2
emotion, while storytelling 242–243
emotional cues 281
emotional tension, articulators and 139–140
empathetic listening 280
emphasis, in message 243–245
energy in words, finding 155–158
enunciating 239
environment, Voice Profile 310–311
environmental awareness: pitch 120–121; tension 139
environmental factors related to stress 53
environmental health recommendations 28
environments, vocally and acoustically challenging environments 4
exercises for: articulators 149; breathing 74–79; constriction 88–90; definitive statements 247; jaws 146–147; lips 148; muscular flexibility 144–158; onset 92–94; pharynx 147; pitch 124–131; pitch range 126–131; posture 38–43; presence 273; projection 194–196; rapid articulatory change 153–155; release of tension 59–63, 88–90, 144–146; resonance 104–108; temporomandibular joint (TMJ/

jaw hinge) 89–90; tongues 148–149; vocal variety 173–176; volume control 189–192
exhaustion and stress 51
experience, stress management 56
eye contact 269–271; in virtual communication 294; while pausing 255

facial expressions 280–281
facilitating meetings, contextual considerations for 288–289
false-consensus effect 210
fast speakers 249–250; strategies for 252
fear of public speaking 193, 217–218; strategies for easing 220–222
feedback 206 , 278; active listening 278–280; assessing vocal variety 168–169; about messages 233–235; models of 235; silencing the critic on your shoulder 282–283; in virtual communication 294
fidgeting 264
fight-or-flight response 51–52, 140, 217–218
fillers 167, 276
final consonants 151–152
finding energy in words 155–158
fire engine/ambulance siren 125
first impressions 209–212; accents 240
fitness 26–27

games: for developing structure skills 228–229; show-and-tell 237; 'What?' 244–245
gastro-oesophageal reflux disease (GORD) 23
gesture 261–262; fidgeting 264; finding your words 263–264; self-assessment 262–263; in virtual communication 295
gliding 125
good posture 33–35; exercises for encouraging good posture 38–43
GORD see gastro-oesophageal reflux disease
Greek rhetoric 224
Griots 224
group eye contact 270–271
group situations, volume 200

habitual gestures 264–267
habitual tension 87

habitual volume 199–200
happy high status 272
hard attack 24
hard onset 90
head resonance 99
head-neck alignment 16
headphones, speaking with 201–202
hearing-loss, age-related 185
helpful posture 35
hoarseness 304
holistic ways to relieve tension 66–67
hormones, vocal change 117–119
hosting a meeting, contextual considerations for 288–289
humour, pauses 255
hydration 20–21

iconic gestures 264
imagery, exercises for release of tension 59
impressions, vocal perceptions 209–210
impromptu speech, improving 237–238
improving, sight-reading 133
infants, vocal folds 11
in-person communication, guidelines for 285–287
intensity of gestures 265
intonation 244, 245–247
introducing/thanking speakers 297–298

jaw hinge, exercises for 89–90
jaws, exercises for 146–147

keeping voice in good shape 80–82
kinaesthetic feedback 138–139
knees 17; helpful posture 35
knowing what to say 236–237

languages, vocal variety 166
laryngopharynx 86
larynx 11, 86, 98; in males 12; see also phonatory system
law enforcement/security guard, resonance 111
leaked gestures 265
lifestyle choices 18–19
lips, exercises for 148
liquid intake 20–21
listening: active listening 278–284; empathetic listening 280
lumbar region, breathing exercises 75–76

males, larynx 12
Marjaryasana-Bitilasana 145
masking 213–215
masks, during pandemic 274
medical referrals 15–17
medium 238–239; body language 205; voice as 239–241
menopause: pitch 117–118; vocal quality 12
mental health: pitch 123; recommendations 29–30
message 223–225; body language *see* body language; emphasis 243–245; feedback 233–235; within the message 232–233; modulating 242–243; storytelling 230; structure models for 225–228
meta communication 165
metaphoric gestures 264
micro expressions 280
microphones 276; posture when using 37; virtual communication 296
mind-body link 14, 19, 31
mindset *see* speaker's mindset
mitigating stress 54–55
modulating messages 242–243
monotony 116–117, 257
mouth, resonance 98
mouth sounds 296
mumbling 142
muscular flexibility 136, 140–141, 161; articulators 138; exercises for 144–158; importance of 136–137; incorporating into daily life 159–160; kinaesthetic and tactile feedback 138–139; practical advice for 143–144; self-assessment 141–142; tension 139–140; tongue-twisters 158–159
music, to relieve fear and anxiety 222

nasal resonance 99; exercises for 106–107
nasopharynx 86
necks, exercises for 42–43, 62–63
negative self-talk 216
nervous tension 49
networking events, contextual considerations for 289–290
noise 205, 274–277
non-verbal communication, on camera 295
nonverbal cues 280–281, 288
nonviolent communication (NVC) model 235

observation, vocal variety 179–180
oestrogen 118
onset 90–91; exercises for 92–94; practical advice for 91–92; strategies for 95–96
oral resonance 99; exercises for 104
oropharynx 86
outward focus 203–204; vocal variety 179

pace of speech 177, 248–253
paralinguistic noise 276
parasympathetic nervous system 218
PASTA (Problem, Alternatives, Solution, Takeaway, Action) 227
pauses 177, 254–257; emphasis 244
PEEL (Point, Evidence, Explain significance, Link) 227
Pendleton's Feedback model 235
performances, pitch 134
performing 215–216
peripheral vision 35
pharyngeal resonance, exercises for 105–106
pharynx, exercises for 147
phonation 10; stress 69
phonatory system 9
physical fitness 26–27
physical health recommendations 29
physical inventory 17
pitch 113–115; ageing 117–120; altering 123–124; changes in 117–118; environmental awareness 120–121; exercises for 124–131; importance of 115–117; monotony 116–117; pitch pattern variation 131–132; pitch under pressure checklist 121; practical advice 123; in presentations 134; reading 132–133; self-assessment 121–122; singing 132; stress 115; transgender individuals 118–119; vocal ranges 113
pitch, giving or pitches, giving 134
pitch pattern variation 131–132
pitch range 117, 119, 123; exercises for 126–131
pitch versatility 114
political leaders, resonance 112
positioning 267–269
positive messages 232–233
postural problems 20
posture 11, 16, 31, 267–269, 276; achieving good posture 33–35;

alignment 33; dynamic posture 31; exercises for encouraging good posture 38–43; first impressions 211; helpful posture 35; importance of 31–33; making change to 37; medical referrals 16; psoas muscle 46; quick prep before speech or presentation 46–47; self-assessment 35–36; self-awareness of 36–37; sitting checklist 43–44; static posture 31; unhelpful posture 34; while at work 44–45; while driving 47
posture inventory 17
power posing 32
PPF (Past, Present, Future) 226–227
PPS (Problem, Process, Solution) 226
preferences for voices 100
PREP (Point, Reason, Example, Point) 228
preparation 171–172; silencing the critic on your shoulder 282–283; vocal variety 180–181
presence 272–273
presentations, pitch 134
pressure 50
primary stressed syllables 244
professional 'mask' 213–215
professional voice users 2–3; keeping voice in good shape 80–82
professionals for whom voice is not an essential part of their work 3
professionals who do not rely on their voices for work 3
projection 192–196, 202
psoas muscle 46
psychogenic voice disorder 48
psychological noise 275
public speaking 224–225

rapid articulatory change, exercises for 153–155
rate of speech 249–253
reading, pitch 132–133
recordings of voice 101–102; assessing vocal variety 168; volume 187–188
relaxation 48–50; breathwork 81–82; environmental factors 53; tools for 66–67; see also release of tension
relaxed readiness 49
release of tension 49–50, 57–58; exercises for 59–63, 88–90, 144–146; holistic ways to 66–67; before speaking events 63–64; see also relaxation

religious/spiritual/political leaders, resonance 112
resonance 10–11, 97–99; awareness 110; exercises for 104–108; feeling 102; importance of 99–100; practical advice for 103; recommendations for developing 109–110; role-specific resonance 111–112; self-assessment 101–102; strategies for 109; tension 103–104
resonators 98–99
resonatory system 9, 97–99
respiratory system 9; ageing 120
rhetorical skills 225
ribcage, exercises for 38–40
Rishis 224
role play 171
role-specific resonance 111–112

safe shouting 196–199
security guard/law enforcement, resonance 111
self-assessment: of breathing 71–73; communication 206–208; constriction 87–88; context 283–285; gesture 261–262; pitch 121–122; posture 35–36; resonance 101–102; stress 56–57; tension 57; vocal variety 167–169; volume 186–188
self-awareness: of breathing 71–73; muscular flexibility 141–142; of posture 35–36; resonance 101–102
self-control, stress management 55–56
self-efficacy, stress management 55
self-perception, recordings of voice 101–102
self-reflection, muscular flexibility 141
shoulders 17; exercises for 40–42, 62
shouting 196–199
show-and-tell 237
sight-reading, improving 133
silencing the critic on your shoulder 282–283
silent breath 84
singing 238; pitch 125, 131–132
sirening 124
sitting bones 17, 34
sitting checklist, posture 43
situation behaviour impact 235
sliding 124–125
slow speakers 251–252
slurring, pitch 125
smoking 22–23, 119, 172

smooth onset 93; strategies for 95–96
smooth voicing, exercises for 92–94
SOAR (Situation, Obstacle, Action,
    Result) 228
social functioning, Voice Profile
    312–313
soft onset 90
sore throats 16
spatial gestures 264
speakers, introducing/thanking
    speakers 297–298
speaker's mindset 216–217; confidence
    219–220; fear 217–218; not liking
    your voice 222–223
speaking range 113
speech, muscular flexibility 141–142
speeches/presentations: contextual
    considerations for 286–288; posture
    prep 46–47; recommendations for
    preparation and delivery 177–178;
    releasing tension before 63–64
speed: of gestures 264; of speech
    248–258
speed variation 253
spicy food 23–24
spinal movement, exercises for 38–40
spiritual leaders, resonance 111
spotlight effect 203–204
square breathing 81
standing position 17
static posture 31
steaming 21–22
stimulating energy, exercises for
    144–146
storytellers 224
storytelling 230–232; with emotion 243
stress 8, 49–50; constriction 86;
    dealing with at work 64–66; effects
    on voice 51–52; environmental
    factors of 53; exhaustion and 51;
    levels of stress checklist 50; pace of
    speech 249; phonation 69; pitch 115;
    self-assessment 56–57; strategies
    for mitigating 54–55; Voice Profile
    306–307; work-life balance 53–54;
    see also relaxation
stress management 54–55; anxiety 56;
    experience 56; self-control 55–56;
    self-efficacy 55
stretching 139, 144
structure models for, message 225–228
structure skills, strategies for
    developing 228–229
style, assessing vocal variety 169

tactile feedback 138–139
teachers, resonance 111
teaching, contextual considerations for
    287–288
tech neck 16
teeth, loss of 120
telephone operators/customer-support
    agents, resonance 111
temporomandibular joint (TMJ/jaw
    hinge), exercises for 89–90
tension 12, 17, 48; emotional tension
    139–140; facial expressions 281;
    habitual tension 87; muscular
    flexibility 139–140; nervous tension
    49; release of tension 178; resonance
    103–104; self-assessment 57; vocal
    variety 171; see also constriction;
    stress
throat resonance 99
throat-clearing 24
tiredness, pitch 123
TMJ see temporomandibular joint
    (TMJ/jaw hinge)
tone 259–261
tongues: exercises for 148; muscular
    flexibility 141; stretching 144
tongue-twisters 140–141, 158–159
'too fast' speakers 249–250
tools for relaxation 66–67
trainers, resonance 111
training, contextual considerations for
    287–288
transgender individuals, pitch 118–119
tunes 246

unhelpful posture 34
upper chest, exercises for 62
upspeak 246
urine 20–21

vaping 22–23, 172
varying intonation, exercises for vocal
    variety 173–176
Vedic tradition 224
VHI see vocal health inventory
vibration of vocal folds 10
virtual communication 290–294; non-
    verbal communication 295
virtual voice 295–297
vision, peripheral vision 34
visual brainstorming 228
visual cues, for vocal variety 181–182
vocabulary, developing 237–238
vocal auditory channel 205

vocal clarity 96
vocal colour 245; definitive statements 247–248; intonation 245–246; upspeak 246
vocal damage 2, 12
vocal demand 2–3, 303
vocal flexibility 178–179
vocal folds 8, 116; hard attack 24; in infants 11; throat-clearing 24; vibration 10
vocal fry 257–258
vocal health 206, 288; Voice Profile 302–303
vocal health inventory (VHI) 13–14
vocal history 304–305
vocal loading 11–12, 86
vocal perceptions 209–212
vocal profiles 15
vocal quality 162–163, 257; changes due to ageing 12
vocal ranges 113
vocal situations, testing 198–199
vocal spontaneity 257–259
vocal status 307–308
vocal tone 259–261
vocal tract 9
vocal variety 162–164; exercises for 173–176; exploring 176–177; importance of 171; outward focus 178–179; practical advice for 189; self-assessment 167–169; strategies for 179–181; tension 168; visual cues 181–182
vocal warm-up 27
vocal-auditory channel 273
vocalisation 22
vocally and acoustically challenging environments 4
voice: changes 11–12; as medium 239; not liking your voice 222–223; virtual voice 295–296; where it comes from 8–9
voice box 8 *see also* phonatory system
voice care 306, 312–313
voice changes, early warning signs and symbols of voice changes 12–14
voice diary 15, 312
voice genogram 308–309
voice health, Voice Profile 297–298

voice production 10
Voice Profile 302–303; anxiety and stress 309; environment 310–311; general health 303–304; how to use 312; social functioning 310–311; vocal demand 307; vocal health 305–306; vocal history 304–305; vocal status 307–308; voice care 306; voice genogram 308–309
voice quality 206
voice recovery strategies, cold remedies 25–26
voice warmups 314–316
voice work 11
voice-loss 304
voiceover artists, resonance 112
volume 85–86, 183–; adjusting 211; ageing 185; control of 193–194; emphasis 244; exercises for 189–192; group situations 200; habitual volume 199–200; importance of 183–186; practical advice for 189; projection 192–193; self-assessment 186–187; shouting 196–199; speaking with headphones 201–202
vomiting 23–24

warming up 27
warning signs and symptoms to voice changes 12–14
weight 17
well-being 28
W-formation eye contact 270
W/H questions 227
'What?' 244–245
whole-body release of tensions, exercises for 60–62
work, dealing with stress 64–65
working from home 49
working voice, practical advice 88
work-life balance 53–54
workplace infections 25
workplace responsibilities 27–28
workshops, contextual considerations for 287–289

yawning 139, 144
yoga 141

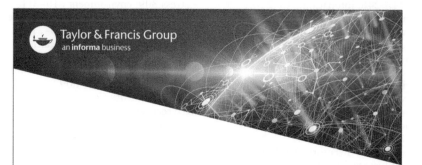